DOMESTIC MOD[
THE INTERWAR
AND E.H. YOUNG

*From Chiara to Rachele, Arianna, Giovanni and the memory of
Marston and Owen
From Kathy to Eva, Bob, Robin and Luc*

Domestic Modernism, the Interwar Novel, and E.H. Young

CHIARA BRIGANTI
Carleton College, USA

KATHY MEZEI
Simon Fraser University, Canada

LONDON AND NEW YORK

First published 2006 by Ashgate Publishing

2 Park Square, Milton Park, Abingdon, Oxfordshire OX14 4RN
711 Third Avenue, New York, NY 10017

Routledge is an imprint of the Taylor & Francis Group, an informa business

First issued in paperback 2018

Copyright © Chiara Briganti and Kathy Mezei 2006

Chiara Briganti and Kathy Mezei have asserted their moral right under the Copyright, Designs
and Patents Act, 1988, to be identified as the authors of this work

All rights reserved. No part of this book may be reprinted or reproduced or utilised in any
form or by any electronic, mechanical, or other means, now known or hereafter invented,
including photocopying and recording, or in any information storage or retrieval system,
without permission in writing from the publishers.

Notice:
Product or corporate names may be trademarks or registered trademarks, and are used only
for identification and explanation without intent to infringe.

British Library Cataloguing in Publication Data
Briganti, Chiara
Domestic modernism, the interwar novel, and E.H. Young
    1.English fiction – 20th century – History and criticism 2. omestic fiction, English
    History and criticism 3.Dwellings in literature 4.Aesthetics in literature 5.Modernism
    (Aesthetics)
    I.Title II.Mezei, Kathy, 1947–
    823.9'1209355

Library of Congress Cataloging-in-Publication Data
Briganti, Chiara.
  Domestic modernism, the interwar novel, and E.H. Young / by Chiara Briganti and Kathy
Mezei.
    p. cm.
  Includes bibliographical references and index.
  ISBN 0-7546-5317-X (alk. paper)
  1. Young, E. H. (Emily Hilda), 1880-1949—Criticism and interpretation. 2. Women and
literature—England—History—20th century. 3. English fiction— omen authors—History
and criticism. 4. English fiction—20th century—History and criticism. 5. Domestic fiction
English—History and criticism. 6. Modernism (Literature)—England. I. Mezei, Kathy,
1947- II. Title.

PR6047.O465Z57 2006
  823'.912—dc22

                                    2005026510

ISBN 13: 978-0-7546-5317-2 (hbk)
ISBN 13: 978-1-138-37909-1 (pbk)

Contents

List of Figures		*vi*
Acknowledgements		*vii*
Introduction: 'And What About the Home?'		1
1	The Interwar Domestic Novel and the Meaning of Home	17
2	Home Lives, Still Lifes	41
3	House Haunting	61
4	Private and Public Spheres: Publication and Reception	75
5	The Turn to Domestic Modernism	95
6	Vicarages and Lodging-houses	111
7	Modern Heroines of the Everyday	131
8	England, My England	153
Conclusion		165
Bibliography		*169*
Index		*195*

List of Figures

Cover	British Domestic Interior: a sitting room in the modern style, 1935 Unnamed artist in the Print Users' Year Book, 1936, with permission, Mary Evans Picture Library (Picture Number 10034360)	
1	Suburban sprawl, *The Ideal Home*, July 1931, p. xxxix	3
2	Labour-saving devices, *The Ideal Home*, January 1924, p. xxxiii	5
3	Bust of E.H. Young by her sister Norah Sanderson. Courtesy of Christopher Fallows	42
4	E.H. Young's house with plaque, 2 Saville Place, Clifton Photo by Kathy Mezei	43
5	The Penguin cover for William, 1935	82
6	The first ten Penguins	83
7	The Isokon, Lawn Rd, NW3. Photo by Kathy Mezei	84
8	Advertisement for *Miss Mole*, *The Publisher and Bookseller*, 17 June 1930, p. 1342	85
9	'Paris Frocks by Air', *The Wonder Book of Aircraft for Boys and Girls*, ed. Harry Golding, London: Ward, Lock & Co., 1920, p. 31	137
10	Celia's House, Royal York Crescent, Clifton Photo by Kathy Mezei	142

Acknowledgements

For their encouragement and support for this project, we would like to thank Ann and Haroon Ahmed, Bob Anderson, Nicola Beauman, Michael Booker, Madeleine Brown, Michael Bott, Robert Carter, Glen Cavaliero, Elizabeth Ciner, Michael Clifford, Béatrice Collignon, Stella Deen, Paul Delany, Rachel De Wachter, Paolo and Rachele Dini, Stephen Duguid, Christopher Fallows, Iben Schmidt Fonnesberg, Mieke Fritz, Alison Hennegan, Susan Knowles, Maggie Lane, Karen Langhelle, Alison Light, Arlene McLaren, Michel Pharand, Bill and Kate Saunders, Dorothy Sheridan, Tamsin and Harriet Somers, Mary-Ann Stouck, Jean-François Staszak, Veronica Strong-Boag, June Sturrock, Gavin Stamp and Sir Tony Wrigley.

We offer special thanks and gratitude to Ann Donahue, our commissioning editor at Ashgate, Meredith Coeyman, desk editor at Ashgate, to Pat FitzGerald, our copy editor, to the anonymous reader at Ashgate, to Dr. Angus McLaren for his excellent advice, and to our first-rate research assistant, Lisa Pitt.

The following institutions and granting agencies have made our project and our collaboration possible, for which we express our sincere appreciation: Social Sciences and Humanities Research Council of Canada (Standard Research Grants Programme), Minnesota Humanities Commission, Carleton College, the Department of Humanities and the Institute for the Humanities at Simon Fraser University, New York University (London), Leckhampton at Corpus Christi and Clare Hall in Cambridge, the Sorbonne, and in particular, Corpus Christi and Wolfson Colleges in Cambridge for our Visiting Fellowships; the Library in the School of Architecture at Cambridge University, the British Library, London Library, Rare Books and Special Collections at the University of British Columbia, Archives and Manuscripts, Reading University Library, Mass-Observation Archives, University of Sussex, and the University Library, Cambridge. For permission to reproduce material, we gratefully acknowledge the following. For his generosity and kindness in making Young's papers available to us, we thank Young's literary executor, Bill Saunders, and his sister, Kate Saunders. The photograph on the cover, 'British Domestic Interior: a sitting room in the modern style', 1935 by an unnamed artist in the Print Users' Year Book, 1936, is by permission of the Mary Evans Picture Library (Picture Number 10034360). The cover and back cover from *William* by E.H. Young (Harmondworth: Penguin, 1935) is reproduced by permission of Penguin Books Ltd. For the photograph, 'Paris Frocks by Air', reproduced from *The Wonder Book of Aircraft for Boys and Girls*, ed. Harry Golding, London: Ward, Lock & Co, 1921, p.31, we acknowledge Cassell & Co., an imprint of the Orion Publishing Group Ltd. All attempts at tracing the copyright holder were unsuccessful. The advertisement for Gre-Solvent, Labour-

viii *Domestic Modernism*

saving devices, *The Ideal Home*, January 1924, p. xxxiii, is by permission of the Gre-Solvent Company. All efforts have been made to contact the original copyright owners of the advertisements in 'Suburban Sprawl' and 'Labour-saving devices'. Christopher Fallows has kindly given us permission to use his photograph of the bust of Young, sculpted by his grandmother, Norah Sanderson. We thank Neill Denny at The Bookseller for permission to reproduce an advertisement for *Miss Mole* from *The Publisher and Bookseller*, 17 June 1930, p.1342. For permission to quote from the E.H. Young and Ralph Henderson letters in the Jonathan Cape archive in the Archives and Manuscripts, Reading University Library, we thank the Random House Group. Material quoted from the Mass-Observation Archive at the University of Sussex is reproduced with permission of the Trustees of the Mass-Observation Archive. We thank the BBC Written Archives, Caversham Park, Reading, RG4 8TZ for the use of material from the ref RCONT1 Gladys Young File 4a. An earlier study of E.H. Young, '"She must be a very good novelist", Re-reading E.H. Young (1880–1949)', appeared in *English Studies in Canada* 27 (2001): 303–31, and some of the material in the Introduction and Chapter one originated in an article, 'House haunting: the domestic novel of the inter-war years', published in *Home Cultures* 1.2: 147–68 in 2004. For permission to quote from the Letters Club Fonds, we thank the Rare Books and Special Collections at the University of British Columbia.

Introduction:
'And What About the Home?'

'And what about the Home?' he boomed. 'The Home is the foundation of all that is good in the national life. Take away the Home and the – the whole edifice collapses. We can't', he looked round at his audience, 'we can't do without the Home.'

Reverend Maurice Roper in *The Vicar's Daughter*: 167[1]

To construct a social world that is ordinary and solid is to quiet doubts and anxieties ... it is to create a world in which one can be at home, or rather, at Home.

Gouldner: 432

And what indeed does Reverend Roper mean by 'Home' in 1934? Is he referring to the English *beau ideal* of nation, to imagined domestic spaces and family life glowing with Christian good will, to a specific vernacular built form, or to an inculcated or atavistic desire for belonging and at home-ness?[2] Taking as a case study Emily Hilda Young, who published 11 novels during the 1920s, 1930s and 1940s and was highly acclaimed on both sides of the Atlantic, we examine how the meaning of home and the narration of domestic space were articulated in the impressive upsurge of women novelists in Britain between the two world wars.

Our project has a dual purpose: to provide analytical tools for reading the works of writers who suffered from the assumption that the experimental modernist techniques are the only expression of the modern, and to make a significant literary contribution to the burgeoning interdisciplinary field of home culture.[3] In the domestic novel written primarily by middle-class women for middle-class women about middle-class and often middle-aged women's daily and inner lives amid the 'tyranny of tea'[4] and dramas of the doorstep,[5] we discover an unrelenting, if covert, search for and creation of the self and a subtle pursuit of the art of living, an articulation quite different from the luminous, agonized portrait of the artistic self in D.H. Lawrence, James Joyce, or Joseph Conrad. The domestic space of house and garden operates as a site of agency and mode of communication for female novelists and protagonists, with the domain of the private, the interior and the everyday replacing the public sphere and the 'great outer life' of 'telegrams and anger' as the focus of attention.[6] In this turn to the domestic sphere, plots centre around the home and women become the subjects rather than the objects within domestic space (Gale: 23). Writers as varied as Virginia Woolf, who 'saw the home as the locus of all great aesthetic, social, and political change' (Morgan: 91), Katherine Mansfield, Ivy Compton-Burnett, E.M. Delafield, E.H. Young and Elizabeth Bowen subjected house and household to critical scrutiny

2   *Domestic Modernism, the Interwar Novel, and E.H. Young*

and contemplated alternative domesticities. Through their deliberate attentiveness to domestic objects, interiors, rituals and their validation of the everyday, these writers, often resorting to inventive narrative strategies in dialogue and focalization, unveiled the extraordinary in the ordinary.

A number of converging factors contributed to the proliferation of the interwar domestic novel: the post-war reification of the home, domestic values and Englishness; the campaign of 'homes fit for heroes'; the mass production, advertising and consumption of domestic goods; the increase in women's magazines; and the implementation of government policies like the marriage bar, National Insurance Acts and dole office practices that removed women from the workplace in spite of their immense contribution to the war effort (Beddoe: 3).

With this turn to the home and the domestic interior between the wars, a corresponding turn in the novel form is hardly surprising. Similar to the conditions that propelled the rise of the novel in the eighteenth century, the interwar period also experienced a domestication, feminization and privatization of society.[7] New Feminism, which gained ground in the 1920s, attempted to 'develop a new, more domestically oriented feminist ideology' and to improve the situation of women in the home to the dismay of Old Feminists like Winifred Holtby, who felt that this was a revival of the traditional image of women as domestic, mother, housewife and wife (Trodd: 5). Social historian John Burnett notes that new recruits to the middle class which increased from 20.3 per cent of the total population in 1911 to 30.4 per cent in 1951 'shared with the older members of the class the belief that family and home were the central life interests and that the house, which enshrined these institutions, had an importance far beyond other material objects' (251). Detached, single-family houses and villas proliferated, engendering a taste for home life and an economy of home-making; middle-class aspirations were reflected in and influenced by accelerating forms of mass media, the establishment of BBC radio, the cinema, women's magazines, mass book publishing and mass housing projects. Within the domestic interiors of these houses and novels, women and children were, however, discovering and forging separate and legitimatized identities. The demand for middle-class housing, the growth of suburbs, garden cities outside London (an attempt to protect the countryside from suburban sprawl) and housing and council estates, along with the shift in focus of women's magazines from high society to homemaking, fostered the private and everyday lives of women, men and children (Figure 1).

At the same time progressive and feminist publications in the vein of *Time and Tide* validated women's point of view and provided venues for publishing fiction; both E.M. Delafield and Young experimented with the domestic genre in the pages of *Time and Tide*. Furthermore, the multiplication of 'gentlemanly' publishing houses like Duckworth and Jonathan Cape, which catered to middlebrow readers, and the escalation of cheap paperbacks and reprints also facilitated the rise of the domestic novel.

The paperback revolution, highlighted by Allen Lane's 1935 revolutionary Penguin books, boosted the publication and distribution of women's novels. For example,

Introduction: 'And What About the Home?'

Figure 1   Suburban sprawl, *The Ideal Home,* July 1931, p. xxxix

4   *Domestic Modernism, the Interwar Novel, and E.H. Young*

one-third of the 'Fiction – orange covers' series in 'Penguin Book's Complete List of Publications to the End of 1938' were popular women novelists including Phyllis Bottome, Susan Ertz, Stella Gibbons, Ethel Mannin, E. Arnot Robertson, Vita Sackville-West, Beatrice Kean Seymour, Angela Thirkell, Sylvia Townsend Warner and E.H. Young (*William*). Although the English pastoral continued to play an important part in fiction and poetry (Mary Webb, Sheila Kaye-Smith, Viola Meynell, E. Arnot Robertson, Dodie Smith), modernity, the metropolis and the home, whether bucolic or urban, replaced the pastoral idyll as a site for the emerging feminine self. As many women architects were guided toward the design of houses and contributed to develop 'a tradition of modernist "social" architecture, with holiday camps and nurseries' (Wilson: 93), so women novelists in the interwar years became increasingly preoccupied with what Nicola Humble has called 'imagining the home' (109–148).

The experience of the First World War, the resultant trauma of instability and desire for recuperation, which coexisted with the resistance to a 'return to normality', both enhanced the idea and meaning of home for returning soldiers and the home front and accentuated that crisis of gender relations which had been brewing for decades. Laurence Storm, Storm Jameson's persona in *Three Kingdoms* (1926), responds to her husband's claim that 'as the world gets more settled, less women will need to work, and one by one they'll fall back thankfully on some man. It's their instinct' (181), by retorting: 'You're wrong ... More and more girl children are being born like me, with an instinct for freedom and to get out ... You talk about our apathy and forget the tradition behind us. Back of men are memories of the outside of the cave. Back of women are only memories of the inside. We're out. We're out now. You'll never push us back' (181).

Not for lack of attempts, though. A 'return to the home' was energetically promoted through the commercial sphere in advertisements, newspapers and women's magazines. These magazines (*Good Housekeeping*, 1922; *Modern Woman*, 1925; *Everywoman's*, 1934; *Woman and Home*, 1926; *My Home*, 1928; *Modern Home*, 1928; *Woman's Journal*, 1927) competed for middle and lower-middle-class women consumers and were 'dedicated ... to upholding the traditional sphere of feminine interests and ... recommending a purely domestic role for women' (White: 100).[8] Featuring articles and advertisements on homemaking, interior decoration and 'labour-saving' devices, they were informed by the same ideology that supported the government-sponsored post-war programme of social reconstruction. Advertising discourses 'turned unpaid labourers into technologically sophisticated craft-workers with special competencies and skills' and gave women's role in the domestic sphere 'a new lease of life' (Macdonald: 51) (Figure 2).

In response to this trend, *The Lady* and *The Queen* shifted their emphasis from society women to the middle class. Events like the 'Ideal Home Exhibitions' and programmes like the BBC's 'Woman's Hour' also glorified the idea of home and women's domestic sphere (Trodd: 5; Humble: 108–118; Chapman and Hockey: 1–13). With the marriage bar, married women had to leave professions like teaching; symptomatically, *The Lady* cut its employment features and substituted homemaking

Introduction: 'And What About the Home?' 5

Figure 2　　Labour-saving devices, *The Ideal Home*, January 1924, p. xxxiii

6 *Domestic Modernism, the Interwar Novel, and E.H. Young*

articles (White: 100). On the other hand, the fact that Young, Woolf, Margaret Kennedy, Lettice Cooper, Vera Brittain, Storm Jameson, E.M. Delafield, Dorothy Whipple, Rose Macaulay and Mollie Panter-Downes wrote for *Good Housekeeping* seems to support John Carey's claim that popular journalism became 'a channel for awareness, independence and self-reliance among women'(referring to D.L. Le Mahieu: 8).

Resisting government propaganda and the facile glamorization of the housewife, domestic tasks and new household equipment, Storm Jameson and Vera Brittain forcefully denounced domesticity. While Brittain's denunciation of the 'stultifying persistence of an unadapted, anachronistic home life' (*Testament of a Generation* 1985: 140) was political, Jameson's was both political and profoundly personal. So, if in her fiction she advocated the freedom of working-class women 'from the pressure of modern villa drudgery' and dissected the conflict of domestic and marital obligations with the appeal of a professional life for a wife and mother (*Three Kingdoms*), in her autobiographical writing she repeatedly declared her 'pathological hatred of domestic life' (*Journey from the North* I, 1969: 88): 'The domestic routine of a house and a settled life wearies me to my death; I can't endure it. This is not something I reason about. ... It is a feeling, an instinct of my body itself, that makes me loathe and shrink from a house, possessions, a domestic life – all of which I have' (*No Time Like the Present* 1933: 116–17).

Other novelists, however, were engaged in thoughtful, often lyrical, sometimes witty representations and reclamations of the everyday that disturbed readers' assumptions about the tediousness of domesticity and the home. They deliberately overrode the attitude of one of the Mass-Observation (M-O) diarists, 'Miss French', writing as Young did in *Chatterton Square* about the Munich Crisis, that 'my home does not occur often in these M-O reports, partly because it is too private, partly because little has been said, the crisis in regard to the home being a subject we all find too deep for words' (Sheridan: 33). They articulated a kind of epistemology of the home in which their heroines interpret being in the world through domestic ritual and the language of the everyday. By writing about and through domestic ritual and the domestic sphere, and by their attentiveness to the mundane, these writers bestowed literary value on domesticity and domestic space.

While in 1909 Cicely Hamilton had noted with displeasure that even that most feminine of occupations, maternity, had always been treated by women 'in exactly the same spirit in which it is commonly handled by men ... from the superficial point of view of the outsider, the person who has no actual experience of the subject' (113), by the 1920s and 1930s domestic novelists had begun to view the world, family and the house from inside the domestic sphere through housework, housekeeping, cooking, cleaning, decorating and to create artistic order out of the disorder of living. They simultaneously privileged and critiqued the home and homemaking. At times they lamented their obligations, like Laura in Mollie Panter-Downes's *One Fine Day* (1947) who, at the sight of a young hiker, is reminded that men have the freedom of 'striding deliberately off, shaking the press of other people from them and climbing the lonely hill', while her own life is limited by 'a domestic chalk line, bound to the

Introduction: 'And What About the Home?' 7

tyranny of a house with its voices saying, Clean me, polish me, save me from the spider and the butterfly' (45). At other times, they suffered from unrealistic dreams fostered by women's magazines in the manner of Julia in F. Tennyson Jesse's *A Pin to See the Peepshow* who, trying to respond with affection to her boorish husband, feels 'terribly like a little wife out of *Home Chat*' (181). However, more often than feminists have been ready to acknowledge, early twentieth-century women novelists from Virginia Woolf to Mollie Panter-Downes drew upon the home and home culture, imbuing them with lyrical qualities.

Embedded within the interwar domestic novelists' interrogation and performance of home and its jarring resonance with Reverend Roper's boisterous and unflagging conviction above, are a series of interlocking questions: how does one configure and interpret the home in relation to nation, political ideologies, the everyday, domestic ritual, built dwellings and social relationships? How is the construction of self and subjectivity connected to one's domestic space? How does the English domestic novel incorporate and position different classes, gender roles and ethnic groups? What does it mean to belong? And by what means do we distinguish between the domestic interior and architectural metaphors as representational or analogical and the architectural and domestic as epistemological and ontological, as ways of thinking, knowing, being? Given the pervasiveness of houses in literature, when is the house emblematic in itself and when is it a structure that shapes human actions (Wall: 351 n.3)?

In order to address these questions, we demonstrate how amidst the interwar revitalization of the domestic novel genre and anxieties about gender, class, domesticity and modernity, Young epitomizes the fictional embodiment and inscription of home within a long, venerable literary tradition of symbiosis between architecture and literature and, more specifically, between house and novel. And it is this potent conjuncture of house, home and novel and its symbolization and encoding that direct our study.

Through our reading of E.H. Young and other British interwar women domestic novelists, we suggest ways of understanding how the meaning of home is located, textualized and interrogated. We also investigate the oscillation between modernity and tradition played out in the domestic novel's narrative techniques, which range from conventional nineteenth-century heterodiegetic realism to multiple focalization, experiments with time and non-linear narrative, poetic language and acerbic modern dialogue. Along with other scholars keen to tackle this issue, we respond to the challenge articulated by Nancy L. Paxton that 'if it is difficult today to know how to read some novels which fall outside modernism, it can also be difficult to write about many of them in a way that conveys their intrinsic value and innovativeness' (26).[9] By detailed attention to the novels of Young and her contemporaries, this study therefore seeks to contribute to the development of modes of reading that we hope will prove useful for interpreting the work of so-called 'middlebrow' writers and for demystifying the great divide between the middlebrow and high modernism.

Emily Hilda Young (1880–1949) was a woman and writer of many surprises. As a young married woman, Emily Hilda Daniell was familiarly known as Lily Daniell; at

8 *Domestic Modernism, the Interwar Novel, and E.H. Young*

30, publishing her first novel, she reverted to her maiden name, Young, and, in consort with other women writers of her generation – E. Arnot Robertson, F. Tennyson Jesse, F.M. Mayor, G.B. Stern – adopted gender-neutral initials.[10] Unlike her more celebrated and openly audacious contemporaries – Virginia Woolf, Katherine Mansfield, Jean Rhys, Djuna Barnes, Sylvia Townsend Warner – Young concealed, rather than flaunted, her defiance of conventional morality and traditional roles for women.[11]

Behind the façade of net curtains and middle-class respectability lurked a woman with a raw, passionate imagination who took pleasure in the imaginative lie; a determined woman who hid her skirt behind a rock, donned a pair of men's breeches and went mountain climbing in Wales, 'mapping out many new trails hitherto accessible only to skilled men rock climbers' (Kunitz and Haycraft: 1564).[12] Widowed in 1917 when her husband, Arthur John Daniell, was killed at Ypres, Young (as we shall now call her) then lived for 22 years in a carefully camouflaged *ménage à trois* with a school headmaster, Ralph Henderson, and his wife Beatrice.

Young's writings perform a similar kind of concealment for, within a realist and heterodiegetic narrative mode, she embedded unorthodox social and sexual ideas and forays into irony, multiple narration, deferral and delay. Her oblique references to sexual transgressions respond to candid post-World War I discourses about sexuality. They resemble Rosamond Lehmann's sexual frankness about premarital sex and lesbianism in *Dusty Answer* (1927), E. Arnot Robertson's expression of female sexual desire (*Cullum* 1928) and depictions of unwanted pregnancies, infanticide, adultery (*Ordinary Families* 1933), or F. Tennyson Jesse's and E.M. Delafield's disclosure of adultery and homicide in *A Pin to See the Peepshow* (1934) and *Messalina of the Suburbs* (1923) – two fictional renditions of the Thompson and Bywaters murder case.[13]

We agree with Bridget Fowler's suggestion that women writers (like Young) who had 'trouble with patriarchy' in the form of love affairs, unhappy marriages, or lesbian attachments possessed an 'understanding of the family ... at odds with the contemporary nostalgia for the patriarchal past'. Such 'personal dislocations' (147) led them to explore alternative domesticities and to express them in the form of independent living or celibacy or the renunciation of domestic comfort. In E.M. Delafield's serialized *Diary of a Provincial Lady* (1930), the narrator finds a respite from family life in the country by setting up her own flat in London; in Stevie Smith's *Novel on Yellow Paper*, Pompey Camilus rooms with her beloved aunt, the 'Lion from Hull' in the suburb of Bottle Green; in Winifred Holtby's *The Crowded Street* (1924), Muriel Hammond escapes the stifling atmosphere of her native village to set up house with Delia Vaughan in London. For Young, such refashioning is effected from within the traditional home. As we shall see, she recasts relationships between mothers and daughters and between women by privileging the homosocial companionship of sisters and female friends in alternative models of home over normalized heterosexual marital or amorous relations.

In her first novel, *A Corn of Wheat* (1910), Young began to explore alternate configurations of home and family and household relationships, exposing the

Introduction: 'And What About the Home?' 9

unheimlich, morally hypocritical and personally stultifying in conventional households and families. Rebellious heroines, wild landscapes and Wordsworthian longings mingle uneasily with depictions of lower-middle-class aspirations. In the later novels, as aware as the heroine of her eponymous novel *Celia* (1937) of the futility of nostalgia for her Victorian past, she abandoned the mystical yearnings for a rural England in order to represent bourgeois home life through an idiosyncratic gaze. This was her method of making it new – of questioning the old.

To position Young's novels and commend their pleasurable qualities, we document the history of the publication and reception of her novels as a paradigm case of the situation of women writers and canon formation during the interwar years. This history is an exemplary model of the dramatic changes in the publishing industry in the early twentieth century as it moved into mass marketing and aggressive advertising. Young, along with Ivy Compton-Burnett, Elizabeth Bowen, Rosamond Lehmann and E.M. Delafield, challenges us to reassess the genre and literary status of the domestic novel and facile assumptions about popular and middlebrow fiction, canon formation, aesthetic value and modernity. Although male novelists participated in and contributed to the domestic novel genre (Arnold Bennett, *The Old Wives' Tale* 1909; E.M. Forster, *Howards End* 1910; Denis Mackail, *Greenery Street* 1925; Henry Green, *Loving* 1945; Norman Denny, *Sweet Confusion* 1947), our emphasis is on fiction by women writers. While we include canonical women writers extending from Katherine Mansfield and Virginia Woolf to Elizabeth Bowen, Ivy Compton-Burnett and May Sinclair, we also discuss a number of lesser-known writers – E.M. Delafield, Stella Gibbons, F.M. Mayor, E. Arnot Robertson, Lettice Cooper, Dorothy Whipple, Rose Macaulay, G.C. Pain and Storm Jameson. Many of these latter writers, popular in their day, have played a crucial role in scrutinizing and validating the home and the everyday in the novel and deserve scholarly inquiry. In drawing attention to the quality of these figures, we follow the recovery of many excellent works by Virago Press and Persephone Books.

Our work builds upon other feminist critics who have revisited and revived underestimated or neglected women writers of the twentieth century from the landmark studies of Nicola Beauman, *A Very Great Profession* (1983) and Alison Light, *Forever England: Femininity, Literature, and Conservatism Between the Wars* (1991) to Nicola Humble, *The Feminine Middlebrow Novel: 1920s to 1950s* (2001).[14] These works have been invaluable in denouncing the shortcomings and myopia of modernist criteria of literary valuation and in providing much-needed contextualization for the reading of writers excluded from the canon. For, as Pulitzer Prize winner Carol Shields observed in 2003, realism has 'trafficked too freely in moments of crisis, searched too diligently for large themes ... passed too quickly through the territory of the quotidian and dismissed ... those currents of sensation that leak around the boundaries of vocabulary' ('Narrative Hunger': 34). Because of this anti-domestic bias, a good part of the world has fallen 'through the narrative sieve' (20) and much 'narrative lint ... is lost to our memory and to the narrative record' (31). Yet the tired negative equation of women writers, domesticity and triviality emerged recently on the front page of *The Guardian*

10   *Domestic Modernism, the Interwar Novel, and E.H. Young*

with the header, 'Women writers: dull, depressed and domestic' in an article quoting the introduction of *13*, a new collection of prose and poems edited by Toby Litt and Ali Smith. This instigated a spirited debate about (and defence of) domesticity (23 March 2005:1). Kirsty Gunn responded that on the contrary, 'despite the burgeoning interesting in houses, gardens and cooking on television ... in literature it seems we continue to gloss over the significance of the home ... The English novel is all about staying at home, or not ...' (*The Guardian* 26 March 2005: G2 36).

To address the significance of house and home to literature in general, and to the English domestic novel in particular, we adopt a multidisciplinary approach to the concept and construction of domestic space. Drawing on studies from anthropology, cultural studies, art history, architectural history, history, cultural geography, feminism, philosophy and literary theory, we postulate the relevance of the idea of home and belonging to the domestic novel. In our inquiry into ideas of home, the everyday and domestic space, we avail ourselves of the findings of Gaston Bachelard, Henri Lefebvre, Michel de Certeau, Georg Simmel, Pierre Bourdieu, Maurice Blanchot and Jean Baudrillard, several of whom were developing their theories of space at the time when feminist scholars and writers were strongly critiquing the home, domestic work and the private sphere. Following the lead of Simone de Beauvoir's utterly negative valuation of household work in *The Second Sex* (1949), earlier feminist criticism was so busy 'rescuing' women from the alleged degradation of domesticity that it has connived in the trivialization of women's everyday experience. We agree with Myra Macdonald that an unintended and paradoxical byproduct of feminist critiques has been that of further lowering the status of the domestic sphere, thus uniting feminism and dominant ideology (2004: 59).

During second-wave feminism, voices proclaiming the pleasures of domesticity have been few and far apart, the prevalent view being that housework has sustained women's oppression; 'female creativity in domestic management continues to be seen as tainted by the pejorative connotations of the private sphere itself' (Macdonald: 60). Only recently have feminist scholars such as Maroula Joannou, Iris Marion Young, Rita Felski, Alison Light, Inga Bryden and Janet Floyd, Lesley Johnson and Judy Giles begun to challenge 'the wholesale rejection of an ideal of home for feminism'.[15] Thus, in *Ladies, Please Don't Smash These Windows*, Joannou has joined the efforts of socialist feminists 'to redress the neglect within the Marxist tradition of the personal, the domestic and the sexual' (3–4); Iris Marion Young has called attention to 'the creatively human aspects of women's traditional household work' and argued for an approach that 'reconsider[s] the idea of home, and its relation to a person's sense of identity' (148); Rita Felski has questioned the banishing of the domestic sphere 'outside the dynamic of history and change' (1999–2000: 19); while Alison Light has invited feminism to complement the 'historical scrutiny [of] woman's place in the home' with an effort 'to discover about the place of home in the woman' (219). In a similar vein, Lesley Johnson refutes second-wave feminism's format of the 'home-and-away story of the modern subject' in which the independent modern woman rejects the suburban idea of home in favour of urbanism and rootlessness (452), and Judy Giles argues

Introduction: 'And What About the Home?'   11

against gendered dichotomies that link woman with home, stasis, the everyday, the private, the traditional and dependency (2004: 141). Our intention, therefore, is to integrate earlier male perspectives of domestic spaces and the everyday with more contemporary feminist rethinkings of domesticity and home.[16]

Writing during the modernist movement, many domestic novelists have been labelled as conservative, old-fashioned, or provincial. Noting their turn to the stuff of common life advocated by modernists, we follow the tug between modernity and tradition in the writers themselves and in the reception of their work. Both in technique and subject matter, domestic novelists negotiated the antipathy of certain modernists to the drearily domestic, as exemplified in Le Corbusier's disparagement of the 'cult of the house', with the celebration of domestic decoration and objects by the Bloomsbury artists of the Omega Workshops (1913–19) and the post-war cult of domesticity.[17]

Neither scornful of domesticity nor uncritically celebratory, interwar fiction is both responsive to the imaginative possibilities offered by the domestic and subtly critical of it. As Heather Ingman notes: 'Inter-war novels even by conservative women tend to demolish the unrealistic and sentimental picture of the housewife's life promoted by the media and advertising and thus make possible a feminist critique' (12). In *Diary of a Provincial Lady* (1930), E.M. Delafield satirizes the harried domestic life of an upper middle-class woman who, like her author, writes herself out of domesticity, while Virginia Woolf in *Mrs. Dalloway* and *To the Lighthouse* and Enid Bagnold in *The Squire* compose lyrical elegies to mothers and wives. In contrast, Lettice Cooper's *The New House* (1936), Elizabeth Bowen's short story by the same title (1923), as well as her novel *The House in Paris* (1935), May Sinclair's *The Life and Death of Harriett Frean* (1922), Radclyffe Hall's *The Unlit Lamp* (1924), Woolf's 'Phyllis and Rosamond', and Young's short story, 'The Sacrifice',[18] dissect the sad lives of women who sacrifice their own desires and suitors in order to fulfill the role of dutiful daughter and keep house for their parents. In Bowen's story, Cecily escapes from her 'new house' and caretaking for her brother to become 'another man's possession' (58), while Rhoda Powell, the heroine of Lettice Cooper's novel, finally breaks from her selfish and manipulative mother to move to London, a bedsit and a job. But the London bedsit is, as Rhoda recognizes, an ambivalent space potentially shadowed by loneliness, discomfort and poverty. Moreover, how private is a bedsit with shared bathrooms and interfering landladies? As North complains to his cousin Sara who, like all the main characters in Woolf's 1937 *The Years*, comes from an 'ordinary', large family living in a large house in London (137): '"Why d'you always choose slums –" he was beginning, for children were screaming in the street below, when the door opened and a girl came in carrying a bunch of knives and forks. The regular lodging-house skivvy ...' (253). The answer to North's question is, of course, the desire of the daughters of the house to cast off their role as angels of the house and revolt against the oppressiveness and totality of those large upper-middle-class houses and families firmly under the patriarchal thumb.[19]

Although wary of labels, because some of the writers we study have been

12   *Domestic Modernism, the Interwar Novel, and E.H. Young*

designated as popular, others highbrow, most middlebrow, we enter into the fray of interwar and current discussions surrounding 'middlebrow' and applaud rather than criticize its elasticity. Having ourselves drawn so much pleasure from reading Young and her contemporaries, we want to introduce the domestic novel genre to a wider audience and to demonstrate that the production of women's artistic texts exists *and* existed in excess in the interwar period, although in a 'hidden and unconsecrated manner' (Fowler: 157). Rather than dooming Young's texts, along with many other domestic novels, to be shelved under 'culturally significant' writing, we claim a literary status for them.

Virginia Woolf's oft-quoted comment that 'on or about December, 1910, human character changed' ('Character in Fiction' 1924: 421) has been interpreted as suggesting that it was time for the Edwardian novel to turn from what she considered to be the staid realism of Arnold Bennett and H.G. Wells towards the more impressionistic representation of subjectivity practiced by writers like herself, E.M. Forster, Katherine Mansfield, Dorothy Richardson, May Sinclair and James Joyce. As recent criticism has begun to note, however, Woolf's categorization of the Edwardians as stubborn survivors of a moribund tradition did more than provide a convenient marker for the birth of modernism; it fostered the false impression of a naiveté and a dated traditionalism which are readily disproved, for instance, by Bennett's interest in new experiments in music and painting (especially Cézanne) and his attentiveness to their influence on the novel, as evidenced in the articles he contributed to the *Academy* as well as in his journals and in works such as *Literary Taste* (1909) and *The Author's Craft* (1914). For though Bennett was no theorist, he not only had 'a deep artistic interest in form and treatment', but he also yearned to transcend the limits of the novel: 'there is a tremendous lot in fiction that no one has yet done ... the mood of the servant as, first thing in the morning, she goes placidly round the house opening the shutters! The fact is, the novelist seldom *penetrates*' (*The Journals* 1971: 146).[20] As we grow more sceptical about the exclusionary aesthetic standards of the modernists and become better equipped to appreciate the achievements of a writer who was able 'to take us inside ordinary, unremarkable houses and show us the ordinary, unremarkable people who live in them' (Lucas: 27), we realize how Woolf's condemnation contributed to obscure the achievement of writers like Young who, inspired by the Edwardians, negotiated their own modernity in ways other than those privileged by modernism.[21]

Our study situates a wide spectrum of authors and texts within interdisciplinary discourses about domestic space, and it is our intention that *Domestic Modernism, the Interwar Novel, and E.H. Young* add a new literary and humanistic note to the active interdisciplinary field of domestic space, the home and the everyday. By means of studied attention to the everyday and the domestic, customary relationships between background (the home as setting) and foreground (the adventures of heroes and heroines) in literary texts are reversed. The reader herself will be positioned by the narrative and in the domestic space since what feminist sociologists call 'standpoint' – the place from which we view the world – inevitably affects the reading of the

Introduction: 'And What About the Home?' 13

interiors of house and characters. It therefore becomes of interest to determine how and to what effect these foregrounded domestic objects and spaces facilitate such positioning through the use of windows, staircases, doorsteps, or a vase or dish that is held, passed along, or observed. In our reading of the interwar domestic novel, we discuss the figural aspect and effect of the house and domestic interiors and objects; we explore how the domestic operates as a narrative device to structure the story and to enter the inner consciousness of characters; and we propose an epistemology of the domestic, what Derrida described as the possibility of thought belonging to the architectural moment, to desire, to creation.[22] Thus, by paying attention to the place of home and domestic ritual within the interwar domestic novel and examining the relationship between domestic space and the space of the novel, we acquire not only a method to re-evaluate the domestic novel genre, but a hermeneutics for the novel.[23]

In Chapter one, 'The Interwar Domestic Novel and the Meaning of Home', we set out the parameters for discussing the meaning of home in the novel. Beginning with a definition and description of the domestic novel genre, we then outline the history and concepts of domestic space, house, home and the everyday through a cross-disciplinary approach and theorize the reciprocity of house and novel. Next, we investigate the positioning of the domestic within modernism, the debate between the turn to the domestic and the disdain for the home, and alternative arrangements and reconfigurations of the traditional heterosexual household as performed in the domestic novel. Chapter two, 'Home Lives, Still Lifes', homes in on Young's background and her evolving ideas and representations of home, the everyday and belonging within the interwar context and in relation to genre painting, French Post-Impressionism and the Omega Workshops. Chapter three, 'House Haunting', traces Young's shift from a romantic, transcendental aesthetic to the domain of the home marked by undertones of the uncanny. It follows her inflection of the rural novel with her interest in the figure of the New Woman and her emancipation from nostalgia for a rural past as championed by Mary Webb and Thomas Hardy. With the publication of *William* in 1925, Young became a popular writer; Chapter four, 'Private and Public Spheres: Publication and Reception' details the paradigmatic history of the reception and publication of her novels, locating it within the context of debates over middlebrow culture, the commercialization of culture and the predicament of 'non-canonical' yet serious women writers. Chapter five, 'The Turn to Domestic Modernism', examines Young's constructions of masculinity and the bourgeois and bohemian home in comparison with her contemporaries. Perusing the hybrid public/private domestic spaces of vicarage and lodging-house, Chapter six analyses married life and the longing for home in *Jenny Wren* and its sequel, *The Curate's Wife*, with references to the genre of the vicarage novel. In Chapter seven, 'Modern Heroines of the Everyday', we discuss Young's middle-aged heroines of the domestic everyday, of whom Celia, in the novel of the same name, stands as a model and whom we consider in relation to Jan Struther's Mrs. Miniver and E.M. Delafield's 'provincial lady'. The crisis of nationhood and the dissection of Englishness, the aftermath of World War I, the sexual, international and national politics of appeasement and the imminence of World War

14 *Domestic Modernism, the Interwar Novel, and E.H. Young*

II frame the discussion of Young's *Chatterton Square* (1947) and Woolf's *The Years* (1937) and *Between the Acts* (1941) in Chapter eight, 'England, My England'. We take the opportunity of the 'Conclusion' to signal the continuation of the trope of the house in the post-World War II novels, the Aga sagas of the late twentieth century and the rewriting of the domestic novel in contemporary fiction and film.

Notes

1   References to novels by E.H. Young in the text will be indicated by the title of the novel followed by the page number in parenthesis. Except for *A Corn of Wheat, Yonder* and *Moor Fires*, references will be to the Virago editions.

2   For a discussion of the English *beau ideal*, see Leonore Davidoff, Jean L'Esperance and Howard Newby, 'Landscape with Figures: Home and Community in English Society', (1976), pp. 139–75.

3   Until recently, the study of home culture and domestic space has been dominated by the social sciences (anthropology, geography, sociology and history). Developing interest in material culture and domestic space has produced exciting new journals such as *The Journal of Material Culture* and *Home Cultures*, cross-disciplinary studies varying from the architectural and psychoanalytic – Anthony Vidler's *Warped Space: Architecture and Anxiety in Modern Culture* (2000) – to the semiotics of everyday domestic objects – Sarah Pink's *Home Truths: Gender, Domestic Objects and Everyday Life* (2004) – as well as wide-ranging essay collections such as *A View from the Interior: Women and Design*, eds Judy Attfield and Pat Kirkham (1995); *Home Possessions: Material Culture Behind Closed Doors*, ed. Daniel Miller (2001) and *Espaces domestiques: construire, habiter, représenter*, eds Beatrice Collignon and Jean-François Staszak (2004). However, an increasing interest in the relationship between literature and domestic space is evident in recent conferences: 'Literature and the Domestic Interior', Centre for the Study of the Domestic Interior, Victoria and Albert Museum, 23 October 2004, 'Architectural Spaces and Literary Interiors', MLA, Philadelphia, December 2004; special issues of journals, 'Literature and Architecture', *Mosaic*, 35/4 (December 2002); 'Interiors', *English Studies in Canada*, forthcoming; and of books, Diana Fuss, *Four Rooms and the Writers That Shaped Them* (2004).

4   E.H. Young, *The Misses Mallett* (1985a), p. 22.

5   'Drama of the doorstep' is John Grierson's phrase to describe the daily lives of ordinary people. It was in fact the aim of the documentary film movement 'to bring the citizen's eye in from the ends of the earth to the story, his own story, of what was happening under his nose. From this came the insistence on the drama of the doorstep', *The Fortnightly Review*, August 1939, quoted in *Grierson on Documentary*, ed. Forsyth Hardy (1966), p. 18. Two relevant studies and a special issue of *Home Cultures*, 'The Domestic Interior in British Literature', have appeared as we were going to press:Victoria Rosner, *Modernism and the Architecture of Private Life*, Jennifer Poulos Nesbitt, *Narrative Settlements: Geographies of British Women's Fiction between the Wars*, and *Home Cultures*, November 2005.

6   In E.M. Forster's *Howards End*, Margaret Schlegel comments to her sister, Helen, 'there is a great outer life that you and I have never touched – a life in which telegrams and anger

Introduction: 'And What About the Home?' 15

count. Personal relations, that we think supreme, are not supreme there' (41).

[7] In *Desire and Domestic Fiction: A Political History of the Novel* (1987), Nancy Armstrong observes that 'domestic fiction ... emerged with the rise of the domestic women and established its hold over British culture through her dominance over all those objects and practices we associate with private life' (3).

[8] For a fuller list of women's magazines that appeared in the interwar years, see White, *Women's Magazines: 1693–1968* (1970), pp. 95–6; Appendix 1, pp. 312–15. See also Margaret Beetham, *A Magazine of Her Own: Domesticity and Desire in the Woman's Magazine, 1800–1914* (1996).

[9] Suzanne Raitt, *May Sinclair: A Modern Victorian* (2000); Nicola Humble, *The Feminine Middlebrow Novel: 1920s to 1950s* (2001); Maud Ellmann, *Elizabeth Bowen: The Shadow Across the Page* (2003); Wendy Pollard, *Rosamond Lehmann and Her Critics* (2004); Liesl M. Olson, 'Virginia Woolf's "Cotton Wool of Daily Life"', 2002–2003.

[10] In the 1920s, Young signed her letters concerning her writing 'E.H. Daniell', or 'Lily Daniell', or 'Mrs. E.H. Daniell'. In the 1930s, she tended to sign off as 'E.H. Young'.

[11] Young's fictional practice can be described by Alison Light's felicitous phrase 'conservative modernity' in *Forever England*: 'by exploring the writing of middle-class women at home in the period (a far from stable category in itself) we can go straight to the centre of a contradictory and determining tension in English social life in the period, which I have called a conservative modernity ... it could simultaneously look backwards and forwards; it could accommodate the past in the new forms of the present; it was a deferral of modernity and yet it also demanded a different sort of conservatism from that which had gone before. It is the women of an expanding middle class between the wars who were best able to represent Englishness in both its most modern and reactionary forms' (10–11).

[12] Young describes how she and her sister astonished people by wearing breeches instead of a skirt as they went climbing in Wales before the First World War ('Reminiscences': 25). We thank Maggie Lane for giving us a copy of this reminiscence by Young. In *Twentieth Century Authors: A Biographical Dictionary of Modern Literature*, eds Stanley J. Kunitz and Howard Haycraft (1942), the editors point out that 'writers were invited to write their own sketch', so it is probable that these are Young's own words (vi).

[13] For the historical context see Diana Wallace, *Sisters and Rivals in British Women's Fiction, 1914–1939* (2000), pp. 5–31 and Margaret Jackson, *The Real Facts of Life: Feminism and the Politics of Sexuality, 1850–1940* (1994). Wallace points out the combination of liberation and control for women advocated by Freud, Havelock Ellis and Marie Stopes.

[14] See also, for example, Jenny Hartley, *Millions Like Us: British Women's Fiction of the Second World War* (1997); Heather Ingman, *Women's Fiction Between the Wars: Mothers, Daughters, and Writing* (1998); Phyllis Lassner, *British Women Writers of World War II: Battlegrounds of Their Own* (1998); Anthea Trodd, *Women's Writing in English: Britain 1900–1945* (1998); Maroula Joannou, ed., *Women Writers of the 1930s* (1999); Clare Hanson, *Hysterical Fictions and the Woman's Novel in the Twentieth Century* (2000); Stella Deen, ed., *Challenging Modernism: New Readings in Literature and Culture* (2002a). Two rich contributions to the demystification of modernism are Andrzej Gasiorek, *Post-War British Fiction: Realism and After* (1995), and John Baxendale and Christopher Pawling, *Narrating the Thirties: A Decade in the Making: 1930 to the Present* (1996).

[15] Iris Marion Young, *Intersecting Voices: Dilemmas of Gender, Political Philosophy, and Policy* (1997), p. 136. The last decade's renewed interest in domesticity has not been

limited to the revival of domestic science as witnessed in Cheryl Mendelson's voluminous *Home Comforts: The Art and Science of Keeping House* (1999) or Nigella Lawson's *How to Be A Domestic Goddess: Baking and the Art of Comfort* (2000), but has also received the stamp of scholarly recognition, as evidenced in studies such as Garber's *Sex and Real Estate: Why We Love Houses* (2000).

[16] See Shirley Ardener, *Women and Space* (1993); Mary McLeod, 'Henri Lefebvre's Critique of Everyday Life: An Introduction' (1997); Laurie Langbauer, *Novels of Everyday Life: The Series in English Fiction, 1850–1930* (1999); Linda McDowell, *Gender, Identity, and Place: Understanding Feminist Geographies* (1999).

[17] For a spirited analysis of the process that led to the exclusion of 'the fanciful eclecticism' of the Bloomsbury artists in favour of a Corbusian anti-home, see Christopher Reed's *Bloomsbury Rooms* (2004), pp. 1–16.

[18] Original titles for *The Years* were 'Ordinary People' and 'Other People's Houses', suggesting the emphasis on the everyday and the domestic in this portrait of upper-middle-class life from late Victorian to 1937.

[19] Unknown publication, 11 August 1911. We thank Stella Deen for sending us a copy of this story.

[20] Storm Jameson showed her appreciation of Bennett's attempts to transcend the limits of the novel in her essay, *The Georgian Novel and Mr. Robinson* (1929), where she notes how while Dickens was no longer interested in a life when 'it ceased to be changeful' and became 'a mere chronicle of little happenings', 'for Bennett the drama lies actually in the domestic simplicity itself. He sees in the ordinary events of life, preparing of meals, making of beds, falling ill, an immense and staggering drama' (16).

[21] See, for instance, Lynne Hapgood and Nancy L. Paxton, eds, *Outside Modernism: In Pursuit of the English Novel, 1900–30* (2000); Andrzej Gasiorek, *Post-War British Fiction: Realism and After* (1995); Carola M. Kaplan and Anne B. Simpson, eds, *Seeing Double: Revisioning Edwardian and Modernist Literature* (1996); Lyn Pykett, *Engendering Fictions: The English Novel in the Early Twentieth Century* (1995).

[22] Jacques Derrida, 'Architecture Where the Desire May Live', in Leach, *Rethinking Architecture: A Reader in Cultural Theory* (1999), p. 319. See Mark Wigley's discussion of Derrida on architecture and his relation to Heidegger's concepts of dwelling, building, thinking, in *The Architecture of Deconstruction* (2002). Like Heidegger, the architectonic for Derrida is figural and rhetorical, but also interrogated and dismantled. The house and built forms are created, artificial forms rather than natural or ideal forms, and thus 'since Plato, the house has always been that tradition's exemplar of presentation ... the house is a presentation of an "idea"' (Wigley 2002: 103). The house, metaphor and presence therefore come into question when metaphysics itself is rendered problematic.

[23] For further discussion of the reciprocity of house/novel/body, psyche and house and objects and agency, see Chiara Briganti and Kathy Mezei, 'House Haunting: The Domestic Novel of the Inter-war Years' (2004), pp. 147–68.

Chapter 1

The Interwar Domestic Novel and the Meaning of Home

Must the novel be a house?

Bhabha: 446

Take the Carlyles, for instance. One hour spent in 5 Cheyne Row will tell us more about them and their lives than we can learn from all the biographies.
Woolf, 'Great Men's Houses', *The London Scene* (1975), p. 23

Defining the Domestic Novel

When one of Young's heroines reflects on the 'simple pleasure she found in the sight of familiar places and people' and 'did not tire of the daily round' because 'some little thing was always happening' (*Celia*: 105), she signals certain intrinsic features of the domestic novel: the everyday, the minute and the familiar. Although some domestic novelists resented the drudgery of domesticity, 'the unspeakable fireside, the gruesome dinnertable', others, like Young, found amusement and pleasure in the drab and the everyday.[1] Setting the model for the genre in other literatures in English, the English domestic novel portrays the social relations and daily life of a contained community (house, village, urban parish, suburb), while foregrounding values and rituals that 'comprise the modern notion of domesticity – separation from the workplace, privacy, comfort, focus on the family' (Reed 1996: 7). Its origins lie in the eighteenth century as economic changes created the leisured middle-class woman; a remarkable number of women novelists rose to prominence (Fanny Burney, Maria Edgeworth, Ann Radcliffe), whose novels featured middle-class heroines caught in the throes of convoluted courtship plots. Encouraged by the increased accessibility of books through subscription (and later in the nineteenth century through circulating libraries), women writers gradually abandoned this residual link to the romance and the picaresque to devise fictional worlds that mirrored the lives of their readers. Women became the subject and avid recipients of a fictional world that paid realistic attention to detail and the everyday. However, as the domestic novel evolved through Jane Austen, Elizabeth Gaskell (*Cranford*), Charlotte Yonge, the sensation novels of the 1860s, Anthony Trollope, Henry James and Edith Wharton, it registered an increasing sense of claustrophobia. By the early twentieth century, in domestic novelists inspired by the New Woman and the suffragette movement with its demand for equality in marriage as well as politics, the code of renunciation and submission that had characterized

18 *Domestic Modernism, the Interwar Novel, and E.H. Young*

the genre was under attack. Marriage became the subject of rather than the solution to the plot (Ida Leverson, *The Little Ottleys*; E.M. Forster, *Howards End*).

With its focus on the lives of women (especially housewives and spinsters) and primarily written by women, about women, for women, the interwar domestic novel encompassed social realism (Winifred Holtby, Storm Jameson), self-deprecatory humour and irony (E.M. Delafield, E.H. Young, Jan Struther), the monstrous (Ivy Compton-Burnett) and the rebellious (Elizabeth Bowen, Rosamond Lehmann). As a genre, the domestic novel runs the gamut from drawing-room comedy (Dodie Smith, Stella Gibbons),[2] golden age detective novel of manners (Agatha Christie, Ngaio Marsh, Dorothy Sayers),[3] lyrical exposé of life in the bourgeois home (May Sinclair, F.M. Mayor, Enid Bagnold) and popular saga (Angela Thirkell) to experimental high modernism (Virginia Woolf, Dorothy Richardson, Katherine Mansfield and Stevie Smith).[4] The meaning of home and representations of houses are obviously central to the domestic novel genre.[5] When theorizing dislocation in his essay, 'The World and the Home', Homi Bhabha queried 'must the novel be a house?'(446); his query surely presupposes its converse: must the house be a novel with its own narrative, characters and plot?

The following discussion tries to untangle this long-standing and intricate connection between house and novel and its implications for the domestic novel and modernism. For example, both novel and house are dwelling places and spaces whose deep structures demonstrate anatomical, psychological and descriptive equivalences and whose 'architecture' can be similarly read as Gothic, or modern, or postmodern. And so, just as the novel is itself a domestic space housing characters and plots in a time–space alliance,[6] domestic spaces exist as 'fictional constructs … stories the telling of which has the power to create the "we" who are engaged in telling them' (Bammer: ix). Within both these spaces dwell inhabitants – the ubiquitous family or household or kinship system that sustains and is sustained by the physical and spiritual structures of the space of houses and novels.[7] As Angelika Bammer suggests, home (and from our point of view, the novel) 'might be thought of as an enacted space within which we try and play out roles and relationships of both belonging and foreignness' (ix). Similar to novels, domestic spaces are texts that organize social relations (Dorothy Smith: 279), reveal and shape their inhabitants and can be 'read'. And in terms of a hermeneutics of literature and architecture, the interplay between these two art forms brings to the fore issues concerning representation, the sign and meaning; each art resorts to the other as a reservoir of metalanguage or metaphor. For example, houses are 'written', that is, drafted as plans and blueprints before materializing as built forms: 'tous les grands architectes … ont beaucoup écrit' (Hamon: 29).

As represented in the novel, home and house are associated with comfort, privacy, belonging and well being, whether present or absent, and most importantly with *control*; in Philippa Tristram's words, the novel is 'invincibly domestic' and 'functions like the house as a little world we think we can control' (268).[8] Authors, like homemakers, arrange and manipulate people, space and objects. Noting, along with Mary Douglas, that the home starts by bringing some space under control (289)

The Interwar Domestic Novel and the Meaning of Home   19

and organizes space over time (294), we observe how, in fiction and everyday life, the house itself is material evidence of the human endeavour to control nature and the physical environment. For many women writers and their characters, the domestic sphere thus offered a site for potential control over material objects, household duties, family members and servants.

In Lettice Cooper's *The New House* (1936), Evelyn, the sister-in-law of the protagonist, Rhoda, smugly reassures herself that 'this was her house, and she was the centre; she was hostess, mistress, mother, and wife ... here in the centre of her house, her child going to sleep behind her, the work that she directed going on behind the scenes, her husband depending on her, she could afford not to be afraid of anyone!' (219).[9] Domestic novelists were nevertheless well aware that, as Douglas contends, the home exerts tyrannous control over mind, body and speech since it is 'a tangle of conventions and totally incommensurable rights and duties' (302).[10] In the unspoken words of one of Young's heroines, the tie of family 'was too close and it was knotted with the conventions that had grown round it' (*Celia*: 86). So while daily rituals ensure continuity, laying down 'a new cobweb of threads ... on top of yesterday's pattern', Rhoda in *The New House* muses that everyday life had been not only her friend but her enemy, confounding life with existence: 'because its various demands had hidden her from herself, its manifold activities had made her think that she was living' (44, 184).

Defining Domestic Space, House and Home

Our understanding of domestic space takes into account the material, psychological, spiritual and social aspects of house and home and garden within the wider context of the everyday and of human relationships within and beyond the house. With its combination of the material, social and personal, domestic space resonates with Pierre Bourdieu's concept of *habitus* (fluctuating though it is) as a system of durable, transposable dispositions that generate and organize both practices and representations (1990: 53). However, like house and home, it remains an ambiguous and polyvalent concept. For domestic spaces may criss-cross and destabilize the already uncertain borders between inside and outside and between the private and public spheres to encompass non-traditional ideas of home such as scientific laboratories, prison cells, the family car, or the heterotopic or 'other' spaces of gardens, boarding schools and rest homes delineated by Foucault as constituting a counter-arrangement to society's hierarchies and institutions (Foucault 1997: 354).[11] As enacted in the interwar domestic novel, domestic spaces were generally secularized. And, although the Victorian angel of the house Virginia Woolf was so eager to kill off persevered in the figure of dutiful daughters and long-suffering wives trapped in the home, no longer was this ideal sanctified by writers of this period

While house and home are often used interchangeably, in order to facilitate discussion of the domestic novel, we distinguish between the *house*, a physical, built

20   *Domestic Modernism, the Interwar Novel, and E.H. Young*

dwelling for people in a fixed location and the *home* [12] which, whereas it may possess the material characteristics of a built dwelling, implies a space, a feeling, an idea, not necessarily located in a fixed place.[13] However, as David Benjamin cautions – and this cuts to the heart of our own experience of the narrating and imagining of home in the domestic novel – 'the home is a symbol, so that even though we recognize it, and "know it", it will always defy a rational deconstruction and complete explication of its meaning content' (3).

In her 1991 review of the literature on the meaning of home, Carole Després points to the necessity of contextualizing interpretations of the meaning of home, succinctly outlining different interpretations. Without, however, distinguishing between house and home, she discusses the conceptualization of home as a 'symbol of how people see themselves and how they want to be seen by others' (98) and as an indicator of status, which is 'decoded through the characteristics of the house', mostly its exterior, its accoutrements and its location (100). Meanings of home emerge from the process of controlling social interaction and 'acting upon one's environment' (98), from a sense of permanence and continuity which connects one's past and future (101), and from its quintessence as a 'place for privacy and independence' (98), a place to own, a place with both a material structure and aesthetic characteristics (99). These sociological factors are evidently played out in domestic novels.

The house is frequently presented as a symbol of the self – a representation much influenced by C.G. Jung and Sigmund Freud.[14] In his memoir, *Memories, Dreams, Reflections*, Jung recounts how his concept of the collective unconscious emerged from Freud's attempt to interpret his house dream:

> I was in a house I did not know, which had two stories. It was 'my house'. I found myself in the upper story, where there was a kind of salon furnished with fine old paintings ... Descending the stairs I reached the ground floo . There everything was much older ... Everywhere it was rather dark ... I came upon a heavy door, and opened it ... I discovered a stone stairway that led down into the cellar. Descending again, I found myself in a beautifully vaulted room which looked exceedingly ancient ... [Jung descends another stairway of narrow stone steps into a cave where he discovers two human skulls]. (158–9)

While Freud obsessed about the significance of the skulls Jung had discovered in the cellar of his dream house, insisting that they represented Jung's death wishes concerning his wife and mother-in-law, an increasingly irritated Jung decides instead that the house represents the psyche, his psyche. For example, the salon symbolizes consciousness, while the lower floors – and cellar – depict levels and layers of unconsciousness.[15]

Freud himself in his 'Introductory Lectures on Psychoanalysis'(1916–1917) describes a 'suite of rooms to explain the structure of the unconscious': 'Let us compare the system of the unconscious to a large entrance hall, in which the mental impulses jostle one another like separate individuals'. Continuing the metaphor, he explains that consciousness resides in the drawing room; a watchman who stands

The Interwar Domestic Novel and the Meaning of Home 21

on the threshold between the two rooms examines the mental impulses and refuses to admit them to the drawing room if they displease him (quoted in Rice: 277–8). It has subsequently become commonplace to interpret houses (in dreams, memories, literature and art) as settings for an emerging interior life (Rybczynski: 36) and as extensions of the psyche and body.

Not only does the house lodge, protect and shelter the human body from the outside elements and from other people, but it is often envisaged as a body. The visceral embodiment of the house prevalent in the Gothic and domestic novel reflects a tradition that perceives buildings in terms of an organic structure, its dimensions and scale modeled on the human body. This tradition originates with Vitruvius's prescription that 'as in the human body there is a harmonious quality of shapeliness ... so it is in completing works of architecture' (25) and that the temple should possess the same symmetry and proportion as a well-formed human body (37). In extending the idea of house and body to include the gendering and sexualizing of the house, Marjorie Garber suggests that the 'house has been simply and directly mapped onto the female body' (49), partly an extension of the cult of domesticity, partly a literal reading of women's sexuality as something enclosed and interior. House, body and mind are in continuous interaction; the physical structure, furniture, social rituals and mental images of the house at once enabling, moulding, informing and constraining the activities and ideas which unfold within its bounds (Carsten and Hugh-Jones: 2). Thus, in Rebecca West's *Harriet Hume* (1929), 'the dumpy windows of the "best bedroom" floor', the 'dining-room windows, broad and slightly protuberant, like the paunch of a moderate over-eater' of the houses in Kensington, are a suitable introduction to a 'fat papa', a 'fat mamma' (7, 8) and fat progeny and do much to conjure up a future of dismal self-complacency for Arnold and Harriet.[16] Straining the metaphor even further, Frank Lloyd Wright complains in his 1931 essay, 'The Cardboard House' that:

> Any house is a far too complicated, clumsy, fussy, mechanical counterfeit of the human body. Electric wiring for nervous system, plumbing for bowels, heating system and fireplaces for arteries and heart, and windows for eyes, nose, and lungs generally. The structure of the house, too, is a kind of cellular tissue stuck full of bones, complex now, as the confusion of bedlam and all beside. The whole interior is a kind of stomach that attempts to digest objects ... The whole life of the average house ... is a sort of indigestion. (51)[17]

Home, as Marx argued, provides the site for reproduction and thus for the production of future labour power; the house shelters parents and children and produces and stores the food that will nurture them, if they are economically viable. The house requires labour power to function, primarily the unpaid labour of women and children; moreover, during the 1920s and 1930s, the house and 'housekeeping' were guided by laws of efficienc , the assembly line and Taylorism, as well as by the imperative to consume the products of the assembly line – stoves, fridges, vacuum cleaners, washing machines – purportedly labour-saving devices.

22 *Domestic Modernism, the Interwar Novel, and E.H. Young*

In Stella Gibbons's *Bassett* (1934), the business partnership between a London working-class woman who is sacked from her job in a dress factory and a decayed gentlewoman in reduced circumstances provides an imaginative solution to the economic upheaval wrought in their lives by the war. By the end of the novel, the joint efforts of Miss Baker and Miss Padsoe have turned The Tower, Miss Padsoe's Edwardian country house, into a successful boarding house, saving Miss Baker from sharing the fate of workers, who are 'dropping reluctantly from their precarious hold on their unnecessary little jobs', and Miss Padsoe from being imprisoned in a relic which 'at once reflected and embalmed, like a mirror and a crystal in one, the happy thoughtlessness of an era gone for ever' (23). Despite its drop in status from an upper-class Edwardian country home to the precariously genteel boarding house, the transformed Tower ensures independence for the two women and enables them to assert a measure of control over their fate, environment and social interactions. Like so many literary houses, it stands as an effective marker of changing social and economic conditions.

Reciprocity of House and Novel

It is by now a commonplace (although a relatively unexamined commonplace) to draw attention to the affinity between house and book. Thus Gaston Bachelard speaks of writing a room or reading a house (14), while Pierre Bourdieu refers to the house as book in which is inscribed a vision and structure of society and the world (Carsten and Hugh-Jones: 2) and Philippe Hamon, whose *Expositions: Littérature et Architecture au XIXe Siècle* (1989) is a comprehensive comparison of the two arts, imagines the novel as a 'maison de papier' (31).[18] Homi Bhabha reminds us that 'the image of the house has always been used to talk about the expansive, mimetic nature of the novel' (446) and Frederic Jameson wonders whether built space (including rooms, corridors, doorways) is a form of language and investigates the renarrativization of domestic space and the family in modernity (261–2). Inga Bryden and Janet Floyd emphasize their interest in the 'representation of interiors *in* texts and also interiors *as* texts' ('Introduction': 9). In his discussion of the sentimental novel, a version of the domestic novel, Bakhtin too observes how the 'specific-temporal zone of Sentimental pathos [is] associated with the intimacy of one's own room' (397).[19]

Throughout literary history, writers and critics have described literature and the process of writing in architectural terms: 'literary architecture' (Walter Pater 1889), *A Room of One's Own* (Virginia Woolf 1929), *The House of Fiction* (Henry James 1934), *The Poetics of Space* (Gaston Bachelard 1957).[20] Several novelists and poets have also turned their hand to architecture and interior decoration: Edgar Allan Poe, 'The Philosophy of Furniture', 1840; Edith Wharton, *Decoration of Houses*, 1902; John Betjeman, *Ghastly Good Taste or, a depressing story of the rise and fall of English Architecture*, 1933; Elizabeth Bowen, *Bowen's Court*, 1942.[21] Thomas Hardy trained and practiced as an architect until he took up writing full time.

The Interwar Domestic Novel and the Meaning of Home   23

Undoubtedly, the abiding tradition of novels and tales named after houses from Jane Austen's *Mansfield Park* (1814) to Mark Z. Danielewski's *A House of Leaves* (2000),[22] in which houses are not merely context and setting for human interactions but the subject itself of the story, is indicative of this reciprocity of house and novel.[23] Although the habit of comparing architecture and literature can be traced back to Plato (Frank: 3), it was during the great age of the English house when not surprisingly house portraiture was a 'favored art form among the wealthy' (Garber: 39) that a recurring phenomenon – the symbolic relationship between house and novel – consolidated itself. The rise of the novel and the idea of the nuclear family home emerged simultaneously during the eighteenth century: the middle-class, moneyed, leisured household is indeed the stuff of fiction. When John Lukacs observes that 'domesticity, privacy, comfort, the concept of home and of the family ... are ... principal achievements of the Bourgeois age' (616), he could well be referring to the subject matter in novels by Jane Austen, Elizabeth Gaskell, or George Eliot as well as in the interwar domestic novel.

Although a novel's focus is normally on characters, these characters' habits, everyday life, conversations and inner life must nevertheless be set against or displayed within specific locales; therefore houses and rooms play a necessary part in creating the effect of realism. The comparatively recent notion of privacy, which emerged in the eighteenth century in Europe and North America, resonates in this new literary form that explores intimate private spaces of the mind and society often set within a middle-class and child-centred household and home.[24] Witold Rybczynski has suggested that the evolution of domestic comfort must be understood in the context of something new in human consciousness; 'the appearance of the internal world of the individual, of the self, and of the family' in which the house is appreciated as a 'setting for an emerging interior life' (35–6). From the late nineteenth century, this correspondence between domestic interior and psychological interior as well as between the individual home and the nation as home assumes increasing prominence in the visual and literary arts and in the rhetoric of nation and empire. As Rosemary Marangoly George contends in her study of the politics of home in postcolonial literatures, 'in the heyday of British imperialism ... England gets defined as "Home" in opposition to "Empire" which belongs to the English but which is not England ... "home" and "home-country" are used to articulate a whole range of political stances – radical, reactionary and revolutionary' (4–5). And Osbert Lancaster remarked in *Homes Sweet Homes,* his lighthearted history of the home in England on the eve of World War II, that while 'all over Europe the lights are going out, old lamps, gas-mantles, electroliers, olde Tudor lanthorns ... the history of the home provides the most intimate, and in some ways the most reliable, picture of the growth and development of European culture' (1939: 10).

People must, as Heidegger might say, dwell in order to be. Arguing for a link between dwelling, building, thinking and being, Heidegger views building not only 'as art or as technique of construction', but traces it back into 'that domain to which everything that *is* belongs', that is, a genuine connection with place, a home,

24 *Domestic Modernism, the Interwar Novel, and E.H. Young*

a dwelling. This dwelling is '"*the basic character*" of Being in keeping with which mortal characters exist' ('Building, Dwelling, Thinking': 100, 109). In '... Poetically Man Dwells ...', Heidegger connected dwelling and poetry, suggesting that poetry is a letting-dwell, a distinctive kind of building (111).[25]

Gaston Bachelard also probed this link between being and dwelling in his *Poetics of Space*, exploring how the image of the house appeared to 'become the topography of our intimate being' (xxxii). By associating houses with childhood, dreaming and memory, he emphasized the significance of dwelling-places in the evolution of a literary imagination – that atavistic desire of the imagination and consciousness to locate themselves in a particular space, find a home and yet also to articulate homelessness, longing for home, sickness for home (nostalgia). For Bachelard, secret rooms and secluded nooks and crannies shelter and protect the daydreamer and inspire her reveries, preparing the ground for poetry; the house is an 'embodiment of dreams' (6, 15).[26] Literally so for the protagonist of *A Day Off* (1933) by Storm Jameson, a writer who harboured a positive dislike of houses and hatred of domesticity, but nevertheless produced a poignant articulation of the longing for home. Her novella, the harrowing chronicle of one day in the life of a conspicuously nameless woman, opens on a lost dream. Staring at the ceiling of the dingy room that she has never had the heart to make into a home, she sees in its cracks the plan of a house, her childhood home, which attracts her with the force of a desire to return to a state of non-existence. At the end of a day punctuated by the effort to resist the assault of memories of her recent miserable defeats, the nameless protagonist finds a momentary respite from despair in a dream that is both a return to the past and to the maternal house:

> The sleeper had descended to her mother's house. At first she was aware only of the room, familiar, darkened by the yard. It was outside her, part of the dream. Then she was *in* the dream, so that she saw the room on another level, not as something remembered but as lived. During the time it took her mind to describe an arc not measured in space, she thought and saw as a child. The part of her that went on while she slept, was actually and only a child. (253, Jameson's italics)[27]

Less sympathetic than Bachelard to the bourgeois home and more steeped in the culture of cities, Walter Benjamin asserted in his reflectio s on the evolution of domestic privacy and consumption that the private citizen's living spaces were characterized by 'phantasmagorias of the interior', which were the result of the separation of living from work spaces in the late eighteenth century.[28] He described this private citizen's drawing room as 'a box in the world-theatre', in which he assembles the distant in time and space and thus suppresses the outer world of business, high capitalism and the public sphere (1973: 167–8). Hence, through his manipulation of space and accumulation of objects, the citizen unwittingly impresses his aspirations – nostalgia and psychology, as well as the influence and demands of the outer public world – upon his domestic interior.

The movement into the domestic interior evident in the modern domestic novel parallels the novel's concurrent preoccupation with the inner lives and relationships of

The Interwar Domestic Novel and the Meaning of Home 25

ordinary people. As 'the traditional figure of an interior divided from an exterior', the house 'is used to establish a general opposition between an inner world of presence and an outer world of representation' (Wigley 2002: 102). With its focus on domestic spaces and, in particular, domestic interiors and 'an inner world of presence', the early twentieth-century domestic novel proposed different ways of perceiving and reading subjectivity. By 1917, Virginia Woolf ('The Mark on the Wall') and Katherine Mansfield ('Bliss' 1918) were engaged in the radical practice of associating private domestic spaces and homemakers with the representation of inner consciousness and materializing the relatively recent concept of personal privacy in domestic life. To accomplish this, they fabricated innovative narrative techniques that drew the reader inside their characters' minds without recourse to an obtrusive and directive narrator.[29] And frequently the medium was the domestic, a 'view from the interior' (Attfield and Kirkham: 1989). In Mansfield s story, 'Bliss' (1918), we enter Bertha Young's modern London house and a modern relationship. As Bertha moves from the dining room up to the nursery, she interacts with various domestic objects – a mirror, a bowl of fruit – unwittingly revealing that which lies beneath the ordinary and the everyday, the unhomely in the home, the strange in the familiar.[30] To establish this atmosphere of uncertainty and ambiguity, Mansfield employs free indirect discourse as an oblique mode of revelation:

> When she had finished with them [tangerines, apples, grapes] and had made two pyramids of these bright round shapes, she stood away from the table to get the effect – and it really was most curious. For the dark table seemed to melt into the dusky light and the glass dish and the blue bowl to float in the air. This, of course in her present mood, was so incredibly beautiful ... She began to laugh.
> 'No, no I'm getting hysterical.' (175)

Through 'hysterical' language Bertha deludes herself about her sexuality, her modernity and her relationship with her husband and her new friend, Pearl who, it turns out, is having an affair with Bertha's husband. In *To the Lighthouse* (1927) at the end of a long day in the Ramsay summer house, the reader accompanies Mrs. Ramsay into the drawing room as she joins her husband and hence enters into an intimate conversation of unspoken words and looks:

> Then, knowing that he was watching her, instead of saying any thing she turned, holding her stocking, and looked at him. And as she looked at him she began to smile, for though she had not said a word, he knew...
> 'Yes, you were right. It's going to be wet to-morrow. You won't be able to go.' And she looked at him smiling. For she had triumphed again. She had not said it: yet he knew. (104)

Other domestic novelists, including Young, Ivy Compton-Burnett, Elizabeth Bowen, Lettice Cooper and Rebecca West, also foregrounded the domestic so that certain objects such as the black bowl decorated with a white naked nymph in *The*

26   *Domestic Modernism, the Interwar Novel, and E.H. Young*

Return of the Soldier (1918), the still life of fruit in 'Bliss', or the stocking in *To the Lighthouse* 'speak' in the place of human subjects. In Woolf's words: 'the mind is freed from the perpetual demand of the novelist that we shall feel with his characters. By cutting off the responses that are called out in actual life, the novelist frees us to take delight ... in things in themselves' (1958: 122).[31] For, as Jean Baudrillard notes, objects are a 'reflection of a whole view of the world according to which each being is a "vessel of inwardness" and relations between beings are transcendent correlations of substances' (317). The domestic sphere thus offered a discourse of interiority to the modern women in much the same way nature did for the Romantic poet or the inscribed, sexualized and racialized body does for many contemporary women writers. Through narrating the home and inventing a lexicon of domesticity, domestic novelists discovered a convenient and familiar medium for investigating self and subjectivity.

At the same time that we observe the prominence of the architectural in fiction, the importance of the home, the personality of the house and how writers place a 'building at the center of a book in order to provide the scaffolding of automatic organization' (Harbison: 74), we also notice how many writers refer to their work as a built form and their writing in architectural terms. Writer after writer reports that the novel or the story is not 'merely a fictional narrative containing representations of architecture within it; rather, it is itself fundamentally architectural' (Hegglund: 401). Among early twentieth-century writers, Arnold Bennett's journal entry on his drafting of *Anna of the Five Towns* (1912) is a case in point: 'The "first process" (imagine the building of a house on a hill) is to get the materials, pell-mell, intermixed, anyhow, to a certain height' (1971: 28). Explaining her radical 'method' in *Mrs. Dalloway*, Woolf too resorts to architectural metaphors: 'her [Woolf's] dissatisfaction was primarily with nature for giving an idea, without providing a house for it to live in... . [For the novelists of the preceding generation] the novel was the obvious lodging, but the novel it seemed was built on the wrong plan' (1928: vii). Maud Ellmann recounts that in a course on the short story given at Vassar in 1960, Bowen compared a story to a house: 'each "has a structure." And within the structures of her fiction, house after house rises up on her imaginary landscape, rampant as those housing-estates which Bowen, from her privileged vantage point, regarded as an eyesore on the British countryside'(2003: 8).

Home and Memory

From Wordsworth's *Tintern Abbey* to Daphne Du Maurier's *Rebecca*, innumerable poems and novels are spun from the memory of places. Often the house performs the function of spatializing time by representing the history of a family, community, or nation; the space within the walls of a house is not an empty space which holds objects, but a 'space saturated with a family's history' which is itself intertwined with a community or nation's history.[32] *Mansfield Park* is not only the site for testing Fanny

The Interwar Domestic Novel and the Meaning of Home 27

Price's moral values and a repository of memories and relationships of the comfortable Bertram family, but also an emblem of wealth accumulated through the slave trade in the West Indies. Describing Bowen's Court, an Anglo-Irish big house built in 1775 that she inherited in 1930, Elizabeth Bowen reflects that 'lives in these houses, for generations, have been lived at high pitch, only muted down by the weather, in psychological closeness to one another and under the strong rule of the family myth ... I know of no [Anglo-Irish] house in which, while the present seems to be there forever, the past is not pervadingly felt (1942: 19).

Even though in Young's lower- and middle-class world we encounter no ancestral homes, Rosamund in *Chatterton Square* rejoices in the thought that her children are the fourth generation to live in the house, for in its rooms and corners echoing with family memories and histories lies what Leonard Woolf called 'a quiet continuity of living' (1967: 15). Speaking about her memoir, *A House Unlocked* (2001), Penelope Lively has said how Golsoncott, the house in Somerset in which her family had lived since 1923, had seemed to her 'like a set of coded allusions to a complex sequence of social change': 'from each object there spun a shining thread of reference, if you knew how to follow it. I thought that I would see if the private life of the house could be made to bear witness to the public traumas of a century'.[33] In other words, house, garden and domestic interior in tandem mirror and generate dispositions of national and community social practices and ideologies (Bourdieu: 53), a case in point being the manifestation of Englishness in the interwar years through the home and domestic rituals as discussed later in Chapter eight.

Inevitably, the spaces of domesticity and of fiction shape the people who inhabit them; conversely, people and characters create and shape the spaces they inhabit. In structural and symbolic ways, houses and novels store and restore memories; 'by remembering "houses" and "rooms" [and stories, we might add], we learn to abide within ourselves' (Bachelard: xxxvii). Not only do these spatial constructs compose and record the past, they also set out a grid for present and future lives and understanding. Houses, rooms, domestic objects and spaces serve as common mnemonic devices for recalling the past, childhood, personal and communal histories. As noted earlier, the nameless speaker's dream of her maternal home in Jameson's *A Day Off* is the device by which she recalls and locates her childhood, temporarily escaping her depressing present.

Home and Away

The idea of home, as several feminist and postcolonial critics (Gillian Rose, Iris Marion Young, Biddy Martin, Chandra Talpade Mohanty, bell hooks, Rosemary Marangoly George, Caren Kaplan, Lesley Johnson) have pointed out, is a contested space of differences and inequities of gender, class, (dis)location and of the 'illusion of a coherent stable self' (I.M. Young: 158). In this light, it is interesting to observe E.H. Young's rejection of a conventional home and domestic space in her early

28   *Domestic Modernism, the Interwar Novel, and E.H. Young*

'New Woman' novels, *A Corn of Wheat* and *Yonder*, her exploration of alternative domesticities in the 1920s and early 1930s in *William* and *Jenny Wren*, and her subtle analysis and apparent acceptance and affirmation of the middle-class home and household in her later novels, *Celia* and *Chatterton Square*. For, as Iris Marion Young (and bell hooks) argue, it is important to recognize the power of home for many women; home 'expresses a bounded and secure identity … where a person can be "herself"… The longing for home is just this longing for a settled, safe, affirmative, and bounded identity' (I.M. Young: 157). But, for others, including Jean Rhys, Elizabeth Bowen, Katherine Mansfield, Storm Jameson and Dorothy Richardson, home is an absence; their heroines are nomads, living in the temporary, transient spaces of hotels, boarding houses, or as guests in other people's country houses. In her study, *Elizabeth Bowen*, Hermione Lee notes that after *The Last September* (1929), her novel about the Anglo-Irish big house during the Troubles, Bowen was preoccupied with:

> places for the dispossessed. Boarding houses, rented cottages, shut-up homes, empty villas, obscure shops one can never find again, parks at dusk … bombed houses … places where people have stopped living or are on their way to somewhere else … . They attract people who have lost their homes or their way … places for 'the disinherited'. (73)[34]

Dorothy Richardson's nomadic *Pilgrimage* begins with Miriam Henderson leaving the family home. The room she finds four years later has multiple symbolic valences: signifying Miriam's downward mobility as well as her progress toward self-development, 'the new room, "half dark shadow and half brilliant light" (II: 13) … becomes itself a metonymic image for the self … that it is a part of her quest to discover' (Radford: 50). For women like Miriam, the lure of the metropolis does seem to fulfil what Elizabeth Wilson describes as the urban sphere of women's emancipation from the everyday world of domestic life and homely existence in the suburbs (Johnson: 450).

    Such it was for Storm Jameson and for her persona Hervey Russell. In the 'Mirror in Darkness' trilogy: *Company Parade* (1934), *Love in Winter* (1935), *None Turn Back* (1936), we follow Hervey as she moves from a depressing suburb to a lodging house to rooms to a rented house. If in Jameson's first trilogy: *The Lovely Ship* (1927), *The Voyage Home* (1930), *A Richer Dust* (1931), houses represent only gestures toward an idea of home – as L.P. Hartley noted in his review of *The Voyage Home*, Jameson's sense of home, 'of something stable and abiding, is weak' (Hartley: 144) – in the 'Mirror in Darkness' home just about disappears. At the very beginning of this trilogy we are told that Hervey's room 'looked as though no one was living in it'; she is only too glad to leave its dreariness to gaze at the 'brightly-coloured web' that is London (*Company Parade*: 10), immersed in the energy and novelty of the crowd, revelling in anonymity. In *None Turn Back*, we are again reminded that 'Hervey made little mark on the places she lived in, as though she were always on the point of a journey, or had not been told she might stay' (11–12). Her few possessions – a child's cot, a few worn clothes, a baby's bath – reflect the narrower circle of her affections and her increasing engagement in the life of the city.

The Interwar Domestic Novel and the Meaning of Home   29

As with Richardson, in Jameson too, the figure of the house is extended to the city (Radford: 52). Resembling their authors, heroines in Bowen's, Rhys's, Jameson's, Richardson's and Mansfield's stories have gravitated to the metropolis, London, from the margins of the colonies – Dominica, New Zealand, Ireland, or the north of England. They suffer from modern urban psychological and physical dislocation; they are in transit, on the move, restless, a restlessness facilitated by the lure of travel, modern transport (cars, trains, steamships, planes), technology (telephones and telegrams) and the inauguration of passports.[35] In Bowen's 1932 novel, *To the North*, the two protagonists, sisters-in-law who share a house in London, are modern heroines always on the go; one, Emmeline, owns a travel agency whose motto is 'Move dangerously'; the other, Cecilia, 'never seems to be happy when she is not in a train – unless, of course, she is motoring' (1999: 15). As Hugh Haughton observes in his introduction: 'travel is paradoxically central to this study of the English at home' (vii).

But for those for whom being away from home or abroad were not matters of choice or leisure, home acquired a different meaning. During the war with soldiers mired in the mud and stench of French battlefields and, between the wars, with so many British citizens serving in administrative or military posts overseas, often leaving children behind with relatives or in boarding schools, England, as represented by the English home and domestic rituals, assumed a powerful symbolic resonance that was often a vital aspect of the domestic novel. As Bryden and Floyd note: 'when colonized space is constructed as marginal, domestic space is thus accorded a position at the centre' (5). Indeed, in his discussion of Bill Brandt's photographs of English life between the wars, which range from a Welsh miner's family and home to the upstairs/downstairs world of the big house, Paul Delany quips that 'England is imagined the biggest house of all' (2004: 16). The dream of this home was fortified by the commercial and industrial investment in housekeeping, decoration and shopping through women's magazines and advertising, repeatedly celebrating Sir Edward Coke's famed observation that a 'man's house is his castle – for where shall a man be safe if it be not in his own house?' There are ironies abounding in this 'imagined home' in that the material comfort of the bourgeois home in England derived to a large extent from exploitation of the working class and of the colonies.

However, strangely enough, the domestic novels of the period rarely refer to family members or friends serving abroad or incorporate issues of migration and foreign domestic spaces into their surprisingly insular portraits of home. Exceptions to the general insularity of the domestic novel are the golden age detective novels that often exhibit old India hands, retired army officers, or prodigals returning from the 'colonies', interwar domestic novels that feature returning shell-shocked or disfigured soldiers (Septimus Smith in Woolf's *Mrs. Dalloway*, Richard in *Celia*, Piers in *Chatterton Square*), or domestic novels set during the war. In Stella Gibbons's unjustly neglected *The Bachelor* (1944), Kenneth Fielding, the bachelor of the title, his sister Constance and their cousin Betty have just been relieved of the inconvenient presence of a billeted family when their placid domestic arrangements are more dramatically disrupted by the arrival of Vartouhi Ammanatta, a young refugee from the imaginary

30 *Domestic Modernism, the Interwar Novel, and E.H. Young*

occupied Balkan nation of Bairamia. The clash between Constance's complacent propriety and Vartouhi's flamboyant personality is captured in Constance's reaction to Vartouhi's gift of a bedspread to Kenneth:

> It was a bedspread, truly, but what a bedspread! It blazed with brilliant yellow, blue, crimson, green, black, and white; it was stiff with massy open flowers and pink silky buds coiling away among their brown leaves in a deep border around its edge ... there was something in the opulent colours and strange bold, easy design of Vartouhi's work that struck at [Constance's] deepest convictions. Propriety, common sense, prettiness – all were nullified by the gorgeous barbarity before her. She felt actually frightened. What idea was in the girl's head – flinging a thing like that across a man's bed? It was really disgusting! The foundations on which Sunglades stood were being attacked. (289–90)

'Small and dark' with 'a lined, ugly face, like a monkey', but with 'so much personality that it did not matter what he looked like', the mysterious foreigner Tori (Count Kristori Czepanskow-Ansdalt) is one of the odd assortment of people dislocated by the war who are billeted at Brede Manor, a large Georgian country house in Jocelyn Playfair's *A House in the Country,* also published in 1944 (7). Tori offers wise, if cryptic, advice to the heroine, Cressida, and is, of course, involved in a dangerous secret mission. In the one novel she wrote during the war, *Chatterton Square*, Young also invokes the alien and exotic by sending Rosamund's husband, Fergus, to France, from where he occasionally, melodramatically, emerges to disturb the tranquillity of the household.

Into the Everyday and the Drama of the Doorstep

> Whatever its other aspects, the everyday has this essential trait: it allows no hold. It escapes. (Maurice Blanchot: 14)

> The story of the modest little suburban housewife who happens to sit next to me in the railway carriage interests me more than famous people ... The little housewife's accounts of her sister's matrimonial difficulties or the story of her husband's losing his place in an office, are more real to me than the affairs of the political, literary, art, or social world. (Young quoted in Kunitz and Haycraft: 1565)

Although Woolf's flamboyant experiments have obscured her connection to more 'middlebrow' domestic novelists, Young's comment indicates a deep affinity with Woolf's project; in other words, this seems a rewording of Woolf's call to women to write about the Mrs. Browns in the corner of the railway carriage (Snaith: 51). And although overshadowed by the canonization of the high modernists, the domestic novel of the interwar years was well attuned to the exigencies of modernity, in particular, to its reclamation of ordinary people, moments and objects. Uncannily, the very words that Freud used to describe the field of exploration of psychoanalysis aptly fit

The Interwar Domestic Novel and the Meaning of Home 31

the concerns of the domestic novel: 'the material for [psychoanalytic] observations is usually provided by the inconsiderable events which have been put aside by the other sciences as being too unimportant – the dregs, one might say, of the world of phenomena' (1973: 52), or to use Pulitzer Prize winner Carol Shields's words, 'the mucilage of daily life that cements our genuine moments of being ... accumulating at the side of the story but not claiming any importance for itself' (*Unless* 2002: 41). Appropriately, therefore, Henri Lefebvre begins his study of everyday life, *Everyday Life in the Modern World* (1971), with a literary example: James Joyce's *Ulysses*. Focusing on the significance of a particular *day* – 16 June in the early twentieth century – to the lives of the Blooms and Stephen Dedalus, Lefebvre underlines how this day was 'narrated in every detail to become ... a symbol of "universal everyday life", a life elusive in its finitude and its infinity and one that reflects the spirit of the age ... as Joyce's narrative rescues, one after the other, each facet of the quotidian from anonymity' (2).

Appealing to a wider reading public in serialized essays, E.M. Delafield and Jan Struther adopted the diary form to reproduce the immediacy of daily life, redefine the heroic, and reconsider the validation of public over private space. With their focus on recording the everyday, their projects were curiously in tune with the Mass-Observation (M-O) Project, begun in 1937 by Tom Harrisson, Humphrey Jennings and Charles Madge, in which the personal diaries of ordinary people played a crucial role in the observation of everyday life. Responding to M-O's appeal for recording their everyday, over 300 people volunteered to keep full diaries during the war; in answering a 1937 questionnaire about their reasons for joining M-O, several women commented on the importance of this task and of observing from the inside: 'Miss Atkinson' wrote that 'the studies of daily lives with every little detail should be very interesting to posterity', while 'Miss Chapman' felt that 'it was something new, something to talk about ... it makes [things I do in the house] important when they have to be remembered and recorded ... It also widens my horizon. I had never really wondered what people had on their mantelpieces' (Sheridan: 18–19).[36]

We argue that domestic novelists so often accused of harbouring reactionary feelings of nostalgia for a more stable society were, on the contrary, joining efforts with modern phenomena such as M-O and the Documentary Film Movement in the 1930s, and the aesthetics advocated by James Joyce and Georg Simmel in rendering vivid the everyday – the drama of the doorstep – 'without its everydayness being remaindered in the process' (Highmore 2002a: 39), that is, without salvaging only what is unique in the everyday. Like the M-O project and the Documentary Film Movement, interwar domestic novelists faced the challenge of finding forms to rescue moments that have been often considered too transitory to catch the eye. This was no easy task; for, though as Henri Lefebvre famously pointed out, 'culture can no longer be conceived outside the everyday' (quoted in Langbauer: 19), 'the everyday is ... the most universal and the most unique condition, the most social and the most individuated, the most obvious and the best hidden' (Lefebvre 1997: 34).[37] This point is taken up by Alice Kaplan and Kristin Ross who contend that the political, like

32 *Domestic Modernism, the Interwar Novel, and E.H. Young*

Poe's purloined letter, is hidden in the everyday, exactly where it is most obvious: in the contradictions of lived experience, in the most banal and repetitive gestures of everyday life – the commute, the errand, the appointment (1987: 3). But then, as Liesl Olson queries, 'how can the ordinary be represented, in fiction, when by virtue of its representation it becomes more than just ordinary?' (52).

Related to this is the predicament of recreating or representing the everyday language of ordinary people who inhabit the domestic novel and of voice, perspective and dialogue. Young's heroines Celia and Miss Mole relish the tactic of ordinary small talk to expose the hypocrisies and pretensions of others in Michel de Certeau's sense of disrupting totalizing and disciplinary strategies through guerrilla tactics (37). On the other hand, as Henri Lefebvre and de Certeau have maintained, the everyday offers moments of possible transformation and resistance. And so, modernist novelists who are 'diametrically opposed both to novels presenting stereotyped protagonists and to the traditional novel recounting the story of a hero's progress' (Lefebvre 1971: 3) turn ordinary events into epiphanies (Joyce), moments of being (Woolf), or intimate 'deserts of vast eternity' by describing 'a boy eating strawberries or a woman combing her hair on a windy morning' (Mansfield 1954: 388). The special quality of the everyday may indeed be 'its lack of qualities. It might be, precisely, the unnoticed, the inconspicuous, the unobtrusive' (Highmore 2002a: 1).

Observing the powerful correspondence between the quotidian, the individual and 'unarticulated norms', James Duncan, following Lefebvre and de Certeau, notes how 'the everyday activity of individuals acting in collectivities produces and to a greater extent reproduces the social structure of the group' and how 'relations in a society can be said to be structured in that so much of everyday life is based on unselfconscious adherence to unarticulated norms' (39). The domestic novel exposes their unexamined acceptance; the witty debunking of 'unarticulated norms', a favourite subject of many domestic novelists, is one of the threads that joins many of Delafield s provincial lady's diary entries: 'Have very often wondered if Mothers are not rather A Mistake altogether and now definitely come to the conclusion that they *are*' (167). Extensions of the everyday, society life and customs are also subject to a new scrutiny, which often reveals their lack of intrinsic merit and exposes their absurdity. In E. Arnot Robertson's *Cullum*, Esther is puzzled by the tacit rules that determine permissible topics of conversation and by regulated domesticity. She shares her lover's distaste for life 'moored to a mutton chop': 'Half the people in the world are moored to a mutton chop… They waste so much time by putting off starting to do something, simply because there isn't time to finish it before the next meal-time!' (78). As we shall see in later chapters, the domestic novel employs ruses such as (not) tidying up or cleaning and narrative tactics of irony, free indirect discourse, interior monologue, or multilayered conversations to undermine the strategies of totality that control the heroines' lives.

The Battle of the Domestic and the Modern

While the everyday would seem to suggest versimilitude and the ordinary, thus placing the domestic novel within the tradition of realism (Langbauer: 2), the investment in the representation of the everyday by modernist writers committed to literary experimentation like Woolf and Mansfield, reminds us that the everyday and the domestic played a complicated role in the evolution of high modernism. As Rita Felski observed, 'the vocabulary of modernity is a vocabulary of anti-home' (48). Cyril Connolly's famous rejection of the literary representation of the domestic and the everyday summarized the view of many interwar intellectuals:

> We take the line that experiences connected with the blitz, the shopping queues, the home front, deserted wives, deceived husbands, broken homes, dull jobs, bad schools, group squabbles, are so much a picture of our ordinary lives that unless the workmanship is outstanding we are prejudiced against them. (*Horizon*, January 1944 quoted in Hartley: 8)

And, as Andreas Huyssen has pointed out, one of the principles of high modernist art has been precisely to avoid this 'contamination with mass culture and with the signifying systems of everyday life' in order to maintain its 'adversary stance' to the 'bourgeois culture of everyday life' and to mass culture, which, at the beginning of the twentieth century, was associated with the feminine and thus further devalued (1986b: 197).

But Felski and others have argued that women writers, by virtue of their link to domestic culture and the performance of everyday life and thus to the repetitive, the cyclical and the immediate, were attuned to the expression of the 'subjective sense of duration' and time that characterizes modernism and the avant-garde (Fowler: 142). Furthermore, as Christopher Reed notes, citing Foucault's 'points of resistance', 'the domestic, perpetually invoked in order to be denied, remains throughout the course of modernism a crucial site of anxiety and subversion' (1996: 16). This dynamic proves central to our reading of English interwar domestic novels and to our argument that, far from being inherently conservative, politically and technically this 'new style domestic novel' (Beddoe: 21) was essentially a discourse of opposition.

Christopher Reed calls this new consideration of the domestic, 'domestic modernism', seeing it as a movement which, opposing the primacy of science and technology as influences on modern design, projects 'the values of home life outward onto the public realm in both its aesthetic and socio-cultural initiatives' (2004: 4, 5).[38] In her article on Young's *William* (2003), Stella Deen speaks of 'domestic modernity', an expression Judy Giles also adopts in her *Parlour and the Suburb* to describe the 'ways in which women negotiated and understood experience and identities in terms of the complex changes that modernization provoked in the so-called private sphere'. Refuting the claims of feminists like Marilyn French that domesticity was unquestionably oppressive, Giles argues that women responded in diverse ways to 'improved housing, suburban domesticity, the demise of domestic service, and the

34 *Domestic Modernism, the Interwar Novel, and E.H. Young*

growth of domestic consumerism' (2004: 6).[39] Lefebvre's Marxist argument that the everyday is a powerful site of the transformation of society (1971: 194–206) helps debunk the myth that the domestic novelist's preoccupation with the everyday signifies her endorsement of the status quo.

In turning to a domestic modernism, many interwar women novelists quietly undid the gendered binary that assumed that the mass culture of serialized feuilleton novels, popular and family magazines, lending libraries and bestsellers and everyday bourgeois culture were 'pejoratively feminine', and that 'woman ... is positioned as reader of inferior literature – subjective, emotional and passive – while man ... emerges as a writer of genuine, authentic literature – objective, ironic, and in control of his aesthetic means' (Huyssen 1986b: 193, 189–90).[40] The trenchant irony of Young, Ivy Compton-Burnett, Stella Gibbons, E.M. Delafield and the innovative narrative techniques of Compton-Burnett, Sinclair, Woolf, Mansfield and Stevie Smith suggest writers in control of their aesthetic means, self-consciously remaining in the territory of the quotidian and committed to giving visibility to the everyday.

However, 'a problem for the critic ... is the sense that there is little to be said about a literary text unless it is expressed in terms of modernism' (Paxton: 26). Indeed, such novels require from the reader and from the critic consideration of 'alternative experimental techniques and forms that, in retrospect, appear to differ from those employed by high modernists' (4). Although most interwar domestic novelists were not interested in the decentred subject of the high modernists, they nevertheless evolved techniques to reflect their ambivalence and their investigation of domesticity, women's agency and subjectivity in relation to patriarchal constructions of the everyday. Like the surrealists or the high modernists, they responded to the shock of the new, but they resorted to muted narrative shocks and tactics to express their responses. Through clever focalization, free indirect discourse and dialogic exchange in the form of the unexpected glance, ironic speech act and narrative sleight of hand with which the gaze of the reader is deliberately redirected or even misdirected, practitioners of this genre disturb readers' assumptions about the domestic, the everyday and the home.[41]

While Young's often omniscient and didactic narrators seem to operate within nineteenth-century modes of realism, they also shift from consciousness to consciousness and playfully withhold information as a strategy of delay, deferral and surprise in the modernist manner.[42] In his role as literary executor, Ralph Henderson, reflecting on Young's novelistic technique, justly points out that 'the author does not tell us all she knows' ('*E.H. Young*, her Muse, her Method & her Message': 6). In the case of Young, as with Woolf and Mansfield, it is often through a character's interaction with or viewing of domestic objects that her consciousness is most successfully revealed. Similar to painters of still lifes, here too the emphasis is on different ways of looking at the same object. While the gaze and the look expose the inner life, oblique modes of eavesdropping and voyeurism – on stairs, at curtained windows, by half-shut doors – complicate the plot. When Young does take advantage of free indirect discourse rather than narrative summary to interpellate characters' habits of mind and language into the narrator's overarching discourse, her fiction becomes livelier and more immediate.

The Interwar Domestic Novel and the Meaning of Home   35

Her unique narrative style contributed to the 'multiplicity of realisms' championed, for instance, by Henry Green and Ivy Compton-Burnett that Andrzej Gasiorek sees as characterizing post-war British fiction (4–5, 13–19). And, although less explicitly than Dorothy Richardson, she was equally attentive to the problem of 'thinking the feminine' (Pykett: 77).

In the hands of some women writers, the domestic novel tended towards the popular and the formulaic, while in others it engaged in a dialogue with the form, often transforming it. The invocation of the everyday was a deliberate tactic, freeing writers and readers from the expectations and constraints of high culture (Langbauer: 15; Harris: 3). The domestic novel throws into question gender roles, sexuality and hierarchical, patriarchal positions in the household and village where everyone knows his or her place – what Bourdieu describes as differential positioning within specific patterns of privilege and legitimacy (Boys: 215). Thus, Compton-Burnett's 1935 novel *A House and Its Head* derives much of its tension and irony from quips on position and power: who is the head of the house? who takes what position at the dining table? who inherits the house, the name and the family fortune? and which wife or which daughter takes precedence in the house? Compton-Burnett's idiosyncratic, cryptic and nasty dialogues – and her novels are constructed almost entirely of direct discourse – enhance and underpin the atmosphere of strangeness and secrecy of her domestic spaces. As late as in her 1955 novel *Mother and Son*, where the narrative unravels a double tale of betrayal and illegitimacy and the home is exposed as a privileged site of secrecy, secrets, rather than blood or marriage, make a family. And so, having discovered that Julius is not Rosebery's father, Miss Wolsey rejoices in her new sense of belonging: 'I will keep [the secret]. I feel it is mine. I feel this makes me one of you' (156–7).

Although the domestic novel flourished between the two world wars, ostensibly reflecting a nostalgia or melancholy for village and domus in the face of the encroaching and alienating metropolis, and a threatening, unknown, exotic other from across the Channel or the far-flung reaches of a restless empire, the domus has a 'bucolic air only from outside, from afar, from the city' (Lyotard: 272). For, inside, we all too often tumble upon tragedy, violence and the uncanny. Compton-Burnett's novels of gentry life are brimming with infanticide, incest, matricide and child abuse; Agatha Christie, the doyenne of nostalgic Englishness, like many other golden age detective novelists whose stories are set in country houses or picturesque, cosy villages, exposes one dysfunctional family after another in her 1930 *The Murder in the Vicarage*; Young's novels depict alcoholic fathers, deceitful stepmothers, violent death and abusive marriages. Through the choice of unusual focalizers – a spinster, unwed mother, middle-aged wife, child, or servant, that is, a view from the margins – in the interwar domestic novel, the familiar household is perceived aslant and transformed into the unhomely. Rituals punctuating the life of house, village and parish mask secrets and deceptions while facilitating their occurrence; certain dedicated spaces (vicarage, manor house, pub, library, garden) constitute ideal venues for the masking and unmasking of 'the little sanctities of a household' (Compton-Burnett 1955: 64).

36 *Domestic Modernism, the Interwar Novel, and E.H. Young*

As Mark Wigley observed, 'violence was concealed by the mask of the domestic, hidden by the very thing that made it possible' (114).

However, although like Woolf, Mansfield and Compton-Burnett, Young can be scathing in critiquing the oppressiveness of the house in the construction of feminine subjectivity, she also reminds us of the importance of discovering more about 'the place of home in the woman' (Light: 219).

Notes

[1] This is how Ida John, in a letter to Dorelia McNeill, referred to the domestic arrangements that must of necessity hamper Augustus's genius (quoted in Tickner, '"Augustus's Sister": Gwen John: Wholeness, Harmony and Radiance' (2004) p. 37).

[2] See Maggie Gale's discussion of women playwrights of the 1920s and 1930s (2000). Gale notes the generally conservative leaning of playwrights like Dodie Smith, Clemence Dane, G.B. Stern, F. Tennyson Jesse and Harold Harwood, but also describes how their domestic and realistic comedies were the 'perfect vehicle with which to place centre stage the issues [for example, work and marriage] directly effecting change in the lives of their female contemporaries' (23); she goes on to comment how their plays, like the domestic novel, investigated 'gender and power relationships within the family' and located 'the private sphere as having great *public* significance (33). Needless to say, domestic spaces – the library and the drawing room – provided the customary settings, reinforcing the significance of the home. The novels of Ivy Compton-Burnett with their staged settings of breakfast room, study, drawing room and stylized dialogue resemble domestic comedies; Stern, Tennyson Jesse and Smith wrote domestic novels as well.

[3] In his outline of the golden age detective story (1920s and 1930s), Stephen Knight notes the significant function of the house and the domestic:

> In social terms most examples on both sides of the Atlantic are set among the comfortable upper-middle-class (only rarely aristocratic) country settings ... Raymond Williams saw the classic murder as a modern evolution of the English country-house tradition, now in capitalist rather than landed gentry form ... [Agatha Christie's *The Mysterious Affair at Styles* (1920)] is largely solved because Poirot can understand why a set of paper spills on a mantelpiece have been disarranged ... Poirot ... represents a heightened version of female domestic knowledge as a weapon against fictional disorde . (87–91)

[4] In England, two publishing ventures have played an important part in rediscovering and reprinting women writers of the domestic genre, and thus have generated interest in and critical attention to this genre. Virago Press, begun in 1973 by Carmen Callil, Ursula Owen and Harriet Spicer, has over 200 titles in its 'Virago Modern Classics' series, including Young, E.M. Delafield, Rosamond Lehmann, Rose Macaulay, Enid Bagnold, Mollie Panter-Downes; Persephone Books (www.persephonebooks.co.uk) started by Nicola Beauman, has published over 54 'forgotten books' by women (and men) of the twentieth century, including Dorothy Whipple, Lettice Cooper, Julia Strachey, Betty Miller. Both publishers feature striking and distinctive book designs and introductions by well-known writers or critics.

[5] For a fuller definition of the domestic novel, see Chiara Briganti and Kathy Mezei,

The Interwar Domestic Novel and the Meaning of Home 37

'Domestic Novel' (1999b), p. 197.

[6] We thank Jean-François Staszak for directing us to this way of phrasing this concept (Colloque Espaces domestiques, Paris, September, 2002).

[7] See Signe Howell, 'The House as Analytic Concept: A Theoretical Overview' (2003), pp. 16–33.

[8] See John E. Crowley, *The Invention of Comfort: Sensibilities and Design in Early Modern Britain and Early America* (2000). Crowley describes how the concept of comfort came to have its 'modern emphasis on self-conscious satisfaction with the relationship between one's body and the immediate physical environment' (ix).

[9] One of the most scathing portraits of domestic manipulators is Leonora in Barbara Pym's *The Sweet Dove Died*, published in 1978 but written between 1963 and 1969. Metaphors of furniture arrangement and house decoration become increasingly emphatic as James reflects that his friend Leonora 'would arrange or adapt' Ned, his lover, 'just as she had arranged Phoebe. Not to speak of the way she had arranged James himself' (149).

[10] As useful and seminal as this article is, we note that Douglas does not distinguish between 'home' and 'household' and that some of her characterizations of home seem more applicable to 'household.'

[11] We note Roderick J. Lawrence's caveat that 'the concept of home is ambiguous, and therefore, it cannot be taken for granted. In particular, the common association between domestic space and home is contentious', although, unfortunately Lawrence does not here elaborate on this contentiousness. (1995: 53.)

[12] The *OED* states that 'home' is derived from the Old English 'hām' and the High German 'heim' and that the Old English and Middle English meaning is 'a village or town; a village with its cottages'; other meanings include ' a dwelling-place, house; abode; the fixed residence of a family or household;' 'a place, region, or state to which one properly belongs, in which one's affections centre, or where one finds rest, refuge, or satisfaction' (1548); 'one's own country, one's native land' (1595). 'Home' also means a reference to the grave (ME) and in games, 'the place where one is free from attack'. The word 'house' – from Old English and Old High German 'hüs' – has equally interesting and complex meanings. These include a 'building for human habitation, esp. a dwelling-place; the portion of a building occupied by one tenant or family; a place of worship; an inn, tavern' (1550); 'a religious house, a college in a university; a boarding-house attached to a public school' (1857); the 'building in which a legislative assembly meets; a place of business, a theatre; the persons living in one dwelling' (OE); 'a family, lineage, race'.

[13] Roderick J. Lawrence's elaboration is helpful in clarifying the slippery and sometimes contentious distinction between house and home:

> Housing evokes a range of images and concepts commonly related to the material and physical nature of one or more kinds of dwelling units … . the meaning of *housing* like the meaning of *home* varies from person to person between social groups and across cultures; houses are commonly attributed an economic value, an exchange value, an aesthetic value and a use value, whereas, in addition to these, a home is usually attributed a sentimental and symbolic value … . [these values] as well as domestic roles, routines and rituals … . are acquired, nurtured, transmitted, reinforced, or modified by interpersonal communication [as well as by individuals]. (1991: 92)

[14] The work of Gaston Bachelard, Clare Cooper Marcus, Bettina Knapp has been influenced by Jung, while that of Anthony Vidler reflects Freud s uncanny.

38   *Domestic Modernism, the Interwar Novel, and E.H. Young*

[15] See Clare Cooper Marcus's elaboration of this concept in *House as a Mirror of Self: Exploring the Deeper Meaning of Home* (1995).

[16] In George Eliot's *Middlemarch*, the young doctor Lydgate reflects on the French anatomist, Bichat in precisely these terms:

> That great Frenchman first carried out the concept that living bodies ... are not associations of organs which can be understand by studying them first apart, and then, as it were, federally; but must be regarded as consisting of certain primary webs or tissues, out of which the various organs-brain, heart, lungs, and so on-are compacted, as the various accommodations of a house are built up in various proportions of wood, iron, stone, brick, zinc, and the rest, each material having its peculiar composition and proportions .... (110)

[17] Parts of this quotation serve as the epigram to Mark Wigley's *Architecture of Deconstruction* (2002).

[18] *La maison de papier* is also the title of a novel by Françoise Mallet-Joris (1970).

[19] The private room, Bakhtin claims, is 'the zone of the letter, the diary. Public-square and private-room zones of contact and familiarity ... are very different, as different ... as are the palace and the private home, the temple and the more house-like Protestant church' (397). When he points out that it is not a matter of scale, but rather of a special organization of space, he recognizes the reciprocity between genre and material built form that characterizes the novel and, in particular, the domestic novel (397). See also Bettina Knapp, *Archetype, Architecture, and the Writer* (1986); Philippa Tristram, *Living Space in Fact and Fiction* (1989); Marilyn R. Chandler, *Dwelling in the Text: Houses in American Fiction* (1991); Sharon Marcus, *Apartment Stories: City and Home in Nineteenth-Century Paris and London* (1999); Diana Fuss, *Four Rooms and the Writers That Shaped Them* (2004) on Emily Dickinson, Sigmund Freud, Helen Keller and Marcel Proust.

[20] Pater in his essay, 'Style', discusses the building of a sentence and the literary architecture and design of a composition (23).

[21] Sara Luria argues that Wharton's domesticity is 'inseparable from her work', as evidenced in the construction and decoration of her home, The Mount, as well as her co-authorship of *Decoration of Houses* (1897). Luria continues with reference to both Wharton and Henry James that 'the house is essential because it physically realizes the aesthetic of deferred and ultimately renounced gratification so prominent in [their] work ... Through physical barriers – walls, doors, secluded chambers – literary architecture provides the tangible support needed to resist transgression ... Architecture for Wharton and James, hence, has the potential to be the space of writing' (I. Bryden and J. Floyd, eds,: 189–90).

[22] Tellingly, this is how Larry McCaffey and Gregory Sinda describe the kind of textual space that Mark Z. Danielewski offers in *The House of Leaves*: 'think of a multistoried house, with many stairways and elevators offering different entryways and exit points, with each room connected to other rooms by various doorways, and with a secret passageway that leads down a long winding staircase into a large, utterly black cellar'. 'Haunted house: An Interview with Mark Z. Danielewski', *Critique* (Winter 2003), 44, 2: 99–135, 99.

[23] We would agree with Diana Fuss that one must be wary of the 'too easy bifurcation between literal and figurative space reinforced by the separate disciplines of architecture and literature. To attribute substance and materiality to architecture and imagination and metaphor to literature, misreads both artistic forms ... A building and a poem are not

The Interwar Domestic Novel and the Meaning of Home   39

substitutable, but they are not oppositional either ... architecture and literature work in tandem for the writer to create a rich and evolving sense of the interior' (2004: 4).

24   One wonders how much privacy there could have been in households with large and extended families and servants? See Moira Donald, 'Tranquil Havens? Critiquing the Idea of Home as the Middle-class Sanctuary', in Bryden and Floyd, eds, 1999: 103–20. Donald points out that the nineteenth-century home was not necessarily the antonym of work if one looks at the home from the point of view of the servants (104). In her discussion of privacy in the Victorian home. Judith Flanders suggests that while in theory the home was the private space of families, in practice they were another aspect of public life, a public exhibition of the family's status (xxv–xxviii). Social historians have also linked the privatization of family life to the growth of machine production, which displaced the 'domestic labour force from the home ... [and which] led to the separation of place of work and the home, which in turn meant the domestic sphere came to be more highly regarded' (Williams: 39).

25   In 'The Domestication of the House', Mark Wigley explains Heidegger's 'turn' to the house in his later work, quoting from his 1947 'Letter on Humanism' : 'Language is the house of Being. In its home man dwells'; Wigley elaborates on Heidegger's architectural rhetoric as applied to philosophy, a 'thinking that houses' (2002: 97–121, 97)

26   There is a paradox underlying Bachelard's poetic evocation of the house; Joe Moran notes that in arguing that the house promises 'far distant voyages into a world that is no more' (143), Bachelard connects the house to an eternalized "poetics of space" that denies its more quotidian realities' (Moran: 608).

27   The nameless protagonist, trapped in a sordid room she is too fearful to leave, her days pouring out 'in an untidy crumpled heap, like clothes emptied from a drawer' is Jameson's last portrait of 'woman in interior': from now on, when her fiction is not characterized by the pointed absence of a female voice, her women will be roaming a cityscape of slums and rat-infested basements, populated by poor socialists, disaffected politicians, industrial sharks, scarred war veterans. With rare exceptions, after *None Turn Back,* the last volume of the 'Mirror in Darkness' trilogy, women will be relegated to marginal roles.

28   'The covered shopping arcades of the nineteenth century were Benjamin's central image because they were the precise material replica of the internal consciousness, or rather, the *un*conscious of the dreaming collective. All the errors of the bourgeois consciousness could be found there' (Buck-Morss, 1989: 39).

29   See Charlotte Grant, 'Reading the House of Fiction: From Object to Interior 1720–1920', November 2005.

30   See Angela Smith's excellent introduction to Katherine Mansfield, *Selected Stories* (2002), pp. ix–xxxii.

31   See Peter Schwenger, 'Still Life: A User's Manual', 2002: 'Particularly in the modern period, the encounter with an object moved, in certain authors' works, from the margins to the center of their narratives. Virginia Woolf, for instance, welcomed the techniques of James and Proust because they offered new possibilities for writing about *things*' (140).

32   Our thanks here to Stefania Forlini.

33   Interview with Julie Batty <http://www.bbc.co.uk/radio4/discover/archive_interviews/34. shtml>.

34   Interestingly, Lee writes in her introduction to the 1991 reprint of this study of Bowen, originally published in 1981, that were she writing it now, she would feel free to spend more time without having to make excuses for it on the 'brilliant use of trivia, of domestic

40 *Domestic Modernism, the Interwar Novel, and E.H. Young*

and social detail, on *things* in Bowen: clothes, furniture, decor, the cinema, travel, meals, drinks, shopping, suburbs' (1991: 4).

[35] See Paul Fussell's *Abroad: British Literary Travelling Between the wars* (1980).

[36] Delafield s *Diary of a Provincial Lady* (1930) was first serialized in *Time and Tide*; Jan Struther's *Mrs Miniver* (1939) was serialized in *The Times*. See also *Mrs Milburn's Diaries: An Englishwoman's Day-to-Day Reflections 1939–45* (1981); *Few Eggs and No Oranges: The Diaries of Vere Hodgson 1940–45* (1999).

[37] We should remember that, although Lefebvre admits that the everyday weighs heaviest on women, it provides the realms for fantasy, desire, rebellion and assertion (McLeod: 18). He also felt that because of their ambiguous position in everyday life, women were incapable of understanding it (Langbauer, 1999: 21).

[38] Geneviève Sanchis Morgan also uses the term 'domestic modernism' in her essay, 'The Hostess and the Seamstress: Woolf's Creation of a Domestic Modernism' (1997).

[39] Nor should we forget that for the middle class, 'modern housing' did not connote the dramatic functional international style of Le Corbusier or even of Wells Coates who designed the Lawn Road Flats where Agatha Christie lived from 1940 to 1946. They preferred the rather 'conservative modernism' of the mock Tudor detached or semi-detached garden city houses, parodied by Lancaster as 'by-pass variegated', 'pseudish', 'stockbrokers Tudor' (1959), or the villas springing up in red rows (Bowen, 1932, 1999: 99), described with distaste by among others Young, Bowen, Cooper, Woolf, George Orwell and D.H. Lawrence.

[40] Huyssen also discusses how connotations of mass culture as essentially feminine are 'imposed from above' (192), a topic which several domestic novelists address, often through irony (Huyssen, 1986b).

[41] For a discussion of focalization, referring to perspective or point of view, see Gèrard Genette, *Narrative Discourse*, trans. Jane E. Lewin (1980), Mieke Bal, *Narratology: Introduction to the Theory of Narrative* (1985) and Shlomith Rimmon-Kenan, *Narrative Fiction: Contemporary Poetics* (1983). Narrative theory distinguishes between the narrator (who tells the story) and the focalizer (the person through whose eyes we see). At times, they may be the same.

[42] Stella Deen has also noted how, in *William*, Young's 'emphasis on changes of consciousness' and 'oblique statements, circumlocution, and elision of events from the plot' indicate her modernity (Deen, 2003: 101).

Chapter 2

Home Lives, Still Lifes

> When a male is included in a Vermeer, one has the sense that he is a visitor – an intruder – for these women do not simply inhabit these rooms, they occupy them completely ... the Dutch women are solidly, emphatically, contentedly at home.
>
> Rybczynski: 71

Reading the Life

'She wants personal details but she is not going to get them', Young wrote in 1933 to Miss Atkinson at her publisher, Jonathan Cape. She was referring to Mlle Claire Engel who was seeking information for a piece in *Les nouvelles littéraires*.[1] Mlle Engel is not the only one whose curiosity has been piqued by Young's intriguing private life and reclusive writer's persona in combination with the unusual actions and unconventional opinions of many of her characters.[2] In his 'E.H. Young – An Appreciation', Henderson, addressing the issue of privacy, oddly commented that Young 'kept the details of her own life away from the public gaze lest, for example, her renown as a rock-climber should prejudice anyone in favour of *Miss Mole* or *Chatterton Square*' (11).

Young was born in 1880 in Northumberland, the third child of six daughters and one son, to William and Frances (Venning) Young. Her father, a ship-broker, was a partner in the firm of Simpson, Spencer and Young. His name and profession suggest that he was a model for William Nesbitt in *William*, and one may very well wonder if her own father was as accepting of Young's unconventional love life, as the novel's William was of his daughter Lydia's affair.

Young first attended Gateshead Grammar School; then, at ten, when the family moved to Sutton, Surrey into a house called Beaconsfield, she was sent as a boarder to Penrhos College, Colwyn Bay, Wales. One of Young's sisters, Norah Sanderson, became a sculptor; there is a photograph of her bust of E.H. Young in the 1950 *The Bentleian* (13), the school magazine for the Bentley Grammar School in Bristol (Figure 3). Another sister, Gladys Young (West), became a renowned actress who first made a name for herself on stage, and then in film and radio.[3] In 1902, Young married a lawyer, John Arthur Daniell, aged 28, who was in practice with his father in Bristol. Daniell had been at Bristol Grammar School with Harold Sharp, who had lived next door to the Youngs in Sutton and had married Young's sister, Margery. At first the Daniells lived in Bristol at Harrington Park, Redland and then Downs Park East, Westbury Park; by 1907 they had moved to Clifton, into a flat in Saville Place (Figure 4) that is commemorated by a plaque erected in 1992 by the Clifton and Hotwells Improvement

Figure 3   Bust of E.H. Young by her sister Norah Sanderson. Courtesy of Christopher Fallows.

Figure 4 E.H. Young's house with plaque, 2 Saville Place, Clifton. Photo by Kathy Mezei.

44   *Domestic Modernism, the Interwar Novel, and E.H. Young*

Society (M. Lane: 7).[4] Clifton, with its Georgian houses, leafy streets, village green and quaint shops, became the vividly evoked Upper Radstowe of the novels. High above the noisy, busy docks of Hotwells, close to Brunel's suspension bridge over the spectacular Avon Gorge, Clifton inspired Young's imagination. Simultaneously symbolizing the separation and the proximity of city and country, the bridge offers her characters the means of escape into the pastoral – the farms, Leigh Woods and enticing, magical pools like Monk's Pool – while the verdant downs of Clifton, with their scenic vistas, invite introspection and consequential chance encounters.

Throughout the years of young married life in Bristol, Young wrote stories, poems and novels. In his memoir, '*E.H. Young*: her Muse, her Method & her Message', Henderson recalled that she began to write in her twenty-sixth year, composing short pieces in the form of fortnightly essays. Until then, he claims:

> Her mind was being stored with the best thoughts from the past, especially Plato. Modern philosophy too formed an important part of her training from Descartes through Locke, Berkeley, Hume, Spinoza, Leibnitz to Kant and Hegel, while a vigorous course of logic was helping to form habits of careful thinking and accurate observation. (2)

A Corn of Wheat was published in 1910 by Heinemann when Young was 30; Heinemann also issued *Yonder* in 1912 and *Moor Fires* was published in 1916 by John Murray. A short story, 'Cow's Tail', appeared in April 1913 in *The English Review*, formerly edited by Ford Madox Ford.

During the war, Young and her sister Gladys groomed horses in a stable and Young, like many other young women, also worked in a munitions factory.[5] In 1916 Daniell, who had been rejected in 1914 as unfit for military service, was called up. As Sergeant-Major, he was sent to France; there he was killed at Ypres in 1917.

The Daniells and Henderson were certainly acquainted by 1906. Young (as E.H. Daniell), recollecting her rock climbing days in Wales for the Pinnacle Club, wrote that she had her first sight of Tryfaen in 1906 'when R.B. Henderson and I left the family party ... took the train to Port Madoc and bicycled up to Pen-Y-Gwryd ...' ('Reminiscences' 1935: 27).[6] We speculate that Young and Henderson became attracted to each other during their climbing expeditions in the pre-war Bristol years. After the war, Young joined Henderson's household in Dulwich, Henderson having been appointed headmaster at Alleyn's, a boy's grammar school, in 1920. An accomplished scholar, Henderson had graduated from New College, Oxford, with a double first in maths; he also studied theology from a liberal religious perspective and published widely in this field, including *The Four Witnesses* in 1933 for which he was awarded a Lambeth Degree in Divinity in 1934. Henderson had married Beatrice Mansfield in 1901 and a son, John Ralph, was born three months later. Although as headmaster Henderson presented a public profile, Mrs. Henderson kept in the background. Young lived with the couple for 22 years in housing provided by Alleyn's School but located at some distance on Christchurch Row, College Road and Sydenham Hill, and it seems that this *ménage à trois* was an amicable, convenient arrangement. The illicit relationship between Young and Henderson was a well-kept secret, handled with discretion, for any whisper of impropriety would have imperiled Henderson's position as headmaster. Mrs. Henderson performed minimal duties as headmaster's wife, appearing at school functions with the more vivacious Young following a few steps behind. In recognition of her presence at the school and her relationship to the Hendersons, Young was given the title of Librarian at Alleyn's, a merely honorific position. We were amused to learn that Henderson, while living this secret and 'immoral life', served as moral advisor to the Archbishop![7]

Mervyn Gotch was on the staff at Alleyn's and, according to their son David Gotch, Young was close to his parents. David Gotch claimed that Young wrote a number of her novels at their house, 4 Hill Rise, Forest Hill; wary about domestic distractions in the Henderson household if the current book was not progressing smoothly, Young felt safe in the Gotch house where such distractions did not obtain. Cyssely Gotch would join Young for a brief chat at mid-morning, bringing in a cup of tea, and the two women would smoke a cigarette together.[8]

During school holidays, Henderson and Young would undertake rock climbing expeditions to Wales, Switzerland, or the Dolomites, accompanied and chaperoned by the Gotches or other friends. By all accounts, Young was a remarkable and intrepid climber; in a short memoir, 'E.H. Young as a Mountaineer', Henderson recalled the accolades she received – 'she climbed like a gazelle'; 'this is the poetry of motion' – and quoted Captain Grenfell: 'never woman climbed like this woman'. In June, 1915, Young led up an entirely new route of the Idwal Slabs, introducing a new era in rock climbing: 'no woman had ever done such a thing before' and the experts (all men) who had tried that cliff had pronounced it impossible.[9] Her great-nephew, Christopher Fallows (grandson of Norah Sanderson), recalls that Emily, who was his mother's favourite aunt, was described by his father and uncle as neat and tidy in her climbing. (E-mail to Kathy Mezei, 1 August. 2005).

During the years in Dulwich, a hilly south London suburb rather like Clifton, Young published eight novels, all, with the exception of *The Vicar's Daughter*, set in Bristol (Radstowe).[10] She joined the Society of Authors and during the 1920s sought their advice concerning royalties and payments for stories and poems she was submitting to magazines.[11] She also participated in P.E.N. where she may have met Lady Ottoline Morrell with whom she maintained a correspondence during the 1930s and to whom she sent copies of *Moor Fires, Yonder* and *Celia*, accompanied by self-deprecatory notes.[12] She did not, however, mingle with London literary society. One biographical entry, quite likely written by Young herself, states unequivocally: 'she goes to no public dinners, knows no celebrities, and does not care for the society of "lions"' (Kunitz and Haycraft: 1564). Biographical entries note her clubs as 'Forum' and 'Writers'. She also published stories in the progressive *Time and Tide*, including 'Lena Maude' (7 April 1923) about a middle-aged servant's odd encounter with a burglar (775–6) and 'An Artist' (18 January 1924) with a story-telling nursemaid (60–61). 'The Sacrifice' was published on 11 August 1911. 'The Stream,' originally published in *Good Housekeeping* in 1932, was reprinted twice in story collections.[13]

46 *Domestic Modernism, the Interwar Novel, and E.H. Young*

'The Grey Mare' (17 February 1948) and 'Cow's Tail' (20 September 1950) were read on BBC.[14]

Young composed her novels in notebooks of marble blue-green or tan, each dated and labelled with an address – one of several of her south London addresses – 74 College Road in the 1920s, Sydenham Hill in the 1930s. At the end of each chapter she scribbled a word count. Unfortunately, her writing is difficult to decipher, a frustrating experience for her biographers and critics. We found at least two versions of some novels; for example, there is an early version of *Miss Mole*, dated 1 May 1928 and what Young called a second edition, dated 30 September 1929. She has working titles and notes for some of the novels; *The Vicar's Daughter* was initially called 'Blunt' and *Celia*, interestingly, 'Middle-age'. In the Celia notebook, Young lists the characters and their respective ages in the present and during World War I.

In 1940, Henderson retired as headmaster of Alleyn's and his wife, Beatrice, decamped to Weston-super-Mare. With the proceeds from her books, Young and Henderson bought a house in Prior's Close, Bradford-on-Avon, close to their friends, the Gotches, who were living in Calne. For the first time, Henderson and Young inhabited their own domestic space and created their own household, although they never married. Now Young's perspective on home and domesticity changed from that of an outsider and observer of other households, who had lived in rented and college accommodation, to one who possessed her own home and would make her own domestic arrangements. Hannah Mole, housekeeper, paid companion, governess, musing in *Miss Mole* about 'a home which was all her own and none of these tangled personalities to deal with' (65), must have expressed Young's own longing. In 1942 Henderson became acting headmaster at Bristol Grammar School for a term and during the war, Young was active in Bradford-on-Avon's Civil Defence.[15] Diagnosed with lung cancer, Young died in 1949. After her death, Henderson took a post at Keele University. Affectionately known to Christopher Fallows' family (the Sandersons and their children) as Bol, Henderson would visit them at Buxton, Derbyshire for long periods after Young's death. He died in 1959 in a nursing-home in Buxton, followed by Beatrice in 1961.[16]

At Home

With the publication of *William* in 1925, Young shifted her focus away from romantic and wild nature and Brontëian households to a contemporary domestic realm – the home and the bourgeois family; here specific and individualized houses play significant roles, exert their own form of agency and invite the frequent expression of domestic fallacy. Whether influenced by the interwar cult of the domestic or by writers like Jane Austen (with whom she was often compared) and the current fashion of the domestic novel genre, or whether she simply settled upon a particular niche suited to her philosophical and ethical concerns, Young gravitated to the home as a site and metaphor for displaying human relations. And it may indeed be a combination of all these factors that compelled her to focus on Bristol and Clifton (or Radstowe and Upper Radstowe as they became in the novels) and their houses, domestic scenes and family relations. When Celia or Miss Mole or Rosamund or William walk through the streets of Radstowe, their observations and experiences reflect a modern, if provincial, consciousness that transgresses its domestic space to briefly enter the public sphere of the city.

Oddly, Young's first three novels, *A Corn of Wheat* (1910), *Yonder* (1912) and *Moor Fires* (1916), although written in Bristol, are mostly set in isolated moors or mountains; only after moving to south London with Henderson and his family did Young turn to Bristol with its tidal waters, busy port, verdant countryside and village atmosphere and to an ironic dissection of middle-class urban domesticity. None of her 11 novels (1910–47) are set in London and, in spite of the fact that she lived in the metropolitan centre, she did not participate in or depict its literary life. Instead, much like May Sinclair in *The Combined Maze* (1913), Elizabeth Cambridge in *Hostages to Fortune* (1933), Dorothy Whipple in *High Wages* (1930), Stella Gibbons in *Bassett* (1934), E.M. Delafield in *Messalina of the Suburbs* (1924), F. Tennyson Jesse in *A Pin to See the Peepshow* (1934), G.C. Pain in *Surplus Women* (1943) and Phyllis Bentley in *A Modern Tragedy* (1934), she wrote about the provincial and suburban lives of the lower-middle-class – housewives, salesmen and salesgirls, men in trade and commerce and men of the cloth. Although *The Misses Mallett* (1922), located in Bristol and the surrounding countryside, a hybrid of the Gothic and the sentimental and haunted by the textual ghosts of many literary big houses, displays a dash of domestic veracity and poignancy, it is with her fifth and most successful novel, *William* (1925), that she begins to perfect the art of the domestic novel through evocative vignettes of domestic life in middle-class Upper Radstowe. It seems as if Young needed to distance herself from her home of 16 years and dislocate her imagination in order to draw from a storehouse of memories.

As if she were participating in the Mass-Observation experiment that saw the modern artist as occupying 'the position of the observer, effectively the Mass-Observer' (Mengham 2001a: 29), she trained her eye upon the space of the home and the shifting human and spatial arrangements and relationships. Although writers never figure as characters in Young's fiction, her narratives are studded with passages that read like poetic manifestoes. So the title character in *Celia* remembers that as a girl she would draw a sharp pleasure in observing people in chapel, 'as though she were eating something she liked very much and knew there was plenty more of it'; as a middle-aged woman Celia now realizes that:

> As a matter of fact, she was storing up what she was too young to recognize or to use, but as she grew older, increasing her store while she fed from it, she understood that her pleasure came from an insatiable interest in men and women and an eye for the ludicrous, the pathetic and the incongruous which she was always ready to turn against herself. (90)

This passage aptly describes not only those traits that equip Celia to be the heroine of her story, but also Young's own apprenticeship as a writer – the way in which the idiosyncrasies and oddities of human behaviour, carefully stored up in youth, allowed her to turn away from the early dabbling in metaphysics of her somewhat unsatisfactory 'rural' novels to focus on the poetic significance of everyday domestic life, sharing the conviction voiced by one of her characters, that 'life, for most of us, is made up of small matters' (1947, 1987): 220). By recollecting and re-imagining the home space of Clifton, the domestic sphere of everyday rituals and the interior life of urban families and houses rather than intoning a poeticized nature or quoting literary or historical references, Young found her artistic niche. Yet at the same time she was also questioning the traditional parameters of domestic space, delving into the many possibilities and meanings of home and offering her readers tentative and radical re-arrangements of house, home and family.

When Young directed her gaze at the pressures of urban life rather than at attempts to escape from the reality of industrial England, she finally succeeded in finding a more convincing form for her philosophical vision. Indeed, her mature works engage in a powerful dialectic between Platonic idealism rooted in nature and the realism of the Depression, impending war, constraints upon the lower middle classes and women seeking to better themselves. Thus, in the later works, instead of constructing a rigid binary opposition between self and society and locating the quest for self in the isolation of moors or mountains, she depicts the self (or selves) attaining agency and subjectivity through interaction with the home, society and the city as well as with the natural world. She also gradually develops a grammar of the home, which serves as the 'magnet' to draw parts of the self together and replaces the sentimentally romantic 'parts of me in every star and ... earthwork' (1912: 190).

The domestic space of specific houses, which even in the early novels is pointedly represented as an embodiment of the psyche and/or the gendered, sexualized, repressed body, eventually transforms into tangible settings where characters negotiate their subjectivities and personal relations. Similarly, the rural world, a nostalgic ideal that in the early novels serves primarily as backdrop 'conducive to spiritual clarity and as a means of character judgement' (Cavaliero: 147), becomes more skillfully integrated into the later novels through the everyday felt experiences of characters. Rejecting conventional romantic endings for her heroines, like Sylvia Townsend Warner's Lolly Willowes, who flees from her well meaning family in London to the village of Great Mop in the Chilterns and an independent life as a 'witch,' or Stella Gibbons's Margaret Steggles who, though admired by three men, does not marry, preferring instead to pursue 'Beauty, and Time, and the Past and Pity ... Laughter, too' (1946: 418, Gibbons's ellipsis), Young explores alternative configurations of home, family and household. She experiments with foregrounding rooms in which arrangements, decoration, furniture, positioning, self/other boundaries, exiting and entering both mimic an interior consciousness and highlight the territorial meaning of home (Després: 99–100).

The interior spaces, furniture and decoration of Young's houses replicate (or deliberately *fail* to replicate) her characters' personalities, situations and mental states.

Home Lives, Still Lifes

In *Chatterton Square*, Mr. Blackett finds that the house he has chosen has the added attraction of a flat-roofed room filling the space between his residence and that of his neighbours. Though an ugly excrescence, in its difference, this room 'matched the difference from other people he felt so strongly in himself' (10). Although it is not until the end of the novel that Herbert Blackett will be able to fathom the extent of his wife's estrangement from him, he gets an early first glimpse by observing her room. Entering Bertha's empty drawing room, he cannot but feel that though he has had no hand in furnishing it, for every object has come from Bertha's old home: 'the room was not like her' and it seems 'almost uninhabited' (56). These correspondences resonate with twentieth-century handbooks on the home as in Elise de Wolfe's injunction that the interior should express the figure and 'personality of its occupants, especially that of the lady of the house' (Forty: 105) or in Emily Post's that the house should express 'your personality, just as every gesture you make – or fail to make – expresses your gay animation or your restraint, your old-fashioned conventions ... or your emancipated modernism' (quoted in Forty: 106).[17] But Young, as well as Elizabeth Bowen, Virginia Woolf and Lettice Cooper, complicated these correspondences to expose gender and class roles and positions. In keeping with her acute sensitivity to her 'questionable' class, Louisa Rendall in *Jenny Wren* withdraws to the basement kitchen, rarely venturing to the upper floors of her lodging-house.

From Jane Austen to Agatha Christie and Barbara Pym, curates and vicars retreat to the masculine space of their studies for privacy and self-reflection, while the doorstep and window offer heroines like Young's Dahlia, Jenny, Celia and Flora liminal spaces at the threshold between inner, private and constricted domestic space and the outer public world of romance, adventure and commerce; tradesmen come to the door, but are not invited indoors. As Rachel Lichenstein and Iain Sinclair put it in *Rodinsky's Room* (1999): 'Doors represent status: those who possess them are allowed a measure of privacy. They can remove themselves from their servants, supplicants or creditors. The door is a border, framed and presented' (184). Of the danger of the doorstep no one is more aware than the fastidious Herbert Blackett: 'here, almost on his doorstep were just such people as he wished ... the whole family, to avoid and Bertha had been to blame for breaking the crust of politeness which was more than enough to offer them' (E.H Young 1947: 25).

The media of houses, doors, windows, the road and the space between allow Young to set in motion conflicting desires for connection and separation. Through her emphasis on ways and angles of seeing, the gaze and eyes, she exposes the masks, self-deceptions and misperceptions which simultaneously conceal and reveal human traits. Perspectives are frequently afforded through stairs where children spy upon adults, conversations are overheard and inappropriate behaviours observed. In *The Curate's Wife* (1934), the garden gate, the front doors of the Rendalls's and Doubledays's households, the windows in the studies and household stairs serve as venues for voyeurism, eavesdropping and intimate encounters. Mr. Doubleday's irrepressible habit of looking out from his study window suggests both a benevolent curiosity in humanity and a rebellion against his wife's coercive personality, providing him with

50   *Domestic Modernism, the Interwar Novel, and E.H. Young*

'a store of somewhat disconnected facts' (19), a welcome distraction from his work and a vicarious escape from his oppressive domestic interior. On the other hand, to peer from outside through a window into one's own house may mimic the process of looking into one's self and entering into one's interior and hidden recesses, reflecting the mental rooms of the interior in psychoanalysis. It may also be, as Bryden and Floyd suggest, that to 'try to read [domestic objects] ... or to stand *outside* a house and see in through its windows "is to write a story of lives one does not know"' (quoting Tristram: 13). Like other domestic novelists, Young was susceptible to the symbolic valences of keys and locked doors for the inviolability of the self. Thus, as in Cooper's *The New House* (1936), Mrs. Powell 'could not bear a closed door in anyone she lived with. She wanted a latch-key to every room in their person' (111), in *Celia,* the equation between room, locked door, key and the concealed or inner space of the self is made explicit through the description of Susan's doll's house: 'its front, which swung back on hinges, to give access to the rooms, could be, and unless Susan was busy with the house, always was firmly locked' (49).

Doors, windows, halls, stairs and beds perform strategic narrative functions. Elderly Mrs. Swithin in Virginia Woolf's 1941 *Between the Acts* alludes to the staircase of life, 'this daily round; this going up and down stairs' (152), a sentiment echoed in *Celia* where the narrator presents her heroine continuously going up and down stairs as a sign of the onerous repetitiveness of her life. Taking on multiple symbolic valences, the stair stands emblematic of social intercourse, the transition between public and private space and the ascent into Celia's domestic web. Celia's ear is 'tuned to every step on the stairs, to each different manner of turning the key in the lock and opening and shutting the door' (1937: 81).

Gradually, Young developed a decorating strategy whereby decoration and narration became metaphorically interchangeable: houses and bodies are adorned and arranged and ornaments judiciously placed and polished.[18] Furniture (notably bureaus, beds, chairs), doors, stairs, windows and curtains – synecdoches of house and body – perform functions of concealment and display and mirror gender roles and the aspirations of upwardly mobile classes, while the social geography of the house itself charts the course of relations between sexes and classes. As Celia, who dreams about the past over trinkets scattered on the floor, and Miss Riggs, the housekeeper who itches to sort and order the drawers, realize through their different approaches to 'tidying up', ornamentation and housework can signal an appropriation of space and control, which in Celia's case takes the form of resistance, delay and deferral.

Furniture and ornaments act as ritualized forms of communication and assume fetishistic roles. In *Jenny Wren* (1932), Jenny's father's bureau becomes a commodity of exchange in the fluctuating relationship between Jenny Rendall and Edwin Cummings, while the heavy bedroom furniture and the 'barbaric bed' in *Celia* replicate Celia's sense of the oppressiveness of her marriage. In E.M. Delafield's *Thank Heaven Fasting* (1932), the décor of Monica's bedroom is 'a silent testimony that violent and radical change held no place in her life'; for though Monica, as a faded woman of 30, has long ceased to be the blooming *débutante* who had filled her parents with pride, she is still surrounded by 'pink silk, brass, and white-painted furniture' (174). In Ada Leverson's *The Little Ottleys* (1908–1916), not only is the phrase 'little Ottleys' that describes Edith and Bruce emphasized by the repeated references to their 'very small ... flat in Knightsbridge' (33), but the affinity between certain characters is suggested by their preference in room arrangements and the taste in decoration they share. Edith's unostentatious unconventionality, reflected in her dislike for traditional dark dining rooms and chilly, ceremonious drawing rooms, is paralleled by Lord Selsey's flouting 'of the ordinary subdivisions of a house': 'he did not see why one should breakfast in a breakfast-room, dine in a dining-room, draw in a drawing-room, and so on' (73). Even more suggestively, the 'feminine curves of the furniture' (394) Edith has chosen are suitably contrasted with the masculine quality of her lover's room: 'it was essentially a man's room. Comfortable, but not exactly luxurious; very little was sacrificed to decoration' (450).

However, domestic novelists have also acknowledged the coercive character of this relationship, what a character in Elizabeth Bowen's *The Hotel* (1927) calls the predicament of people 'living under the compulsion of their furniture' (119), a predicament that the spinster protagonist of Bowen's story, 'The New House,' knows only too well: 'Why, even the way the furniture was arranged at No. 17 held me so that I couldn't get away. The way the chairs went in the sitting-room. And mother' (1980: 57). In Bowen's fiction, furniture and household objects do more than determine a pattern for living and display an uncanny ability to become interchangeable with the people they surround. As Maud Ellmann has noted apropos of *The Last September* (1929), furniture embodies 'the unknown but resurgent past' as 'past acts lie petrified in household objects, like the imperialist loot bestrewn around the stately rooms'. Household objects can also 'scrutinize their own beholders, usually with an evil eye' (2003: 6). In Bowen's *The Death of the Heart* (1948), Matchett the housekeeper has gained immunity to the malicious scrutiny of furniture by virtue of a lifelong bodily experience of polishing and cleaning objects that are as familiar to her as her own face; but she knows its ghostly resilience ('chairs and tables don't go to the grave so soon') and the potency of its unnerving surveillance: 'Not much gets past the things in a room, I daresay ... Unnatural living runs in a family, and the furniture knows it, you be sure. Good furniture knows what's what' (81).

On the one hand, houses and objects serve as an archive of memory, repression and desires while on the other hand, specific domestic spaces position characters and readers with theatrical effect (Schwenger: 140).[19] Since many stories open by entering a house, it also makes a difference to the story whether we enter by the front door or the side door and who stands where on the staircase: how we tour rooms and where we are placed in the room influences our point of view.[20] Young gradually came to invoke the house as a tool for analysis of the human soul and so house, home and the domestic everyday – shopping, cooking, repairing the gurgling cistern – became the scaffolding of her novels. Her earlier aspiration after the noumenal slowly shifted towards everyday and domestic phenomenal objects invested with meaning. It is as if Young's growing interest in the anatomy of domestic relations and the increasing

52   *Domestic Modernism, the Interwar Novel, and E.H. Young*

complex psychology of her characters were most successfully realized by their grounding in domestic spaces and realities. By thematizing architectural design and architects, Young investigated the symbolic potential of architecture as a vehicle for determining and consecrating domestic and spiritual life.

Exerting agency over the characters' lives, thoughts, decisions and moods, Young's houses are overtly endowed with human qualities; the embodied house with a distinct personality and agency recurs as an emblematic feature. On 12 November 1945, Young's sister, the actress Gladys Young, appeared in an episode of the BBC programme 'Home Life' called 'The Way You Look at It'. Correspondence between Gladys Young and James Langharn of the BBC suggests that E.H. Young was requested to write the '6 minute script about the home … which you have "once lived in, and loved and left"'.[21] The script describes an anthropomorphized house in the country, a sanctuary from the war, which 'looked like a lady with skirts outspread who was just rising from a curtsey, but a grave lady who through all the chances of life had kept the fine manners of her character'. At first the house represents truth and beauty for the narrator, but as mice, night and solitude encroach and the enemy is 'already within' her gates, the house, with its history and long-dead inhabitants, begins to press on her and turns evil and threatening. It (and the narrator) regain happiness only when children evacuees arrive and fill the house with laughter. As the interviewer, Lionel Gamelin, commented, 'no one shall say, after that … that a house hasn't a personality of its own' (n.p.).

Two typescripts among Young's manuscript papers also indicate her predilection for symbolic houses in which the house is perceived as an organic, living being that animates the contemplation of the meaning of home, family and community; in Baudrillard's words, 'the house itself is the symbolic equivalent of the human body, whose potent organic schema is later generalized into an ideal design for the integration of social structures' (317). In a short lyrical piece, 'On Empty Houses', two houses are transformed into human bodies endowed with feelings. The first, foreshadowing Woolf's personified empty house in the 'Time Passes' section in *To the Lighthouse*, laments its loneliness: 'bereft of its occupants, with vacant rooms and wall-papers smudged with the outlines of departed furniture, it gives a little sigh of relief and settles down to sleep awhile … [the house] metaphorically shakes itself, looks pleasant and prepares to watch' (Young Papers: 1). The second house or cottage possesses more risqué qualities for it was 'a meeting place of the emotions: here were great unwieldy passions born … Here, too, was a total lack of the conventions … there was tennis-playing on the Sabbath and the woman of that house dried her hair in the sun' (2, 3).[22]

In another typescript in which romance and the domestic converge, 'On Window Curtains', Young enters the narrative world of houses by means of the ornamental and the decorative – the curtains which separate the private, inner space from the outer, public world. Through windows, one looks out upon the public world; however, windows and drawn curtains invite the passerby to gaze in and to imagine the intimate life beyond the curtains, and then perhaps to write the story of lives one does not know (Bryden and Floyd: 13). Young envisions a poet walking by houses and observing a variety of curtains – from velvet or brocade to severe serge hangings – whose material

Home Lives, Still Lifes 53

and shape are indicators of class and the inhabitants' personalities. Drifting in a Bachelardian reverie, the poet conjures up romances and fascinating lives for their occupants. The closing lines pose a question that fittingly echoes Young's fictional practice: 'yet why should not romance live even in drab-coloured surroundings and if the poet can turn the drabs to purples life is but so much the lovelier for him' (4).[23]

Still Lifes, Dutch Domestic Interiors and the Idea of Home

> She realized that she, too, should be an artist in her own sphere, that, indeed, she was already doing almost her best to be one, and that the results of her labours, if they were good, were no more to be despised than was a painting of a Dutch interior because it did not deal with gods and goddesses. (*Miss Mole*: 167)

> She wanted to ... get some sort of beauty into the house. (81)

These references to painting and beauty are not accidental and emphasize that imagination and the aesthetics of the everyday give the heroine of *Miss Mole*, like the painter Lily Briscoe in *To the Lighthouse*, the ability to escape the destiny of the superfluous spinster. Young's heroines Margaret Stack, Celia Marston, Hannah Mole, Dahlia Sproat and Rosamund Fraser all study and practice the art of living not as goddesses but as artists of everyday life who transform the life of a dreary housewife or housekeeper into drama and adventure. In the above quotation, Hannah Mole's comparison of the results of her labours to a painting of a Dutch interior suggests an identification with her author and calls attention to Young's self-conscious vision of herself as an artist working in the tradition of Pieter de Hooch and Johannes Vermeer, whose depictions of domestic activity in the second half of the seventeenth century were crucial in making Delft one of the principal artistic centres of the Northern Netherlands. In her review of *The Curate's Wife*, Mary Ross draws the reader's attention to this special 'Vermeer-like quality' in Young; her work is 'akin to a Vermeer painting' because it is 'luminous and exact in detail, narrowly limited in setting, concentrated on the everyday lives of everyday people ... [It has] the coherence of a well loved room' (*New York Herald Tribune*, 21 October 1934: 8).

In these Dutch domestic interiors, as in the domestic novel, houses, their objects and the ephemera of everyday life perform as 'effective ideological carriers' of culture and society (Langbauer: 7). Thus, Vermeer's and de Hooch's Dutch interiors with their symbolic mirrors, doorways, women reading letters and cast-aside brooms and buckets not only imply the routines and comforts of domesticity, but also hint at illicit sex and the desire to escape the confinement of domesticity and Protestant morality. Richard Shone notes how in Vermeer's picture of a woman pouring milk, 'temporal erosion and the boredom of domestic continuity give tension to [a] superficially tranquil image of daily life' (2000: 56); each of these works, he adds, 'encapsulates the slog of daily life, the tussle between compulsion and habit' (2000: 57)).

Likewise, the domestic novel both embraces and critiques the routines of domestic

54   *Domestic Modernism, the Interwar Novel, and E.H. Young*

customs and ritual: in *Crewe Train* (1926), Rose Macaulay satirizes the futility of the battle against disorder, for 'house management largely consists of trying to keep the things in the house from behaving as is natural to their species' (154). The narrator of *The Misses Mallett* seems to express a similar impatience for domestic rituals when showing Rose hurrying home 'under the tyranny of tea'; the next sentence, however, significantly alleviates the oppressiveness of routine: 'the meals were exquisite, like the polish on the old brass door-knocker, like the furniture in the white panelled hall, like the beautiful old mahogany in the drawing-room, the old china, the glass bowls full of flowers' (22–3). In *Celia*, the menial chore of cleaning the bathtub provides Celia and her son with the opportunity for an intimate conversation. Like the seventeenth-century Dutch artists who had found their most effective medium by moving away from portraying 'gods and goddesses' (*Miss Mole*: 167) and the momentous events of history to focus on the small-scale and trivial acts of everyday life in genre painting and still lifes, Young, after abandoning the romantic elements of her early fiction, learnt to combine the homeliness of her scenes with the compelling realism of depiction. As Miss Mole reflects on the home where she has become housekeeper, 'here was a little society, in itself commonplace enough, but a miniature of all societies, with the same intrigues within and the same threatenings of danger from outside' (*Miss Mole*: 74).

In 'The Novel Démeublé', Willa Cather claimed that the novel has 'been overfurnished' (47), criticized the realism of Balzac and Lawrence and praised Tolstoi in whose novels 'the clothes, the dishes, the haunting interiors of those old Moscow houses are always so much a part of the emotions of the people that they are perfectly synthesized' (52). Cather's critique resonates with Woolf's much-quoted anti-Edwardian manifesto, 'Character in Fiction' (1924), where she lambasted Arnold Bennett for his penchant for submerging his characters in a barrage of material details. Woolf lamented how our acquaintance with Hilda Lessways of the eponymous novel (1911) is continuously hindered by her author's obsessive need to describe her surroundings: since 'Hilda not only looked at houses and thought of houses' (1924: 430) but lived in a house, so Bennett must proceed to give us a full description of this house she lives in and pretty soon Hilda herself has disappeared. Though Bennett claimed to aspire to a form of '*synthetic impressionism*' (1971: 23, italics Bennett's), this phrase is better suited to the techniques of Woolf and Mansfield and indeed of most interwar domestic novelists.

With the important exception of Dorothy Richardson, whose extremely detailed descriptions unnerved both Woolf and Mansfield, interwar domestic novelists refrained from describing houses, rooms, or interior décor in great or specific detail.[24] Their pared-down response to the home, while in part the manifestation of the modernist resistance to the opulent descriptions of the Victorians and Edwardian novelists, may also indicate the authors' assumption that readers would naturally decode the class, status and location of these domestic spaces and objects through the domestic symbol systems of net curtains, terraced housing, the number of servants, or the 'stoppered, sand-filled lighthouse' on the mantelpiece (Oliver: 189, 186). In novels from Dorothy Whipple's *High Wages* to George Orwell's *Keep the Aspidistra Flying* (1936) to

Home Lives, Still Lifes   55

G.C. Pain's *Surplus Women*, the ubiquitous aspidistras glimpsed between stiff white
Nottingham lace curtains, red plush curtains and stuffed birds are effective objective
correlatives for the drabness of lower-middle-class neighbourhoods; in like fashion,
a rusty fern and a green serge cloth in *Miss Mole*, a cistern in *The Curate's Wife*, a
bureau in *Jenny Wren*, the garden in *The Vicar's Daughter*, Rosamund's balcony and
Miss Spanner's cluttered bedroom in *Chatterton Square* and a doll's house in *Celia*
are prosaic objects and places transformed into potent metonyms of domestic life. In
Mollie Panter-Downes's *One Fine Day* (1947), the memory of a trug basket, which
the gardener 'had arranged like a Dutch painting with crisp lettuce heads, sweet corn,
white beans and aubergine' (18), captures for Laura the gracious living that has been
destroyed by the war. In the arrangement and decoration of these small domestic spaces,
we experience small gestures of control and appropriation and of the 'housewife as a
modern artist of the domestic interior' (Tiersten: 18).

In much the seventeenth century, when the very familiarity of still life subjects
accounted for the low status of genre painting, at the turn of the [nineteenth] century
'the linkage between domesticity and modernism has been obscured by ... the idea
of the "avant-garde"' (Reed 1996: 7). Christopher Reed has noted how when in
1929, Raymond Mortimer, 'friend and patron of Bloomsbury artists' and Dorothy
Todd (future translator of Le Corbusier) collaborated on the book *The New Interior
Decoration*, they were able to ignore the only too evident schism dividing the styles
of which each of them was promoter. However, only a few years later, 'the fanciful
eclecticism of the Bloomsbury artists was cast beyond the pale' as a new aesthetic
developed through a sequence of choices within 'a cascade of oppositions'. To the
list of dyads that includes 'functional/ornamental, pictorial/decorative, machine/body,
masculine/feminine', Reed significantly adds 'heroism/housework', noting how Le
Corbusier's claims for modernity were proffered in a rhetoric that 'enacts the hero's
victory over the home' (2004: 1–3).

In much the same manner as Bloomsbury aesthetic was exiled outside modernist
design for its preference for housework over heroism, the domestic novel has been slow
to gain recognition because of its disregard of great events in favour of the validation
of everyday reality and its less than radical experimentalism. However, as the work
of literary historians of the last decade has persuasively demonstrated, modernism
is anything but monolithic and the affinities between authors as different as Woolf
and Young are due to be teased out. Like Virginia Woolf, Young, too, developed 'a
poetics of domesticity', forging 'a new type of modernism responsive to the female
artist' (Morgan: 94). And as with Woolf's sister Vanessa Bell, she finds that what
makes form significant is 'the eruption of intimate and domestic life and memory into
expressive form'.[25] Following in the footsteps of William Morris and inspired by the
idiosyncratic style of Augustus John's Alderney and Fryern Court, Bloomsbury artists
of the Omega Workshop launched with gusto into domestic decoration. Roger Fry,
Vanessa Bell and Duncan Grant's still lifes, influenced by the cunningly animated
paintings of Cézanne, 1913–1915, may have seemed to 'proclaim the unadventurous
status quo of the English middle classes',[26] but they, like the domestic novel, while

56 *Domestic Modernism, the Interwar Novel, and E.H. Young*

delighting in material realities and presenting a contained world of rich associations, were also preoccupied with the artist's métier itself (Shone 1999: 34).

Although, as we observed earlier, Woolf objected to Arnold Bennett's smothering of his characters in domestic details, she certainly did not think lightly of houses; indeed, though she may not gone as far as to claim, like Leonard, that the houses one has lived in matter more than 'school, university, work, marriage, death, division, or war', she may well have agreed with her husband that not only are houses occasionally imprinted with the personality of their inhabitants, but they, in turn, have the deepest and most permanent effect upon oneself and one's way of living: 'The Leonard and Virginia who lived in Hogarth House, Richmond, from 1915 to 1924 were not the same people who lived in 52 Tavistock Square from 1924 to 1939' (L. Woolf 1967: 14). Nor indeed was the Virginia who lived in the paternal house in Hyde Park Gate the same person who lived with her siblings in Bloomsbury. Such fresh interiors as 46 Gordon Square and Mary Datchet's flat near the Strand in Woolf's *Night and Day* were conducive to freer living; that freedom to 'grow up as one liked' (1906: 24) and the frankness in conversation which the two 'daughters at home' in her story 'Phyllis and Rosamond' (1906) can only glimpse during rare forays outside the irreproachable rows of South Kensington and Belgravia.[27]

Responding to the summons of the Nabis, who had refused to abide by the limits of the easel and saw every wall as a space to be painted, bohemianism (not limited to Bloomsbury) contributed to invest the home with meaning and personal expression and provided the domestic novelist with a ready code for freer living. Charles and Sophia, the newly-wed art students in Barbara Comyns's *Our Spoons Came from Woolworths* (1950), turn indigence to advantage when they paint all their furniture 'duck-egg green with a dash of sea green' and give a general makeover to their basement flat:

> We decorated the flat ourselves. Because the room was rather dark we painted the walls a kind of stippled yellow, lots of black hairs from the brush got mixed with the paint, but they looked as if they were meant to be there almost.
> We had white walls in the kitchen, and Charles painted a chef by the gas cooker. (12)

Bohemianism, figured through the use of solid primary colours, 'with its heady blend of personal liberty and decorative originality' (Wilhide: 6) became a ready trope for the free, modern woman. Thus, when Katharine Burns, the heroine of G.C. Pain's *Surplus Women*, moves from Barton Street where she has lived with her grandmother to the much less respectable Camellia Street, she revels in the brightness of her bedsit. While in the past she had had a mild preference for pastel shades of colour, now she craves orange and tawny browns, greens and golds:

> Instead of pictures she bought mirrors for her new home and her yellow walls and orange curtain were reflected several times.
> She had found a new bookcase, a chunky thing that left off abruptly and started

Home Lives, Still Lifes

again lower down. She stood a blue bowl of marigolds on it and a little green dog. She went to bed on a divan of orange and green. (37–8)

As we will see in our discussion of *William*, Young, too, was conversant with the language of bohemianism, particularly through Lydia and her modernist decorating strategies. Young's closest affinity, however, was with artists of the interior such as Bérthe Morisot who, alone among the Impressionists, 'made virtually nothing but private, domestic images' and, wherever she painted, 'looked for signs of home',[28] as well as with the French Nabi/Post-Impressionists, Pierre Bonnard and Edouard Vuillard, who were roughly her contemporaries and for whom, too, the interior 'is not merely a place to be recorded but an idea to be expressed' (Higonnet: 71). Vuillard's words, 'I don't make portraits. I paint people in their homes',[29] could have been uttered by Young, whose subject can only be grasped by carefully untangling the texture of familial relationships. For the fascination of the domestic, family networks, attentiveness to mundane tasks and simple acts was not felt solely by the seventeenth-century Dutch artists. There is a continuing tradition that leads from The Netherlands to the England of Duncan Grant, Vanessa Bell, Gwen John ('a sort of modern Vermeer')[30] and her brother Augustus, and to the France of Vuillard, Bonnard and Bérthe Morisot and of Picasso and Braque. The latter's 'belief in the eloquence and validity of material things was continued and developed by subsequent movements from Dada to Surrealism to Pop' (Moorhouse: 60) and carried on with works such as Giorgio Morandi's profoundly evocative still lifes of dust-laden drab objects and Jean Dubuffet's *Matière et mémoire* 1945 lithographs depicting everyday life. It is a sign of the inexhaustible quality of the ordinary that, as Rod Mengham has put it in his survey of the domestic preoccupations of contemporary artists such as Louise Bourgeois and Rachel Whiteread, 'one of the most persistent obsessions of the public art of the past decade has involved an assault on, a redefining of and an affective relocating of the idea of domestic space' (2000: 39).[31]

Notes

1   Letter to Miss Atkinson. 5 February 1933, E.H. Young files, Jonathan Cape Correspondence, Archives and Manuscripts, University of Reading Library, University of Reading.

2   Sally Beauman's introduction to the Virago republication of *The Misses Mallett* was the first source to reveal details of Young's unusual life history. We thank Sally Beauman for passing on information to us.

3   The BBC's Home Service offered serial readings of *Miss Mole, William, Chatterton Square* and *The Curate's Wife* by Gladys Young on 'Woman's Hour', along with two short stories in the 'Short Story Sequence' from 1946 to 1960. Gladys Young's prominence as a full-time radio actress, respected for her versatility and professionalism, no doubt facilitated these dramatizations of Young's novels and stories. When Gladys was invited to speak on a BBC programme – 'Let Up' on 'Home Life' – the producer wrote her to ask her sister for a sample. When Gladys was interviewed on 'Women of Today' in 1950, she concluded

58   *Domestic Modernism, the Interwar Novel, and E.H. Young*

with readings of Katherine Mansfield, Walter de la Mare and Young's *William* (Gladys Young Files: File 4a, BBC Written Archives Centre, Caversham Park, Reading).

[4] At the first International E.H. Young Conference, organized by Maggie Lane and Stella Dean, Ms. Lane led a tour through Clifton to the sites of houses in Young's life and novels (17 June 2000).

[5] See Ruth Adam's discussion of 'The Munitions Girls' who replaced skilled male workers in munitions factories, provoking Lloyd George's comment that it was a 'strange irony that the making of weapons of destruction should afford the occasion to humanise industry' (*A Woman's Place: 1910–1975*, 1975: 65).

[6] We thank Maggie Lane for giving us a copy of this article.

[7] Letter from Michael Booker to Kathy Mezei, 10 January 2002.

[8] Letter from David Gotch to Glen Cavaliero, 2 June 1969 or 1970. We thank Dr. Glen Cavaliero for passing this letter on to us.

[9] Jonathan Cape Correspondence, Archives and Manuscripts, Reading University Library, Reading, n.p.

[10] 'If London had its Dulwich, Richmond and Edgware, the same single-class exclusiveness was to be found in Bristol's Clifton, Cotham and Redland' (Burnett, 1986: 193).

[11] See Emily Hilda Daniell (Young) Correspondence, Society of Authors Papers, Vol. XXV, 1921–1942, British Library, Manuscripts Division, ADD 63230. ff. 66–73v.

[12] See P.E.N. Archive, Department of Special Collections, University Archives, McFarlin Library, University of Tulsa, Oklahoma; also Harry Ransom Humanities Research Center, University of Texas at Austin, Texas, Box 35, File 2.

[13] *Twelve Best Stories from Good Housekeeping*, ed., Alice M. Head, 1932; *The Best Short Stories: 1933*, ed., Edward J. O'Brien, 1933.

[14] Scripts, BBC Written Archives, Caversham Park, Reading.

[15] In recognition of Young's interest in philosophy, Ralph Henderson established an annual 'E.H. Young' Lecture at Bristol University in his will. Begun in 1961, this series presents speakers who address the subject 'Truth is worthy of pursuit for its own sake' from different disciplines. Henderson also created the E.H. Young Prize Fund at the Bristol Grammar School where he had been a student along with Young's husband, Arthur Daniell. This prize was awarded for an essay on Greek thought. For this information, we gratefully thank Mr. Michael Booker, Bristol.

[16] Christopher Fallows' e-mail correspondence to Kathy Mezei, 1 August 2005. We thank Christopher Fallows for permission to quote these biographical details.

[17] Elsie De Wolfe, *The House in Good Taste* (1913); Emily Post, *The Personality of a House: The Blue Book of Home Design and Decoration* (1930).

[18] The phrase 'decorating strategy' emerged out of Kathy Mezei's 2002 English 804 English graduate class (Simon Fraser University), thanks to Lesley Selcer.

[19] In 'Still Life: A User's Manual', Peter Schwenger refers to Michael Fried's 'Art and Objecthood', in which Fried criticizes the theatricality of minimal sculptures, that is, the 'disposition of the object designed to provoke (mental) events in temporal sequence'; Schwenger also mentions Robert Morris's description of the dynamic 'experienced in the spectator, initiated by the object and the way it is positioned' (140). The effects of these dispositions are relevant to the relations among objects, characters and readers.

[20] This, as Ellmann has noted, is particularly true of Bowen: 'her stories typically open by entering a house, often by illicit means, where a dream-future springs into being' (2003: 28).

Home Lives, Still Lifes

59

21 Langharn to Gladys Young, 5 October 1945, Gladys Young Files: File 4a, BBC Written Archives Centre, Caversham Park, Reading.

22 The name on this typescript is Helen Garth, a name Young used for an unpublished novel written just before or during World War I, while living in Bristol with Daniell (Young Papers).

23 A similar animation occurs in Elizabeth Bowen's 1923 story, 'The Return', when the housekeeper, Lydia, reflects how 'during her six weeks of solitude the house had grown very human'; with the return of the owners, Lydia feels the house 'drawing itself together into a nervous rigor, as a man draws himself together in suffering irritation at the entrance of a fussy wife' (1980: 28). In *The Last September*, furnishings 'often show more sentience than their possessors: chairs are "dejected", beds "confidently waiting", and the dinner table "certain of its regular compulsion"', (Ellmann 2001: 9). And the burning of Big Houses by the Sinn Fein are described in terms of 'the death – execution, rather – of the three houses, Danielstown, Castle Trent, Mount Isabel' (Bowen 1982: 206).

24 Jean Radford reads Miriam Henderson's continual attention to details of rooms and furnishings in *Pilgrimage* and the 'facticity' of the descriptions as both part of Miriam's hermeneutic quest and as Richardson's deliberate strategy to impede the reader's interpretive activity as well as her reminder to the reader 'that things and objects exist independently of human appetites and desires' (*Dorothy Richardson*, 1991: 17, 52).

25 Lisa Tickner, 'Vanessa Bell: *Studland Beach*, Domesticity, and 'Significant Form'', *Representations*, 1999: 63–92, 71. 'Like Woolf, [Vanessa Bell] embraced the consciousness of everyday life as something to be caught and held in new forms of expression' (76).

26 T. Hilton, 'Who's the Subject, You or Me?', *Independent on Sunday*, 26 April 1998: 24, quoted in Richard Shone ('A Cast in Time', 1999), p. 35.

27 Significantly, it is through design styles that Woolf articulates the difference between Hyde Park Gate and Gordon Square in 'Old Bloomsbury': 'Needless to say the Watts' Venetian tradition of red plush and black paint had been reversed; we had entered the Sargent-Furse era; white and green chintzes were everywhere; and instead of Morris wallpapers with their intricate patterns we decorated our walls with washes of plain distemper', in *Moments of Being* (1976), p. 163.

28 Anne Higonnet, *Berthe Morisot's Images of Women*, 1992: 79, 63. Higonnet notes how in Morisot's paintings the inside, doubly contained by doors and windows is rendered 'all the more clearly interior because it is not what is shown to lie beyond' (71).

29 Quoted in Judy Collins and Sophie Howarth's display caption for Edouard Vuillard's 'Jeune femme dans un intérieur' (1910) in the permanent collection of Tate Modern, London.

30 'A sort of modern Vermeer' is how Gwen John was described in a review in 1926. However, Lisa Tickner who quotes the review, notes how, even though Gwen John was influenced by the Dutch artists, in contrast to them she painted a room that was also her studio ('"Augustus's Sister": Gwen John: Wholeness, Harmony and Radiance', 2004: 29–45; 29, 31).

31 Works such as Rachel Whiteread's 'Ghost' (The Saatchi Gallery, London, 1990) and 'House' (1993–1994), Gary Simmons's 'Ghost House' (Ruby Ranch, New Mexico, 2001) and Michael Landy's 'Semi-detached' (Tate Britain, London, 2004) point to home as the place where not only are the seeds of identity sown but where the past acquires a materiality as it lingers in objects that carry 'the residue of years and years of use' (quoted in 'Breakthrough Sculpture by Rachel Whiteread Acquired By National Gallery Of Art',

60 *Domestic Modernism, the Interwar Novel, and E.H. Young*

National Gallery press release, 15 October 2004). The Italian artist Graziano Pompili has devoted his career to the affective relocation Rod Mengham describes: in his sculptures and etchings, houses, made of marble, granite, wood, iron and tin, while insistently modeled on the basic structure of a child's drawing, thus reflecting an atavistic desire for belonging at the same time, are studiously presented as natural shapes organically emerging from the earth as though such desire belonged to the earth itself. At once welcoming and inaccessible, they are proof of the human impulse to read the world symbolically and of the stoniness and impregnability of nature; they are, above all, evidence of the resilience of the idea of home, for these houses may exist anywhere – perched on steep cliffs or on top of trees, immersed in water, travelling on horseback or carried in a boat.

Chapter 3

House Haunting

One need not be a chamber – to be Haunted –
One need not be a House

Emily Dickinson: 274

Like Elizabeth Bowen's houses, the houses of Young's early novels are haunted by death, the heavy hand of the past and the coercion of convention. We find these early texts inhabited and inhibited by ghosts of other writers and the phantom of nineteenth-century realist prose. A restless disembodied omniscient narrator prowls through these stories seeking to draw together the strewn parts of the self. As is the case for Woolf in her first two novels, *The Voyage Out* (1915) and *Night and Day* (1919), Young has yet to settle into her subject and technique.[1] The prevalence of characters who mourn lost or absent mothers or confront repressed sexual desires and fears, and of spectral others who return to haunt fragile and troubled selves, suggests a Freudian uncanny. This drift seems to reflect both Young's uncertain narrative strategy and the too evident traces of the Romantic poets, the Brontës, Eliot and Hardy.

Glen Cavaliero was right in noting that to pass from Young's fi st novel, *A Corn of Wheat* (1910), to her last, *Chatterton Square* (1947), 'is to move from youthful idealism to tolerance and considered wisdom' (146). The idealism of Young's early writings was nurtured by her reading of modern philosophy and immersion in Romantic poetry. In the commemorative speech he wrote after Young's death, Henderson praised Young's early dabbling in metaphysics as the effort of a writer 'for whom to hold up the mirror to society was not enough: To her there was behind it all what Plato called the Form of the Good ... she had a mission – to portray the truth, but to portray it in the light of a Divine illumination'('E.H. Young: her Muse, her Method, her Message': 4). In her three early works, *A Corn of Wheat*, *Yonder* and *Moor Fires*, Young endeavoured to move beyond the world of appearances to attain the 'Form of the Good' by focusing on individual characters' 'quest and craving for personal fulfilment (Cavaliero: 146), often expressed as yearning for a home and belonging exacerbated by a literally sick home, but also as a desire to escape from home and domesticity in order to wander in spectral landscapes.

As is quite natural in a beginning novelist, Young tested different genres, including the pastoral, Romantic and Gothic, often in earnest and awkward combination. In her first novels, Young attempted to navigate the currents of modernity, the ethos of the independent New Woman and the construction of a self wavering uncertainly between a unitary self and fragmented and multiple selves. Her early works show an unfortunate affinity with Mary Webb's and Sheila Kaye-Smith's rural novels and

62 *Domestic Modernism, the Interwar Novel, and E.H. Young*

Storm Jameson's experiments in this genre, exhibiting a kindred feverish atmosphere, elemental conflict and fascination with moors, along with a sense of destiny and foreboding that replaces psychological complexity. The identical thunder of hooves galloping in the night in Webb's *Seven for a Secret* (1922) and Young's *Moor Fires* (1916) and *The Misses Mallet* (1922) carries intimations of reckless and dangerous sexuality. Often overwrought and uneasily balanced between an unabashedly romantic vision expressed in breathless, quasi-archaic prose, Young's early novels, like Sheila Kaye-Smith's *Sussex Gorse* (1916), Mary Webb's *Gone to Earth* (1917) and *Precious Bane* (1924) and Storm Jameson's *The Pitiful Wife* (1924) and *The Moon Is Making* (1938), burn with dark and primitive passions. They are inhabited by characters larger than life who strive clumsily after a vision of the kinship between man and nature that easily lent itself to becoming an inspiration for Stella Gibbons's famous mockery in *Cold Comfort Farm*. In her tongue-in-cheek foreword to 'Anthony Pookworthy', who is a satiric combination of D.H. Lawrence and Mary Webb, Gibbons acknowledges her 'debt' to this 'great' novelist in phrases that could apply to the early novels of Young:

> For your own books are not ... funny. They are records of intense spiritual struggles, staged in the wild setting of mere, berg or fen. Your characters are ageless and elemental things, tossed like straws on the seas of passion. You paint Nature at her rawest, in man and in landscapes ... You can paint everyday domestic tragedies (are not the entire first hundred pages of *The Fulfilment of Martin Hoare* a masterly analysis of a bilious attack?) as vividly as you paint soul cataclysms. (8)

While we cannot prove that Mary Webb read Young, we are struck by the similarities between the inchoate longings and revulsion against adult sexuality experienced by the heroines in *Gone to Earth* and Young's *A Corn of Wheat* and *Yonder*. More particularly, the description of Hazel Woodus's mother in *Gone to Earth* as a Welsh gipsy who hates marriage and a settled life (12) is reminiscent of Judith's mother in *A Corn of Wheat*, a gipsy-like figure, 'such unlikely daughter and granddaughter of teachers and clergymen' that another character wonders whether the women in the family had all been 'wild, passionate women, too' (18); Hazel herself, with 'so deep a kinship with the trees, so intuitive a sympathy with leaf and flower, that it seemed as if the blood in her veins was not slow-moving human blood, but volatile sap' (163) has much in common with Judith, whom Young repeatedly compares to some primeval woman, 'a creature of the woods' (3). As Cavaliero observed of Young, 'carefully depicted though her landscapes are, it remains a spectator's portrait merely' (149); the reader therefore remains positioned outside the literal and psychological domestic interior. Only later, as Young turns to a domestic modernism does she, like Woolf, Mansfield and Bowen, find a space of writing and a genre that achieves authenticity and complexity.

During this period, Young's novels are marked not only by pastoral and romantic ghosts, but also by contemporary politics and ideologies. While living in Bristol, Young apparently supported the vote for women and the suffragette movement.[2] Her first two novels, whose heroines express commitment to independence, sexual freedom and professional fulfilment and who attempt to live their lives according to ideals and principles and are therefore inflected by contemporary ideas on the New Woman and women's suffrage, bear some resemblance to Virginia Woolf's *The Voyage Out*, which also portrays a young woman's revulsion at the idea of marriage, and *Night and Day*, which examines the lives of young women seeking to fulfill themselves through social action, education and artistic creation. Both writers were publishing their first novels in their early 30s

'Untrammelled by Husbands and Houses': *A Corn of Wheat*

> Verily, verily, I say unto you, Except a corn of wheat fall into the ground and die, it abideth alone: but if it die, it bringeth forth much fruit. (*John* 12: 24)

A Corn of Wheat, which Young later repudiated and never allowed to be reissued, tells the story of an eccentric heroine, Judith – a young orphaned woman living in a vicarage with her brother's family. She becomes pregnant by Roger Halsted, a young socialist, refuses to marry him, goes to live in a remote village, meets a preacher and accepts his offer of marriage for the child's sake. But the baby is stillborn and Judith, with no reason to remain in the marriage, leaves to join Nell, the sister of her lover, who has founded a house for girls who have 'gone wrong' (290).

Judith is driven by a 'fierce love of the open air' (4) and domesticity represents to her the very negation of life because she sees the world as made 'of those who dwelt in houses and those who really lived' (5). In Vita Sackville-West's *All Passion Spent*, Lady Slane voices the thoughts of many domestic heroines when she reflects that a house is 'not merely a systematic piling-up of brick on brick', but 'a very private thing' (90), which has as much a claim to a soul as that collection of atoms that goes under the name of man. For Judith, on the contrary, a 'house and its furniture' are precisely no more than 'so many bricks and nails and tiles, so much mortar and wood, where bodies might be sheltered and seated' (6). She cannot be persuaded to eat her meals indoors and in the summer prefers a little tent in the corner of the garden to her bedroom. She, of course, puzzles the vicar's wife, who cannot understand why anybody should prefer 'a roof of white and azure to a papered ceiling' (4). The vicar, on the other hand, has a glimmer of understanding of his sister and talks kindly about communing with nature and seeking God in common things. Judith, however, has no use for religious piety; a distinctly romantic character, she shares the pantheism of the early Coleridge rather than Wordsworth's religious piety. Like Coleridge, she is played upon by the forms and colours of nature, 'passively, like an Aeolian harp' (5). In this first novel, Young already sets in place the contrast between figural domestic spaces which represent characters' psyches, mental states, bodies, the tangled web of familial relationships and the countryside, whether pastoral or mountainous, where characters seek freedom, transcendence and romance.

Nature, however, not only nurtures, it also threatens often in response to distasteful sexual experiences. Judith's sexual encounter with Roger Halsted disrupts her communion with nature and, significantly, it is only after this encounter that, sleepless in her tent, she thinks wistfully of the house where she does not belong: she pictures its lights being lowered one by one, the maids upstairs, her brother Charles smoking his pipe while the little vicaress, her hair in curl-papers, tucks the children in bed. This touch of the banal everyday captures the ideal of the Edwardian home as sanctuary from the public sphere and as the repository of domestic and moral value. To Judith, the shelter of the house appears now uncharacteristically welcome; the bedroom, formerly perceived merely as a storeroom for her scant possessions, beckons as a place of peace and for the first time 'seemed to have some personal relation to hersel ' (96).

From the ritualized narrow domesticity of the vicarage, a pregnant Judith flees to 'a small red cottage, with a thatched roof, through which the disproportionately tall chimneys poked' (137), a blatant image of male and female sexual organs and thus of Judith's unwelcome sexual experience. Here, in the first of Young's symbolic houses of repressed fears and desires, surrounded by a spectral landscape of dunes, Judith feels that she will finally gain that loneliness 'entire and unassailed' for which she had longed all her life (137). If the tiny red cottage seems to suggest the dreamy domesticity of a fairy tale, it also bespeaks a view of female sexuality as enclosed, claustrophobic space and we are soon reminded that Judith has no use for comforting domesticity: 'she almost regretted the existence of the little garden, with its hint of confinement (144).

Although Young goes to great lengths to characterize her as a timeless image of femininity, Judith more readily recalls that icon of modernity that was the New Woman. As Sally Ledger reminds us, the New Woman as a category was by no means stable – she may champion sexual purity and motherhood or free love or sexual circumspection (10). What remains constant in Young's characterization of the New Woman is her problematization of marriage, which shifts from emphatic rejection to a refusal to abide by the rules of conventional morality: 'Why should people want to marry her? To Halsted, who loved her, she had opened out as a bud opens to the sun, but a flower longs, too, for the loneliness of light ... she had no need of him anymore (192).[3] Despite Judith's halo of 'tragic, necessary timelessness' (163), she shares the same difficulties that the New Woman experienced in claiming her own sexuality 'without being claimed by it' (Ardis: 111). In refusing marriage to the man who made her pregnant, Judith pursues the challenge to conventional morality that gained the New Woman movement its notoriety: 'to her it was so natural and desirable to bear a child that she had always failed to understand why hands of horror should be uplifted when it had been unprefaced by a superfluous ceremony' (110). This is no simple advocacy of sexual freedom, for by choosing celibacy Judith also echoes the preoccupations of the sexual purity movement; her sentiments for Halsted are painfully detailed as 'no loathing nor distaste, but an abhorrence which shook her body and mind' (155). For her, as for the New Woman, celibacy is a necessary shield against the loss of self (Ardis: 110).

The destabilization of gender roles and the stubborn determination to protect her

House Haunting 65

private self, initiated by the encounter with Halsted, continues when Judith meets Joseph Beales, the preacher. She agrees to marry him because he does not threaten her independence since 'he had no more personality than a streak of lightning or a thundercloud' (259). On first entering his house, a draper's shop, Judith falls and loses consciousness.[4] She wakes up in a drab room, described in a way that makes tangible the revulsion Judith feels toward a domestic life: the dingy white curtains 'plainly told the eye how dusty they would feel to the fingers that touched them, how musty they would smell' (310). She finds out that her fall had caused the child to be stillborn. On coming home from one of her solitary excursions in the countryside, she finds a letter from Halsted's sister, Nell, who plans to open a place (she is careful not to use the word 'home') where 'girls who have "gone wrong"', as they call it, 'could get right with themselves again' (290). Nell, who feels that women ought to be free, 'untrammeled by husbands and houses' (293) is determined that she will not be herding these women together in houses and 'teaching them the domestic virtues' (291). The novel ends with Judith leaving Beales to join Nell: 'she had no doubt of her welcoming for she had taken Nell into the inner part of her where there were no doubts, where her faith in Nature lodged and where now there was enshrined her belief in the God dwelling in herself' (392). Judith enters a community of women that is the harbinger of the female society and alternative domesticities Young will develop in more nuanced fashion in *The Misses Mallett, Miss Mole* and *Chatterton Square*. In the novel's closing line, 'Nell, with a deepening wonder on her face, opened the garden-gate' (392) and Judith passes through this symbolically liminal space, the boundary between a natural and a domestic world, into a newly configured social space.

Unlike other sexually rebellious young women, for example, Rose Macaulay's Denham Dobie in *Crewe Train* (1926) or Lallie Rush in E. Arnot Robertson's *Ordinary Families* (1933), Judith does not succumb to the marriage plot and to a subdued wifely role. In her rebelliousness, she more closely resembles Helen Schlegel in E.M. Forster's *Howards End* (1910), Sue Brideshead in Thomas Hardy's *Jude the Obscure*, or Mary in May Sinclair's *Mary Olivier: A Life* (1919), who refuses marriage and, after her domineering mother's death, devotes herself to writing poetry.

Because Young, like Judith, seems repulsed by sexual experience, marriage and the messy interaction of personalities, in this first novel the home, rather than offering a Bachelardian integration of thought, memories and dreams, harbours a Freudian uncanny. It is nature in keeping with Young's neo-romanticism that offers spaces for intimacy and dreaming, although, as we have seen, it too is infected by the uncanny and the repressed. With each succeeding novel, Young, however, resorts more and more to the 'house and its furniture', to the bodies that seek shelter there, to the domesticity so scorned by Judith.

The Wind, the Blue Hills and the Typewriter: *Yonder*

Published two years after *A Corn of Wheat*, *Yonder* begins as the story of Edward

66   *Domestic Modernism, the Interwar Novel, and E.H. Young*

Webb, a travelling salesman with the soul of a poet, whose only solace in a life driven by economic necessity is the occasional wanderings in the countryside, from which he brings tales of adventures to his favourite daughter Theresa. During one of these excursions, Edward makes the acquaintance of the Rutherford family who live in the hills of Cumbria, in a house 'which seemed long and dark and cavernous' (4). The boy, Alexander, shares Edward's love for Keats and Milton, but especially 'a love of the wind … a greater bond than a whole library' (14–15); the father, James Rutherford, is a Byronic hero afflicted with dipsomania.[5] It seems that Young, like the young Catherine in Elizabeth Cambridge's *Hostages to Fortune* (1933), is 'writing a long novel in the Wessex manner, full of strong-minded dark women and farms in lonely places and Nature and Destiny and a great many other things which she knew nothing whatever about' (18). Clara, Alexander's mother, 'born to cradle men and children, to caress them and buffet them at her wise will' (28) and their neighbour Janet Beaker, a 'good witch', who sits 'as though she held in her lap the cup of wisdom whence all might drink' (84) might very well have added fuel to Stella Gibbons's portrait of Judith Starkadder in *Cold Comfort Farm* as 'a woman without boundaries … wrapped in a crimson shawl to protect her bitter, magnificent shoulders from the splintery cold of the early air. She seemed fitted for any stage, however enormous (2000: 34).

The opening of the novel is distinctly romantic, with the boy Alexander alone in nature, followed by the appearance of the lonely wanderer of whom he immediately asks, 'Did you – see things?' (3). The lofty atmosphere is somewhat disturbed by the jarring discovery that when not wandering on the hills Edward is a rather unsuccessful commercial traveller, doomed to spend his days journeying about the country 'with samples of ugly things, incidental to the dressmaking art' (7). The friendship of Edward Webb with the Rutherford family will last for many years, during which Edward continues to nurture the hope that one day his daughter, Theresa, and Alexander will meet. They come together, but only near the close of the novel after Edward, in an improbable turn of events, is killed by James Rutherford.

The reviewers of *Yonder* remarked on the crudity and immaturity of this ending, which contrasts with the imaginative power and sincerity of the prose. They also noted a 'strange detachment from social backgrounds' (*The Nation*, 6 March 1913: 232), but indeed such detachment is no longer as conspicuous as it was in *A Corn of Wheat*. If the Rutherford family seems suspended in time and enveloped in a vaguely supernatural atmosphere, Edward's family, solidly grounded in lower-middle-class surroundings in Radstowe (Bristol), offers a sobering touch to his Wordsworthian musings. While the gloomy, Gothic atmosphere of the Rutherford house offers an unconvincing backdrop for its equally unconvincing inhabitants, the more finely wrought description of the Webb's home suggests Young's growing interest in a 'house and its furniture'. The sparse allusions to the 'rheumatic' chairs, to the 'little-used drawing-room', to a clock that nobody remembers to wind comprise a ready grammar of neglect that has no need of a heightened rhetoric.[6]

As the narrating consciousness shifts from Edward to his daughter, *Yonder* gradually becomes Theresa's story. Theresa develops from the unconvincing elf adored

House Haunting

by her father, vaguely reminiscent of George Eliot's Maggie Tulliver, into a modern woman whose search for truth passes through tests of marriage proposals, work and the untimely and violent death of her father. In *A Corn of Wheat*, the echoes of the New Woman novel were limited to Judith's fierce sense of sexual independence and to Nell, one of those politically radical women who, in Carroll Smith-Rosenberg's words, 'used the loving world of female bonding to forge a network of women reformers and social innovators into a singularly effective political machine responsible for the many social reforms we associate with the progressive Era' (267). With *Yonder* such echoes become more distinct in the emerging character of Theresa.

After the death of her mother and the marriage of her sister, Theresa becomes the mistress of the household. Although she continues to fancy herself a writer, as did Catherine in *Hostages to Fortune*, she finds that 'with a cake in the oven it was not easy to compose her mind to the calm necessary for her first arresting lines' (117). One may detect autobiographical undertones when Theresa tells her father that her sister Grace 'wants to be a lady in a pantomime', whereas she will have 'to be something where I don't show. I have decided to write books' (61). She trains as a secretarial clerk and relinquishes both her yearnings after divine illumination and her vague writerly ambitions when she comes into contact with 'young women with the independence of their generation and scorn or frank comradeship for men … older women jerked into the necessity of earning bread, with the sheltered look on them … and elderly women, making a last effort to cheat fate' (155).

Employed by an eccentric philanthropist, she begins 'a little feminist movement of her own' (196) which may not placate 'a hankering … of the spirit' (196–205), but provides her with ample opportunity for an exploration of her situation as a woman. Although she does not despise marriage and indeed seems to want 'the other things – a home, and love, and …' (263), she refuses to have herself 'hemmed in by it' and longs for 'wide spaces' (206). A paradigm of the New Woman with her office and typewriter and an interest in 'causes', Theresa is also a throwback to the female salvationist who 'stretched the boundaries of a working woman's space and prerogatives within the community … able to travel through a range of social spaces' and wielded 'a certain amount of power and prestige in poor neighborhoods' (Walkowitz: 74, 85). Theresa rejects marriage to Basil Morton, who feels she should follow a 'life fitted to a woman' (214), choosing instead Alexander, whose disdain of the flesh comes from a desire 'to be unhampered, untrammelled, the servant of nothing but his mind and spirit' (227). These are concerns that Theresa would be only too ready to share for, like Judith, she lives her womanhood as a threat.

One cannot disagree with the *Times Literary Supplement* reviewer that this is 'an overloaded novel, overstrained and overworked' (1 August 1912: 307), but it does constitute an important stage in Young's apprenticeship as she moves away from an exploration of 'the emotional life centred upon a response to natural scenery' to one 'centred upon people' (Cavaliero: 147). Although the novel lacks the psychological depth of E. Arnot Robertson's *Cullum* or Stella Gibbons's *Westwood, or the Gentle Powers*, Theresa, like Robertson's Esther and Gibbons's Margaret, discovers a cultivated, moral and independent self.

68   *Domestic Modernism, the Interwar Novel, and E.H. Young*

Burning Down the House: *Moor Fires*

Moor Fires (1916) was not published in the United States until 1927; thus, predictably, the American reviewers were disappointed that this novel lacked the calibre of *William*. Carl van Doren, one of the few who was aware that this was an earlier work, nevertheless lamented the fact that what surrounds the Caniper family 'is not the human wisdom of William, but the careless geologic fatalism of the moors ... When she wrote "Moor Fires", for all its art and incidental precision, she was still trying another's element' (*New York Herald Tribune,* 9 October 1927: vii 6–7). One would certainly have to agree that Young had reverted to the noumenal world of *A Corn of Wheat* and *Yonder*. This was, however, a world in which she was becoming increasingly uncomfortable as is only too evident in the erratic ending of *Moor Fires* when Helen burns her house and her illicit love in a symbolic purging of her conflicted inner self

If *A Corn of Wheat* was self-consciously romantic, *Moor Fires* is an awkward mixture of Victorian and Gothic. Pinderwell House, the home of the unusual Caniper family, consists of a cold stepmother and four adult children: twin sisters, Helen and Miriam and brothers John and Rupert. Set in isolation amidst the moors, its nearest neighbour being Halkett's Farm, Pinderwell House is disturbed by the ghost of Mr. Pinderwell, his dead bride and the children he had hoped to have. Recent death, betrayal and violence stalk the house, unsettling the meaning of home and family. For Helen, this anthropomorphized 'long house with its wise unblinking eyes' (364), whose rooms are named after Mr. Pinderwell's unborn children, embodies her tormented family history. In contrast to the earlier works, house and domestic space are foregrounded here down to the details of housekeeping, cooking and meals:

> The efforts of Mildred Caniper, Helen and Mrs. Samson produced a brighter polish on floors and furniture, a richer brilliance from brass, a whiter gleam from silver, in a house which was already irreproachable. (33)

Whereas for Judith the reciprocal relationship with nature is only imperilled by the interference of men, for Helen nature is a power both to be worshipped and feared. Although she has no compunction in acknowledging that 'the white nursery had no attraction for her: she was more than satisfied with her many-coloured one; its floor had hills and tiny dales, pools and streams, and it was walled by greater hills and roofed by sky' (18); she also thinks of nature as 'always waiting near to demand a price' (186). The house, on the other hand, hides a secret, a Jamesian figure in the carpet which shadows the Caniper children and which Young only gradually discloses to the reader. When Helen, in a ludicrously melodramatic act, sacrifices her love for Zebedee the doctor and marries George, the farmer from Halkett's Farm in order to save her twin sister from the consequences of imprudent behaviour, such sacrifice seems only preposterous – until we recall how in an earlier scene 'George's gaze had hemmed her in and made her hot' (63). Young has thus complicated the ostensibly obvious contrast between the two sisters – one selfish and shallow, the other given to self-annihilation and apparent saintliness. Woken by the sound of galloping on the moor, it is not so much worry for the reckless Miriam that robs Helen of sleep, but rather the 'mysterious allurement of George's image' (205).

Critics of *Moor Fires* were not insensible to the ideological challenges this novel posed to the bourgeois literary tradition. The reviewer for *Times Literary Supplement* was disturbed by the recognition that the heroine is 'sane ... maternal ... [and] wis[e]' but also 'an adulteress of a strange sort.' Tellingly, this reviewer would not have objected to this duality had the purpose of the novel been to expose 'these heretofore revered qualities in woman'. What is unacceptable is that 'here we find not bitter exposure, but disquieting transmutation' (7 December 1916: 587). Indeed, the novel makes no concessions to conventional morality and is relentless in exploring Helen's agonizing process of self-knowledge. Helen's own mixture of desire and revulsion push her to the edge of hysteria through the everyday vocabulary of domesticity – 'an egg, perhaps. Boiled, baked, fried, poached, scrambled, omeletted? Somehow, somehow. What shall I say next? Hey diddle diddle, the cat and the fiddle, and all that kind of thing. That will take a long time. I know I sound mad, but I'm not' (282). This invocation of ordinary domestic language has a more powerful rhetorical effect than the narrator's habitually excited prose; for example, the narrator resorts to melodramatic verbs and adjectives in reporting how Helen contrasts her two relationships through the houses that represent them in: at Halkett's Farm, 'the larch-lined hollow would half suffocate her, she believed, but she would grow used to George and George to her ... and she would have children: not those shining ones who were to have lived in the beautiful bare house with her and Zebedee, but sturdy creatures with George's mark on them' (343).

Once again, Young found herself resorting to a rather crude sensationalism to untangle the threads of her plot. Tortured by her memories of Zebedee and her disturbing intimacy with George, Helen decides that 'she was going to end the struggle. She could not burn Zebedee, but she could burn the house. The rooms where he made love to her should stand no longer, and so her spirit might find a habitation where her body lived' (366). Metaphorically unleashing the volatile power of the moor fires upon the domestic realm, Helen unwittingly destroys not only a symbolic physical space but also a human life, for George dies in the fire. Pinderwell House, like Poe's House of Usher, is consumed by its own inner corruption and sexual ambivalence. That which has been repressed returns. The self, however, remains elusive and the inner consciousness is awkwardly splayed before the reader who remains positioned at a distance from the inner lives of the characters by a heavy-handed narration.

By the end of the nineteenth century, even Hardy had abandoned the rural world. However, Oxford did not bring him good fortune and after *Jude* he bade farewell to the novel. For Young, however, the city of Bristol offered an ideal site to explore the art of living. The Clifton Suspension Bridge, spanning city and countryside and the picturesque Avon Gorge connecting land and sea, city and empire were fitting symbols of the ongoing dialectic in Young's work between urban modernity and untamed nature

70 *Domestic Modernism, the Interwar Novel, and E.H. Young*

in all their contradictions. Like Viola Meynell, who abandoned the classless brooding characters and wild landscapes of *Martha Vine* (1910), *Cross-in-Hand Farm* (1911) and *Lot Barrow* (1913) to turn to the comedic lives of the *petite bourgeoisie* in *Modern Lovers* (1914), Young turned her wit and her observant eye to play upon the bits of ivory that were implied in everyday middle-class family life, staging minor dramas in the inhabited spaces of the vividly evoked homes and streets of Bristol recollected in tranquillity in south London, where she had joined the Henderson ménage after the war. After much straining after the transcendental and the mystical in the early novels, Young may well have asked herself the question posed by Vuillard: 'Why is it always in the familiar places that the mind and the sensibility find the greatest degree of genuine novelty?' (quoted in Thompson: 5). She may have agreed with Arnold Bennett that 'the spirit of the sublime dwells not only in the high and remote, it shines unperceived amid all the usual meannesses of our daily existence' (1899: 224).

'The Tyranny of Tea': *The Misses Mallett*

Near the end of this novel, Henrietta, the youngest of the four Misses Mallett, muses that 'life was tragic: no, it was comic, it was playful' (245), a pertinent description of the novel itself. Published in 1922 by Heinemann, *The Bridge Dividing* was reissued by Jonathan Cape as *The Misses Mallett* in 1927 and again in 1931 as part of Young's 'Collected Works'.[7] It marks an important transition in Young's career. More evocative than *The Misses Mallett*, the original title *The Bridge Dividing* reflects an incontrovertible paradox in which love, family and longing for home divide rather than unite families, lovers and houses. In this first of seven novels set in Bristol, the bridge of the title also refers to the Brunel suspension bridge which Rose and Henrietta Mallett frequently traverse to meet their shared lover and to experience the freedom of 'the strange, unbridled, stealthy wildness' of the other side (181). As Sally Beauman notes in her 'Introduction' to the 1985 Virago edition, the novel, like the two contrasting worlds on either side of the bridge, 'has a schizophrenic quality, as if two sides to its author's nature – Emily Young and Mrs. Daniell as it were – fought to control material of such subversive vitality that it refused to submit' (xv). Appearing in almost all her Bristol novels, the monumental Brunel Bridge functions both as a significant architectonic metaphor and a narrative device to connect and separate country and city, people and destinies; it exhibits, as Georg Simmel argues, the human will to connection, the passive resistance of spatial separation and the active resistance of a special configuration (66).

This story of a community of women, two sisters, a half-sister and a niece living a comfortable but stifling bourgeois existence, proposes an alternative to the similar evocation of the unfulfilled lives of unmarried women trapped by duty, poverty and propriety in F.M. Mayor's *The Third Miss Symons* (1918) and May Sinclair's *The Life and Death of Harriett Frean* (1922). Four houses – Nelson Lodge, Sales Hall, a boarding-house and a little house on the green – mirror and shape the lives of their

House Haunting

inhabitants. In Nelson Lodge live the four Misses Mallett: elderly Sophia and Caroline caught up in nostalgic memories of youth; the beautiful, reserved Rose, 'meant for something better, harder' than 'perpetual chatter, tea and pretty dresses' (20) and their young, lively and egotistical niece, Henrietta. This house, located in the desirable district of Upper Radstowe (Clifton) and graced with a small walled garden, is not a large establishment, but it displays character and quiet self-assurance (22). Like its mistresses, it has an 'outward life' that is 'elegant and ordered', where carpeted stairs and passages muffle the sound of feet and doors are quietly opened and closed. To Caroline and Sophia, locked in an imagined past, domestic rituals such as dressing for dinner and dining by candlelight are 'deliberately repetitive, thus denying the passage of time and the fearfulness of change' (Cooperman: 5).[8] With its orderly rituals, elegant interior decoration and nostalgic imagined past, Nelson Lodge presents a public display of class and status, enacting a meaning of home which visitors and readers may interpret and read, and which must not be disturbed lest the fragile construction of the public face of the self be shattered.

Set among the woods and fields of the wild side of the bridge, Sales Hall, in contrast, is the residence of ironically named Francis Sales, handsome, weak and inarticulate.[9] Rejected by Rose, he brings home a Canadian bride, Christabel. In short order Christabel, who resembles the supernatural, serpent-like Geraldine rather than her gentle namesake in Coleridge's poem, falls off her new mare in a hunting accident and ends up an invalid, confined to her couch. Resembling the prototype of the suffering Victorian invalid and the outsider who disrupts a home and its comfortable pathologies, Christabel, imprisoned in her crippled body and mind, is symbolized by the pink, feminine, overheated boudoir which pointedly contrasts with the masculine character of Sales Hall, 'a big, square house with honest, square windows ... the odd delightful mixture of hall and farm' (16). From within her Gothic chamber with only a malevolent cat for company, Christabel weaves a web of malice around Rose, Henrietta and Francis.

Francis almost runs off with winsome Henrietta, whose jealousy of Rose has driven her to seduce Francis. Christabel, however, conveniently dies that same evening, as does Caroline, followed a few months later by Sophia. Henrietta will marry Charles Batty, an awkward but artistic young man, one in a line of odd marriage partners in Young's novels. Rose, resigned, marries Francis, who is described by Charles as 'the slaughterer of music and of birds' (171), a pointed epithet that presages Young's evolving comic mode.

Despite the impression created by this brief plot summary, it is in the relationship between Henrietta and Rose that erotic tension is to be found. In the free indirect discourse through which the narrator gives us Rose's thoughts and words, Rose admits to caring 'more passionately for Henrietta' (187) than for Francis. Focalization shifts back and forth between Rose and Henrietta who voyeuristically watch each other in conversation or passionate embrace with Francis. As in all Young's novels, optical tropes dominate: spying, being seen and unseen, invisibility. Henrietta spies Rose and Francis in the woods and Rose, in a replication of that scene, comes upon Henrietta

72   *Domestic Modernism, the Interwar Novel, and E.H. Young*

and Francis embracing. Within this erotic triangulation, which recalls that of *Moor Fires* and indeed Young's own personal situation, Rose sacrifices herself by marrying Francis in order to save her niece from an error of judgement.[10] Oddly, given Young's earlier feminist position, neither Rose nor Henrietta exhibits New Woman tendencies or sympathies. Although Rose wants to play 'a larger part' and Henrietta craves the 'big sport of life', both seem to feel that this can only be accomplished 'through the agency of some man' (13). The phrase 'The Malletts don't marry' serves as a slogan for the Misses Mallett, but 'the idea of qualifying for the business of earning her bread did not occur to Rose' (23). Henrietta did work as a cook in the boarding house, but clandestinely and only until rescued by her wealthy aunts. Nevertheless, there is sexual openness in the novel as Rose reflects on the cost of having avoided physical relations with Francis and as Henrietta brandishes her sexual power.

Why has Young regressed in her portrayal of women's independence from the earlier novels? Has she been influenced by interwar propaganda and the cult of domesticity, or is she shifting her attention to a more domesticated world of compromised love and the realities of married life? How much was this shift to a more nuanced and localized examination of the home affected by her own settled and long-term domestic arrangement, unusual though it was, where she apparently had her own separate flat in the Henderson household and which permitted her to pursue her writing professionally?

Within houses like Nelson Lodge and Sales Hall, haunted by the spectre of heterosexuality and marriage,[11] the ghosts of dead mothers and fathers and a stuffy Victorian heritage, the Mallett women begin to forge alternative domestic arrangements. Although spinster sisters living together was not uncommon in the period and in the domestic novel, the supportive, if stifling, environment created by the four Malletts seems to suggest domestic alternatives to marriage and to offer a vantage point from which to examine the complex negotiations and compromises that married life entails. The quietly sardonic narrator, focalizing through Charles, recognizes that Henrietta is 'made to have a home, to be busy about small, important things, to play with children and tyrannize over a man in the matter of socks and collars' (226).

Not only do the houses in this novel offer vividly-realized settings for dialogue and interactions between family members and symbolize the bodies, beliefs and personalities of their inhabitants, but they are vividly anthropomorphized; waiting for Henrietta and Charles to resolve their differences, the little house on The Green, with its symbolic 'red roof like a cap and windows that squint', mirroring their uncertain relationship 'stood empty, squinting disconsolately, resignedly surprised at its own loneliness' (245). Characters are also continually compared to domestic objects and ornaments. The difference between Rose and Christabel resembles that between 'a Heppelwhite chair and an affair of wicker and cretonne' (38). In another example, 'the sight of Caroline was like a gate leading into the wide, uncertain world and the sight of Rose ... like a secret portal leading to a winding stair' (83). Thus, houses, their decoration and ornaments furnish a vocabulary intimate relations and feelings,

House Haunting

implying that Young has come to recognize the power of the home as a site and trope for exploring human relations. Reviewers, while expressing reservations about the plot, complimented Young on her style: 'often subtle ... sensitive writing' and 'a beautiful manner of telling' (*Springfield Republican*, 4 September 1927: 7f; *The Spectator*, 12 February 1927: 253). Indeed, Young has shed her hyperbolic, romantic descriptions of characters and nature. Although nature is still rendered anthropomorphically – 'the tall elm-trees looked over it [the wall] as though they wanted to escape' (32) – the descriptions of the countryside and Bristol itself are grounded in specific locales and language: 'where an aged city had tried to conquer the country and had failed, for the spirit of woods and open spaces, of water and trees and wind, survived among the very roofs' (76–7). Sally Beauman rightly notes that 'here there is still the sense of a writer trying to discover her own voice. The form has not yet stretched enough to accommodate the content; her solipsistic vision is at odds with a narrative convention that demands equal authenticity in a variety of viewpoints' (1985a: xv). Nevertheless, we see the beginnings of the acerbic, witty conversations and comic turn that give Young's later novels their charge along with the honest and ironic self-reflexivity that characterizes her later heroines. They record an apprenticeship in which Young gradually replaced the Gothic and melodramatic overtones of the early narratives with the more measured exploration of human relationships within the narrow boundaries of the bourgeois home and adopted a modernism tinged with conservatism and domesticity.

Notes

[1] In *Apartment Stories* (1999), Sharon Marcus notes that the omniscient and often impersonal third-person narration that 'constituted a hallmark of nineteenth-century British and French realist and naturalist novels was ... aligned with the public sphere because such narrators spoke from a generalizing point of view to a general public, and because those narrators' boundlessness and bodilessness paralleled the open structure of public spaces and the immateriality of the public sphere. On the other hand, omniscient narration consistently focused on the delimited, concealed, inaccessible spaces of private subjects and domestic spaces' (10).

[2] Meike Fritz to Kathy Mezei, e-mail correspondence, 20 December 2002.

[3] See Jane Eldridge Miller's discussion of the marriage problem novel in *Rebel Women: Feminism, Modernism and The Edwardian Novel*, 1994.

[4] In *Celia*, Celia's father also owned a draper's shop, which in Young's class-conscious novels seems to imply the interstices of class: gentility, trade, respectability, upward mobility. As Mary in May Sinclair's 1919 novel, *Mary Olivier*, reflects 'She was glad she had seen it [Cleveland School] through to the end when the clergymen's and squires' daughters went and the daughters of Bristol drapers and publicans and lodging-house keepers came' (146).

[5] Young, in what will become a characteristic narrative strategy, builds up suspense over why there is tension in the Rutherford house. Eventually, Jim's alcoholism and story are revealed through narrative summary.

74   *Domestic Modernism, the Interwar Novel, and E.H. Young*

[6] Young offers an interesting insight into reading and domesticity in her description of Edward's wife, Nancy:

> Nancy, seated in her rocking-chair, would read her endless novels. Following the indolence of her body, which was the result of more ill-health than anyone but herself suspected, her mind had gradually refused to exercise its natural, homely criticism in literature, and she read greedily, almost mechanically, any novel, not too serious, she could procure. Her method at the circulating library was to work methodically along the shelves, and the attendant, without question, would put the next book into her hands. Often she did not know its name, sometimes she could not have retold the tale. Reading and rocking had become twin habits which were alike soothing and effortless. Meanwhile the mending-basket would be filled to overflowing. (5

[7] It was published in the US in 1927 as *The Malletts* by Harcourt, Brace.

[8] On repetitive aspects of daily life, see Rita Felski's illuminating discussion in 'The Invention of Everyday Life' (1999), especially pp. 18–22.

[9] St Francis de Sales, 1567–1622, Bishop of Geneva, was canonized in 1665 and proclaimed Doctor of the Universal Church in 1877.

[10] In her study of homosocial desire, *Between Men: English Literature and Male Homosocial Desire* (1985), Eve Kosofsky Sedgwick discusses with reference to René Girard's *Deceit, Desire, and the Novel* how in an erotic triangle the bond that links two rivals is as intense as the bond that links either of the rivals to the beloved (21), a fitting description of the intense relationship and rivalry between Rose and Henrietta, Rose and Christabel and Henrietta and Christabel over the weak and vacillating figure of Francis

[11] For this phrasing, we thank Joshua Lovelace.

Chapter 4

Private and Public Spheres: Publication and Reception

The Battle of the Brows

> no one agrees with any one else about brows. (Rose Macaulay, *Time and Tide*, 16 July 1936: 1089)

> Friday 6 September 1935
> Reading Miss Mole: fair, but soft; & Stella Benson but I'm hard on novels. (Woolf, *Diary* IV 1982: 339)

> [To Lady Ottoline Morrell Saturday 19 February 1938]
> I bought a book for 6d in the Penguins called William by E.H. Young, and, for a wonder, enjoyed it greatly. She knows how to put in, and yet remain readable: so minute and yet so alive. And as its the kind of book I generally dislike, I think she must be a very good novelist, and wonder she's not far more famous than dear old voluble Hugh, and Wells and so on. (Woolf, *Letters* VI 1980: 216)

The publication history and reception of Young's novels are paradigmatic of the middlebrow novel that attracts 'legitimate' readers across the problematic divide of aesthetic judgement. Moreover, this history is a prime example of the dramatic changes in the publishing industry in the early twentieth century as it moved into mass marketing and aggressive advertising.[1]

With the appearance of *William* in 1925, the first of her novels to focus on middle-class domesticity, Young was warmly received on both sides of the Atlantic.[2] An American reviewer, Mary Ross, noted that after *William* sold out in the US, 'its reputation was spread almost solely by word of mouth … until there was an expectant group on the lookout for the next work of this almost anonymous author' (*New York Herald Tribune*, 28 September 1930: 6). Yet Woolf's tempered response highlights the difficulty of positioning novelists like Young in terms of readership and the canon and resonates with our own queries. What significance for the history of women's writing and reading can we draw from 'this very good novelist', whose works are now difficult to obtain but whose novels, *Celia* and *Chatterton Square*, delighted undergraduate and graduate students alike in recent classes we have taught? Why, as Woolf wondered, was Young not more famous than Hugh Walpole and H.G. Wells, famously middlebrow novelists?[3] In fact, as the following discussion will show, Young was lauded in her time; however, together with other practitioners of the domestic novel genre, she was

76   *Domestic Modernism, the Interwar Novel, and E.H. Young*

affected by changes in the marketing of books and taste, institutional forces which form and legitimize the canon and presuppositions which attempt to pigeonhole books and readers as either popular, middlebrow, or highbrow.[4] Why is her presence more shadowy than Elizabeth Bowen's, Rosamond Lehmann's, or Vita Sackville-West's? Did Young's insistence on privacy and her refusal to engage with the public sphere and literary London hamper recognition of her talents?

Archival letters reveal that Young participated in P.E.N., joined the Society of Authors, spoke to the British Federation of University Women in 1934 and, despite her disclaimer in *Twentieth Century Authors* that she knows no celebrities (1942: 1564), corresponded with Ottoline Morrell and met with other James Tait Prize winners like Helen Simpson.[5] However, unlike Winifred Holtby, Storm Jameson, Rose Macaulay, or E.M. Delafield, she did not write columns or book reviews for periodicals or newspapers or engage in progressive political activities. Although a popular and amusing writer, she did not settle into a literary niche and become a household name like Delafield, Jan Struther, Stella Gibbons, or Margaret Kennedy, nor as yet have her novels been turned into successful films [6] Evidently, Young was also less adept at marketing and promoting herself through journalism and a public persona than Delafield and Struther. Henderson's observation that she kept the details of her life away from the public gaze lest her renown as a rock climber should prejudice anyone in favour of her novels is revealing. Would headlines about a daring woman climber not have drawn the attention of publicity hounds?

In *The Enjoyment of Literature,* Elizabeth Drew, a contemporary of Young, writing in 1935, explains the wide appeal of 'the literature of escape' as the result of 'the common human craving for 'something different', for a 'refuge from the dullness and drabness, the harshness and baseness and emotional poverty of much of the real world ... where ... human experience is inevitably circumscribed' (x). This passage is striking in that the very words Drew uses to describe the world from which literature allegedly provides an escape portray the world of Young's novels. Although reading for Young's audience may have been a form of escapism, it was not escape into imagined lives more lively or interesting than their own, or into fictional spaces where 'feminine' values are granted more weight than is often the case in 'real' life; furthermore, because of the class to which her characters belong – shopkeepers, clerks, salespeople, impoverished clergymen – her novels would not have had the same attraction as the polished world of the upper-middle classes depicted by Bowen, Lehmann, Delafield, or Struthe .

With the exception of this perfunctory gesture by Woolf, Young was ignored by literary London. Nor is there any evidence that Ottoline Morrell, despite receiving copies of Young's books and exchanging polite notes, invited Young to Garsington Manor. What, therefore, does an examination of her publishing history and her reception by reviewers, the literary world and academia reveal to us not only about Young's personal and professional choices but also about the response to women writers and the popular and proliferating domestic novel genre during the interwar period? For, as Claire Hanson, among others, has noted, many women writers such as

Private and Public Spheres: Publication and Reception 77

Katherine Mansfield, Rosamond Lehmann and Elizabeth Bowen, and more recently Elizabeth Taylor and Barbara Pym, have 'been thought of as somehow minor or trivial' because of their commitment 'to a common language, the small change, as it were, of gesture and speech through which, for most of us, the deeper things of life are intimated and expressed' (1990: 301).[7] A striking example of the dismissal of a certain class of readership who do take pleasure in the domestic novel is a review of *Chatterton Square* by George Woodcock, who qualifies his praise of Young as 'a capable craftsman' by adding that 'for those who like it, she knows pretty thoroughly the technique of this kind of provincial novel' ('New Novels', *New Statesman and Nation*, 6 August 1947: 134).

In 1935, Winifred Holtby distinguished between middlebrow novels that 'provide the main material of the circulating libraries' and 'flourish as "Best Lenders"' and the highbrow, which appeals to 'private purchasers' who 'enjoy sufficiently the aesthetic experiences provided by these novels to possess them in order to re-read and discuss them' (1935: 112).[8] Our reading of Young finds her novels falling into both categories, thus defying simple notions of classification. As the reviewer of Young's second novel, *Yonder* (1912), commented with the public library patron in mind, her novels are 'not for the average reader' (*American Library Association Booklist*, March 1913: 301). Self-conscious, yet not opaque, a 'good read', yet not formulaic, Young's work is a perfect example of what Hilary Radner has called 'the woman's novel', a novel that refuses obscurity, but at the same time defies the classification of popular culture. This kind of novel 'challenges the categories of high Modernism, reflecting the ambiguous position of its preferred reader – the educated woman' (1989: 256), acknowledging her as *une soeur semblable* and guiding her reading pleasure through the staging of symbolically charged scenes of reading. Nicola Humble's term 'feminine middlebrow', along with Alison Light's 'conservative modernity' and Marion Shaw's 'progressive middle-brow novel' (35), serve to elucidate and validate novelists like Young, whose works are complex, yet pleasurable.[9]

Reading practices have recently been the object of much fruitful investigation with literary scholars examining in detail how these practices are constructed by the marketplace and how taste is greedily commodified. In the interwar period, reading practices were influenced by increasingly aggressive marketing strategies such as the launch of Penguin paperbacks in 1935 in the UK and the creation of the Book-of-the-Month Club in the US in 1926, quickly followed by its UK counterparts, the Book Society (1929) and Book Guild (1930), directed at the so-called middlebrow reader. In her analysis of the Book-of-the-Month Club in *A Feeling for Books*, Janice Radway details how the Club applied marketing principles and advertising practices associated with industries such as tobacco, soap and canned goods to book production and distribution. Radway goes so far as to affirm that such commodification posed a threat to 'the essential concepts and forms structuring the bourgeois literary realm, including those defining the book, the author, the reader, and the proper relations among them' (128). While we do not know how Young responded to the relatively low-key marketing of her novels, her correspondence with Cape indicates her eagerness to

78   *Domestic Modernism, the Interwar Novel, and E.H. Young*

be published in the different, cheaper editions and to enter the American market and she, quite naturally, inquires about her sales in both America and Britain; she needed the money.

In her discussion of Woolf's advocacy of the 'common reader' (an amateur and wide-ranging reader) and the 'democratic highbrow', Melba Cuddy-Keane demonstrates how the fight for readership, respect and legitimization in the face of mass production, consumption and communication intensified the debate over high, middle and lowbrow in the early twentieth century (2, 21). Writers like Young, who were forging a niche focused on the everyday lives of women, were popular and published by well-known, large publishing houses; yet, worried about their cultural prestige (21), they sought to address just such a 'common reader' who, similar to the writers themselves, experienced regulation of women's lives and lack of access to higher education (although Young, in contrast to Woolf, did attend college and study philosophy).

The 'Summary and Conclusions' of a report by Mass-Observation on 100 working-class readers, which corroborates other records of reading habits, libraries, booksellers during 1937–1945, state that the 'vast majority of readers prefer [light] fiction but note that 'there is a definite, if not very large, group of people who prefer the more serious types of fiction, especially the sort that is described as being "like real life"' (30). Readers of Young and other domestic novelists would fall into this latter category. And indeed, a list of 25 books taken out by women include Young's *Celia* at the top of the list, followed by novels by Stella Kaye-Smith, Georgette Heyer, Ethel Dell, Ernest Raymond, Charlotte Brontë (*Jane Eyre*), Jane Austen (*Sense and Sensibility*) and Naomi Jacob (17). A.J. Cronin's melodramatic *Hatter's Castle* (1931) was also very popular, as were detective stories by Agatha Christie and Edgar Wallace, Daphne du Maurier's *Rebecca* and Margaret Mitchell's *Gone with the Wind*.[10]

Young published in, and was reviewed by, publications directed at middle-class women and/or the middlebrow reader such as *Good Housekeeping* and *Punch* as well as in journals and newspapers that drew upon a more selective readership (*Time and Tide, Times Literary Supplement, The English Review*). Her novels were issued by established British and American presses (Heinemann, John Murray, Jonathan Cape, Harcourt Brace) with fiction lists that ranged from popular detective novelists to renowned authors such as E.M. Forster, Ernest Hemingway, Sinclair Lewis, T.E. Lawrence and Robert Graves. She was marketed, packaged and promoted by republication in cheaper series like the Travellers' Library, the Reprint Society, selections by the Book Society (*Chatterton Square*), advertisements in *The Publisher and Bookseller* and the usual laudatory cover blurbs. The latter, scripted by successful 'middlebrow' writers such as E.M. Delafield and Hugh Walpole (who, along with J.B. Priestley, served on the selection committee of the Book Society), and *Punch*, deflator of the highbrow, set this most private of writers in the midst of the expanding commercialization of publishing.

Reviews and reviewers also served to situate and classify Young, not only by their commentary, but also by the influence and power of their publication site as well as their presuppositions about audience and readers.[11] Woolf's reading of *Miss Mole* as

Private and Public Spheres: Publication and Reception 79

'fair but soft', her aesthetically-charged judgement that it was the kind of book she generally dislikes and her qualification that she is hard on novels are all revealing comments that continue to speak to our own current reading practice as educated readers. They also reflect Woolf's desire to transform the materialist Edwardian novel as articulated in her 1924 essay, 'Character in Fiction' and her fatigue with the proliferation of sentimental domestic and middlebrow novels in the 1920s and 1930s. In an unsent letter to the editor of the *New Statesman*, Woolf castigated the middlebrow, who unlike the highbrow in pursuit of art and the lowbrow in pursuit of life, mixes life and art 'rather nastily, with money, fame, power or prestige'. What the middlebrow call 'real humanity', she continues, is a 'mixture of geniality and sentiment stuck together with a sticky slime of calves-foot jelly' (115, 117).[12] By comparing Young with Hugh Walpole, H.G. Wells and Stella Benson, Woolf assigns her a position among the middlebrow novelists, yet her comments also imply a perplexed admiration for Young and unease about her place in the battle of the brows. Woolf's prevaricating observations reflect our own discomfort about distinctions latent in 'middlebrow' and 'canon', a discomfort reinforced by publishing practices and by unmediated aesthetic judgements.

At the same time, while highbrow writers like Woolf and George Orwell shot barbs at the stickiness of the middlebrow, several domestic, and supposedly middlebrow, novels were also casting a satiric eye upon middle-class reading practices, highbrow literature and the London literary scene.[13] Storm Jameson's *Three Kingdoms* (1926) bristles with jibes at the publisher Andrew Marr's 'stable' of would be highbrow writers, 'effete young men who write about nothing' and have the wrong habit of talking about art 'when they're no good at life' (203, 204). Stella Gibbons in *Nightingale Wood* (1938), which she calls a 'romantic comedy', mocks both middlebrow and highbrow readers. She punctuates the novel not only with satiric references to the 'meringues of the intellect, those mental brandies-and-sodas – *novels*' (119), to the popular novelist, Berta Ruck, 'a lovely story ... the young man in it was such a darling' (51) and to Dorothy Sayers, thrillers and detective stories, 'Don't want anything heavy when you settle down after dinner' (166), but also to the romanticized view of the highbrow: 'Hetty was also a discontented, queer girl whom nothing pleased but rubbishy books by immoral highbrow authors. So the sooner Hetty married, the better' (39). On the other hand, in *Westwood, or the Gentle Powers* (1946), Gibbons implicitly defends novelists such as Young by aligning herself with those writers who 'pride themselves on being able to perceive romance and beauty in the common scene' (20). In Rose Macaulay's *Crewe Train* (1926), the narrator mocks the young London publisher Arnold Chapel, whose first novel has just appeared:

> Arnold cared very much for this book, which probed very deeply into human psychology, recording thought and emotion in that particular fashionable medium which some consider an accurate transcription and others do not. Arnold hoped it would make a good deal of stir ... and establish his name among the highbrow novelists, for no one wants to be thought only a publisher. (112)

His 'barbarian' wife prefers guide books which do not have people in them.

Macaulay's *Keeping up Appearances* (1928) not only mocks the pretensions of highbrow intellectuals, but also makes the battle of the brows its very subject. Daisy Simpson, a Bloomsbury type, pens columns for the *Sunday Wire* on subjects such as 'After Love's Rapture – What?' or 'The Best Age for Woman' and publishes romantic fiction under the pseudonym of Marjorie Wynne (a likely pun on Elynor Glyn, who at the end of the 1920s was 'the reigning queen of popular love literature').[14] When Daisy visits her 'common' mother and her new family in East Sheen, a suburb that represents the quintessence of lowbrow life, she is 'Mother's clever girl, petted and admired' (18); however, Daisy was raised in London by her upper-class aunt and here, in the eyes of the London set, the young woman who earns her living by writing 'such bright, clever pieces, that people always like to read' (18) is only one 'of those vulgar little journalists' who are 'not realized by nice highbrows, and only recognized by less nice highbrows as a target for unkindly jests'. Yet, East Sheen, where her mother reads P.G. Wodehouse and, soon renouncing the impulse to 'improve her mind', settles for 'another Wallace' (75)[15], though a warm and welcoming place, embarrasses Daisy. She regretfully reflects that, 'it was the highbrows one chose: this environment that annihilated, that relegated one's activities and one's true self to the slums where common people move' (18). Eventually her conviction that 'the impregnable security of one class of writer from another class of reader is more than the security of snails from British cooks, of pigs from Jewish butchers, of the skunk from the squeamish hunter' (91) proves to be wrong and the high wall of partition that Daisy had erected between East Sheen and Bloomsbury starts to crumble.

The argument that Macaulay voiced through Daisy's musings anticipates by many decades the current debate about literary categorization: although Miss Wynne 'was not surely, on the lowest levels? ... to highbrows these slight differentiations between one lowbrow and another are not obvious, all appearing to be submerged in a common lack of intellectual distinction and commonplace sentiment, style, and thought' (126). Citing the evidence of public library loans in the 1990s in the UK, Bridget Fowler has noted that the structures and organization of the literary field (prizes, fellowships, grants) have resulted in a greater number of women turning to 'the despised middlebrow and popular literary genres' (144). Accordingly, she cautions against 'too restrictive a view of the middlebrow' which then 'risks contributing to the very reification of cultural divisions that Bourdieu desires to expose' (148). We would agree with her questioning whether 'these so-called middlebrow novels represented ... a repressed tradition of the new' and 'whether they were suspect in literary terms precisely because, despite the freshness of their subjects, they sold well' (148). Young certainly fits the profile of the popular 'middlebrow' authors to whom Fowler refers and who lived outside the traditional ruling elite, did not inhabit metropolitan or country houses and did not attend major public schools or Oxbridge (148–9). But neither Young or the domestic novelists discussed here capitulate to Woolf's anxiety about the middlebrow as an ungainly mixture of geniality and sentiment.

Private and Public Spheres: Publication and Reception   81

The Paperback Revolution

When Woolf bought *William* 'in the Penguins,' she was participating in an experiment in publishing, for *William* was one of the first ten Penguins mass-produced as cheap reprints by Allen Lane (Figures 5 and 6).[16] Other publishers had certainly previously produced low-cost editions – the shilling railway editions, the 'yellow backs', the 'sixpenny blacks'. However, with this paperback's arresting combination of the penguin insignia and modern, functional and vivid orange design, Lane hoped that his marketing innovation would attract lower-middle-class readers and convert book-borrowers into book-buyers. In the 22 May 1935 number of *The Bookseller* Lane, echoing Winifred Holtby, explained that the Penguin Books were designed to reach people who did not feel at home in a bookshop and preferred the tuppenny library, but whose taste had improved:

> In choosing these first ten titles, the test which I applied to each book was to ask myself: Is this a book which, had I not read it and should I have seen it on sale at 6d., would make me say, 'That is a book I have always meant to read; I will get it now?' (497)

By attempting to reach a wider audience, the 'new reading public', through an eclectic list of titles, Lane also gave greater visibility to the middlebrow. As we know, this experiment, which Jonathan Cape, Young's publisher and one of the publishers of the moment in the 1920s, prophesied would 'go bust', instead revolutionized book publishing and bookselling (Howard: 164). One hundred and fifty thousand copies were snapped up within four days and the first Penguins released in July sold out quickly (*The Bookseller*, 8 August 1935: 767). By making these books affordable, Lane may have unwittingly contributed to blurring the boundary between high and middlebrow literature – between what Winifred Holtby called 'Best Lenders' and books that appeal to 'private purchasers'.

Interestingly, the 2003 'History of Modern Design in the Home' exhibit at the Design Museum in London linked the modern home to the Penguin paperback, claiming that both the Penguins and the Lawn Road Flats, London service flats built in 1932 in the continental international style, were infused with the same democratic spirit of improving the quality of people's lives (Figure 7).[17] Coincidentally, Allen Lane conceived the idea of a good quality paperback, which would only cost the price of a packet of cigarettes, when returning to London after a weekend at the Devon home of Agatha Christie; waiting for a train at the Exeter station and seeking something to read, he found only reprints of nineteenth-century novels. From 1940 to 1946 Christie lived at No. 22 in the Lawn Road Flats, which she compared to a giant ocean liner without any funnels.[18]

Young's first novel was published by Heinemann, although it is not mentioned in *William Heinemann: A Century of Publishing, 1890–1990*, nor are her books listed in the Appendix A of authors and titles. This may corroborate Young's desire to disown her first novel, or it may be an indication of her subsequent lack of status. By 1925

Figure 5   The Penguin cover for *William*, 1935

Figure 6   The first ten Penguins

Figure 7   The Isokon, Lawn Rd, NW3. Photo by Kathy Mezei

with *William*, her fifth novel, Young moved to Jonathan Cape, who had started his publishing house in 1921 – an appropriate move since Cape believed that the fifth book was the critical measure of an author.[19] Edward Garnett, a colleague of Cape's at Duckworth, joined his new company as reader and since Garnett scrupulously vetted every manuscript submitted to Cape (Howard: 33), he reviewed Young's submissions. In response to his comments, she appears to have revised *The Vicar's Daughter*. As a result of the success of *William* in both the UK and America, Cape reprinted her novels (*Moor Fires* (1916); (1927); *The Bridge Dividing* (1922) as *The Misses Mallett* (1927); and *William* (1927)) in cheap editions like Florin Books and the Traveller's Library, a reprint series begun in 1926 which Michael Howard defended as a series that included no book 'which has not already proved its worth and run the gauntlet of the critics' (76). Both *Moor Fires* and *The Misses Mallett* as *The Malletts* were also published in America in 1927, again in response to the success of *William*.

The advertisement for *Miss Mole* in *The Publisher & Bookseller*, 27 June 1930, announced 'An Important Literary Event' in 'the publication of a new book by a well-known and popular writer. E.H. Young whose work has always been successful since her novel *William* was published in 1925, has now written a further book, following up the success of *The Vicar's Daughter*' (1342) (Figure 8). The market-driven language of this advertisement, with its commonplace catch-phrases, 'well-known',

Figure 8   Advertisement for *Miss Mole*, *The Publisher and Bookseller*, 17 June 1930, p. 1342

86 *Domestic Modernism, the Interwar Novel, and E.H. Young*

'popular', 'success', situates Young and *William* in the tradition of the middlebrow and the associated commercialization of novels and reading; seemingly, it caters to the standardization of taste, what Q.D. Leavis so scornfully called the 'herd instinct'. Reviewers, nevertheless, were intrigued by the novel's unusual and audacious treatment of the *pater familias*, adultery and bohemianism.

Then, in 1930, *Miss Mole* won the coveted James Tait Black Fiction Prize. One of the two oldest book prizes awarded annually for best fiction and best biography, it has also honoured: E.M. Forster, *A Passage to India* (1924); Siegfried Sassoon, *Memoirs of a Fox-Hunting Man* (1928); Kate O'Brien, *Without My Cloak* (1931); Robert Graves, *I Claudius* (1934); and Winifred Holtby, *South Riding* (1936). *Miss Mole* subsequently underwent six reprintings in 1930 alone. In 1931, Cape began issuing a collected edition consisting of *Moor Fires, The Misses Mallett, The Vicar's Daughter, Miss Mole* and *Yonder.* Following Young's death in 1947, Cape again reprinted her novels as the 'Collected Works of E.H. Young' up to 1950. According to Michael Howard, Jonathan Cape 'paid particular regard to E.H. Young'; he

> encouraged her with admiration and affection, but she wrote with difficulty and had little confid nce in her ability, and he had to urge her on continually. 'Pegasus,' he would tell her, 'needs the whip!' ... Throughout her writing life she had drawn constant support from Jonathan, his appreciation of her humility and integrity, and his understanding of her need for the encouragement he gave her to the end. (217)

In another anecdote, Howard recalls that Young, already mortally ill, began writing *Chatterton Square* after the war and would send Cape a few chapters at a time.[20] Mysteriously, one batch disappeared and Cape ordered the entire staff to stop work immediately and search for it until eventually, to everyone's relief, the chapters were found in a cupboard (217).

With the exception of her first novel, *A Corn of Wheat*, all of Young's novels were published in America, mostly by Harcourt Brace, who held shares in Cape. In 1941, *William* was reprinted in America in 'The Press of the Readers Club' edition with a foreword by Carl Van Doren, who also reviewed *Moor Fires* for *The New York Herald Tribune* in 1927. Her children's books, dedicated to her nieces and nephews, *Caravan Island* (1940) and its sequel, *River Holiday* (1942), were published by Adam and Charles Black.

Reading Pleasure

> [A] cake ... of delightful nutty and fruity consistency with bits of spiced surprise and a richness of starch base which makes it thoroughly palatable. (Margaret Lawrence on *Miss Mole* 1936: 300)

> Look, biscuits by the bed, rather a good idea, and some light novels by female authors. (Barbara Pym, *Less Than Angels* 1955: 210)

Private and Public Spheres: Publication and Reception 87

Young Digby's appreciation of the combination of light literature by women and comfort food is not the only self-ironic stab Barbara Pym takes at the class of literature to which her critics assigned her during her lifetime. Digby's friend Catherine, herself a writer of stories and articles for women's magazines, experiences a feeling of 'safety and comfort' when entering the Swans's home: here the music on the wireless, a bright fire, chintz-covered chairs and sofa and 'Mabel Swan sitting with her feet up on a pouffe reading the latest work of a best-selling female novelist' (234) create a sense of domestic cosiness that Catherine misses in her bare fl t strewn with papers. However, the fact that Catherine is the character who, through her profession, observing eye and extensive literary knowledge, most resembles her author, invites us to read this passage ironically as an astute commentary on the prejudices that confront many of the women novelists mentioned in this study. References such as Pym's are part of an intertextual discourse that runs through their fiction, often as a response to reviewers and which raises pertinent, perplexing questions concerning reading pleasure, aesthetics, value, canon formation and genre and gender privileging.

As we perused the numerous contemporary reviews of Young's novels, we noted repeated references to pleasure, categories of readers (middlebrow, women), the woman's novel and the provincial novel, modernity versus tradition and the devaluing of the domestic and the private, in comparison with the public, sphere. We found ourselves beset by conflicting modes of reading and positioning Young's works. For her wide-ranging critical reception by reviewers impedes a simple codification of taste and pleasure in that the generally laudatory responses in the UK and America cover an array of audiences from *Times Literary Supplement, The New Yorker, The New York Times Book Review, Spectator, Time and Tide* and *Nation* to *Country Life, Tatler, Englishwoman, Punch* and *Daily Mail*. Reviewers include Graham Greene, Hugh Walpole, E.M. Delafield, V.S. Pritchett, Carl Van Doren, Gwendolen Raverat and George Woodcock. With the exception of *A Corn of Wheat*, which, however, *Punch* had hailed as 'a literary debut of very considerable promise' (17 August 1910: 108), all her novels were extensively reviewed both in Britain and in America. The responses to *Yonder* and *Moor Fires* were understandably cautious, objecting to the 'tedious pseudo-poetical personification and communings with trees and moors' (review of *Moor Fires, TLS*, 7 December 1916: 587) or the flirting with the supernatural.

However, after *William*, which represented Young's first foray into the exploration of domestic modernism, it is not unusual to encounter phrases such as 'sheer pleasure', 'extraordinarily gifted' and 'front rank of present-day English novelists' in the wide spectrum of Young's reviews. Although some reviewers express scepticism regarding the aesthetic possibilities of the everyday, 'the mere succession of familiar, everyday incidents is poor material for imaginative study' (review of *William, TLS* 30 April. 1925: 298), many insist on the pleasure that Young's fiction offers its readers. The emphasis on pleasure, the discriminating reader, the importance of emotions and the activity of daily, domestic living challenges the *Punch*–ian concept of middlebrow as people getting used to the stuff they ought to love (see n. 3) and underlines the difficulty of labelling a writer as complex as Young as 'middlebrow'. Thus we are

88 *Domestic Modernism, the Interwar Novel, and E.H. Young*

left to surmise that either the term 'middlebrow' does not serve Young well or the conceptual limitations of the term itself should be revisited. Our uneasiness finds an echo in Bridget Fowler's response to Bourdieu's cultural theory and her query whether, in the case of women, cultural production has taken forms different from Bourdieu's polarization between art and entertainment to sit uneasily with the kinds of commercial production he identifies: bourgeois art, middlebrow pastiche and the naïve political moralism of industrial art (143). In other words, Fowler invites us to reassess the criteria that define and valorise genres preferred and perfected by women writers and to propose more appropriate terms. We consequently feel that Christopher Reed's 'domestic modernism' (2004: 4) succinctly captures the validation and foregrounding of the domestic and the everyday as it is represented with an unrelenting view from the interior in many novels by women writers between the wars.

When attempting to define the quality of pleasure that Young's fiction provides for the reader, most reviewers can only proceed analogically, comparing Young to Charlotte Brontë, Thomas Hardy, George Eliot, Anthony Trollope, Mrs. Gaskell and repeatedly, Jane Austen. The most sustained attempt to define what exactly is 'Austenian' in Young's fiction comes from Basil Davenport, who, writing about *The Curate's Wife,* recalls not only the 'power of illuminating the humdrum lives of a little provincial circle' and its 'most delicate conception of all the currents of thought and feeling in [Young's] chosen section of suburban society, the tiny social distinctions and the intricate human relationships', but also the remarkable degree 'of sense and sensibility' that distinguishes this novel, in which a moral is drawn 'inoffensively, by showing ... that to behave according to her moral is the only sensible things to do' (*Saturday Review of Literature*, 17 November 1934: 291). Among her contemporaries, Young is compared to Ivy Compton-Burnett, F.M. Mayor, Emily Eden, E.M. Forster and of course, as noted earlier, Virginia Woolf.

Young's quirky, unsentimental representation of domesticity struck a responsive chord in her readers; her fans plead for a further sequel to *The Curate's Wife*, the 1934 sequel to *Jenny Wren* (1932): 'Please don't leave us in despair. Such interesting lives ought to be followed up. Yours in pleasant anticipation. Reader' (Letter undated, Young Papers). Another fan, Mary King, writes that she is left wondering what these characters 'will do next and, above all, wanting to know what happened after you laid down your pen' (Letter, 16 October 1934, Young Papers). In an undated letter, Maud Cameron sends 'greetings to the mother of my best friends' (Young Papers). Reviewing *The Curate's Wife*, E.M. Delafield, herself an adept practitioner of the sequel, in her *Diary of a Provincial Lady* series and a writer who pursued the validation of the quotidian as deliberately as Young, expresses delight at this sequel and does not hesitate to identify herself as part of a fan club (*Now and Then*, Winter 1934: 34). These fan letters appear to corroborate Young's success in appealing to the middlebrow whereby 'readers are left with the agreeable sensation of having improved themselves without incurring fatigue' (Leavis: 44). Yet Young also disturbed conventional notions and offended against received values; the coincidentally named Mrs. Mallett, a vicar's wife who wrote to Young protesting her unkind portrayal of

Private and Public Spheres: Publication and Reception 89

vicars in *The Curate's Wife* while conceding to the fitting comparison of Young to Jane Austen, added reproachfully 'I am not sure of the "without a sting"' (Letters, 11, 20 November 1934, Young Papers).

Readers and reviewers, in general, seem to derive pleasure from identification with the charm and humanity of the everyday, the home and on the part of American readers, the Englishness of these novels as well as from the ironic wit of Young's dialogues and descriptions. It is certainly true that the recurrent use of the Austen tag may indicate, as Cecilia Macheski remarked à propos of Elizabeth Taylor, a desire on the part of the critic to find a '"safe" line of descent void of passionate threats of mad women in attics, women of dubious morals, or even worse, sexual heretics and suicidal depressives' (5). One could argue, however, that Austen not only provides a safeguard here against the threat of unruly femininity, but also a lexicon to define those qualities that make good literature. If we agree with Stanley Fish that 'paying a certain kind of attention ... results in the emergence into noticeability of the properties we know in advance to be literary' (10–11), then Austen's name can be seen as providing the reader with the means to legitimate one's taste and to appease the anxiety the reader feels *vis-à-vis* texts that are not amenable to being interpreted according to those categories that modernism has identified with highbrow literature

A Question of Gender

While several reviewers (of the earlier novels) assume the identity of E.H. to be male, others place Young firmly within the class of 'women novelists'. Thus, for V.S. Pritchett 'Miss Young is within her limits the most satisfying of women novelists' (review of *Jenny Wren*, *New Statesman and Nation*, 26 November 1932: 660–62); she 'excels, as the best women novelists always do excel, in such differentiation of character' (review of *The Curate's Wife, New Statesman and Nation*, 8 September 1934: 296). Although the reviewer for *Times Literary Supplement* finds a heroine like Judith in *A Corn of Wheat* baffling for the male reader, making him feel that he is 'either hopelessly awkward and insensitive for the situation, or that Judith is so rare a being that her case must be resigned to the specialist' (20 June 1910: 226), Graham Greene appreciates 'the authentic nature of [Young's] feminine material and the grace of her style (long sentences trailing down the pages like a rather unfashionable but timeless dress)' and predicts that such qualities will ensure the survival of her novels (*Spectator*, 7 September 1934: 336). Even in those reviews which do not explicitly place Young in a feminine tradition, recurring terms resonate intriguingly with particularly valued female virtues: sympathy, charm, warmth, delicacy, subtlety and insight into character all receive their due. Metaphors used to describe Young's world, even when not pointedly feminine or referring to her deliberately small compass, belong in the domestic realm: so, for instance, *The Curate's Wife* 'has the coherence of a well loved room' (Mary Ross, *The New York Herald Tribune*, 21 October 1934: 8).

90   *Domestic Modernism, the Interwar Novel, and E.H. Young*

While some reviews note that, although the scene of her novels is a modern English town, the manner in which it is painted is that 'of another age' (review of *The Curate's Wife*, *The Commonweal*, 4 January 1935: 296) others claim that *William*, for one, 'carries its modernity with a beautiful ease'; because of its interest in behaviour and in the contact of differing outlooks, this novel 'could not have been written in any period but our own' (*Spectator*, 30 May 1925: 896). Attempts to place Young in the modern tradition compare *Jenny Wren* to Rosamond Lehmann's *Invitation to the Waltz*, while others invoke Dorothy Richardson as an influence to which *William* may have responded consciously or unconsciously, although the reviewer is careful to point out that 'Mr. [*sic*] Young is a more normal person than Mrs. Richardson' and for this reason the novel has a larger appeal than any by Richardson (*Boston Transcript*, 2 September, 1925: 6). Here, we pause to ask ourselves how the assumption of male gender might have determined the reviewer's sense of normalcy?

Yet the retrospective view of Young's modernity is divided. While Sally Beauman comments on 'a narrative experimentalism quite remarkable for its period' (1984: xi), John Bayley categorizes her novels as *passé*, although this observation is not meant as criticism (1988 v). Carmen Callil, who rediscovered Young for Virago, suggests that she was 'more of a writer of her time from the narrative point of view'.[21]

Young's later novels, *The Curate's Wife*, *Celia* and *Chatterton Square* follow the trend of the domestic novel to navigate the troubled waters of matrimony and family life rather than the romance and foreplay of courtship. Marriage is found to be sadly devoid of romance, a minefield of continual negotiation, compromise and misunderstandings. More covertly than Rosamond Lehmann, Radclyffe Hall, Virginia Woolf and Katherine Mansfield, Young explores homosocial relations between women and illicit or adulterous sexual encounters; she also proposes a redefinition of masculinity through the gentle and empathetic characters of Alexander in *Yonder*, William in *William* and Piers in *Chatterton Square*. Although William is a successful businessman, Young focuses only on his sphere of influence within his domestic world, endowing him with unusual insight into, and sensitivity towards, his children and their dilemmas, while Piers's limp and disfigured face serve as a powerful reminder of the way in which the Great War had complicated constructions of masculinity by rendering the wounded soldier both more masculine and feminized.[22]

It is intriguing that Young was the subject of academic discussion in the 1930s: the Letters Club was formed in 1920 by Professor Thorlief Larsen at the University of British Columbia in Vancouver to encourage 'the study of English as a joy'. In this early twentieth-century version of a reading club, undergraduates in their third and fourth year discussed contemporary English literature, probably to compensate for the absence of modern literature from the curriculum. At the Club's bi-weekly meetings, one or two students would read papers. The collection for 1932 contains papers on Siegfried Sassoon, Willa Cather, Wilfrid Owen and E.H. Young.[23]

When we turn to the reception of Young in our time, we find responses that echo the judgements of the interwar years. Virago reissued eight of the 11 novels in their Virago Modern Classic series, with The Dial Press of New York publishing the Virago

Private and Public Spheres: Publication and Reception 91

edition of *The Misses Mallett*. [24] Carmen Callil, founder of Virago Press, explains how Young was chosen:

> I would have included her in the list because I loved her work ... what distinguished her for me was the quiet irony, and the quiet intensity of her writing, and the tradition of British women writers she belonged to – beginning with Jane Austen.[25]

The several productions of Young's work on BBC radio and television attest to her popularity and/or to her sister Gladys's perseverance. *William, Miss Mole* and *Chatterton Square* were dramatized during the 1940s and 1950s on BBC radio. In 1985, *Miss Mole* was read in ten parts on BBC's 'Story Time', probably as a result of the Virago reprint in 1984, and adapted for television as 'Hannah, A Love Story' in 1980. A script of *Chatterton Square* is currently being prepared for television by Alan Butland and Stephanie Skye. *William, The Vicar's Daughter, Miss Mole* and *The Curate's Wife* are available in cassette form and *The Misses Mallett* can be found online.[26]

Young received little scholarly attention even in the 1930s when she was at the height of her popularity. In two studies, *The School of Femininity* (1936) and *We Write As Women* (1937), Margaret Lawrence (Greene) includes E.H. Young in a chapter entitled 'Sophisticated Ladies' in the former and 'A Dream Walking' in the latter. With journalistic crispness, Lawrence discusses *Miss Mole* in both books, referring to Young's irony, her skill with everyday living and the independence of her protagonist. However, other than allying Young once again with Austen and with contemporaneous women writers, Mazo de la Roche, Margaret Kennedy, E.M. Delafield and Victoria Sackville-West, etc., Lawrence does not venture much beyond plot summary or generalizations about gender.

Among the mounting number of studies on twentieth-century women writers, only Joannou, Trodd and Wallace, however, refer to Young.[27] A pioneer exception to this neglect was Glen Cavaliero's insightful *The Rural Tradition in the English Novel: 1900–1939* (1977), which details the rural experience and presence of nature in Young's novels, noting her 'mastery of dialogue, a sensitivity to domestic life and an intrinsic wisdom' (154). In a recent article, Diana Wallace points out that the debates around marriage in the 1930s provide 'a way of beginning to reassess the work of E.H. Young, a fine novelist whose work has much in common with that of Rosamond Lehmann in its anti-romantic analysis of class and gender' (66). And indeed, Meike Fritz's doctoral dissertation on Young, 'The Apostle of the Quiet People', which has been issued by Peter Lang in German (2002), and Stella Deen's three recent articles on Young (2001, 2002a, 2002b, 2003) show that Young is slowly being recognized and studied.

Nevertheless, academic criticism has been less willing than Young's contemporary readers and publishers to acknowledge the contradictory desires elicited by the perusal of domesticity. In our reading of Young, we join in the current challenge to this trend; we step into a domestic space that elevates a private, feminine space into an ironic blueprint for the art of living the everyday.

92   *Domestic Modernism, the Interwar Novel, and E.H. Young*

Notes

1   For a discussion of women writers and the marketplace, see the collection of essays in Judy Simons and Kate Fullbrook, eds, *Writing: A Woman's Business? Women, Writing and the Marketplace* (1998).

2   For a detailed discussion of the publication and reception of Young, see Mezei and Briganti, '"She Must Be a Very Good Novelist": Re-reading E.H. Young (1880–1949)' (2001), pp. 303–331.

3   The term middlebrow became current just as Young's writing career took off. *The Oxford English Dictionary* traces the first appearance of the term to a 1925 article in *Punch*, which noted that 'the B.B.C. claim to have discovered a new type, the "middlebrow." It consists of people who are hoping that someday they will get used to the stuff they ought to like' (Radway: 219). According to Rosa Maria Bracco, the 'term "middlebrow" represented a symbol for the centre in more than one sense.' Produced by middle-class authors for a middle-class audience, middlebrow fiction 'mediated between conflicts and extremes,' with balance as its alleged trademark' (*Merchants of Hope: British Middlebrow Writers and the First World War, 1919–1939*, 1993: 10). See also Joan Shelley Rubin, *The Making of Middlebrow Culture* (1992); Q.D. Leavis's 1932 classic, *Fiction and the Reading Public*, and Leonard Woolf's pamphlet, *Hunting the Highbrow* (1927). In *Virginia Woolf, the Intellectual, and the Public Sphere* (2003), Melba Cuddy-Keane explains the unpalatable origin of the terms, 'high' and 'low' brow. They refer to the height of the forehead, with a high forehead signalling an intellectual (16). See also Cuddy-Keane's useful discussion of the debates over 'high', 'low' and 'middle' brow in the chapter 'Democratic Highbrow: Woolf and the Classless Intellectual', pp. 13–58.

4   The recent reissue of *Miss Mole* in large print in 2000 by Isis (Oxford) presupposes an audience of seniors.

5   See Harry Ransom Humanities Research Center, University of Texas at Austin; P.E.N. Archive, University Archives, McFarlin Library, University of Tulsa; Society of Authors Papers, British Library; Young Papers. We thank Michel Pharand for his assistance here.

6   *Mrs. Miniver*, dir. William Wyler, Metro-Goldwyn-Mayer (1942); *Cold Comfort Farm*, dir. John Schlesinger, BBC (1995); *The Constant Nymph*, dir. Edmund Goulding, Warner Bros (1943); *I Capture the Castle*, dir. Tim Fywell, BBC (2003); *The Weather in the Streets*, dir. Gavin Millar, BBC (1983); and *The Heart of Me* (based on *The Echoing Grove*), dir. Thaddeus O' Sullivan, BBC (2002).

7   Recent biographies and studies on Bowen (Ellmann 2004) and Lehmann (Hastings 2002; Pollard 2004), May Sinclair (Raitt 2000), Olivia Manning (Braybrooke and Braybrooke 2004) however, suggest that these women writers are beginning to receive due recognition.

8   'An experiment conducted in 1902 by Ernest A. Baker, librarian of Woolwich public libraries, divided literature in three classes – authors deserving 'to be well represented in public libraries', 'popular mediocrities' as well as 'doubtful cases' and finall , novelists 'decidedly below the standard admissible in a rate-supported library', making no mention of 'brows' (Derek Hudson, 'Reading,' in Simon Nowell-Smith, ed., *Edwardian England*, 1964: 310).

Private and Public Spheres: Publication and Reception   93

[9]   Radner's essay, although focusing in particular on the 'dissertation novel', provides an illuminating commentary on the effect of the academic polarization of the writerly and readerly text on canon formation.

[10]   Mass-Observation File Reports, Mass-Observation Archive, File 48, 'Selection and Taste in Book Reading', Fulham Study (January–February 1940).

[11]   Joan Shelley Rubin describes how American reviewing since the nineteenth century had taken the form either of news – blurbs, factual information, or of criticism – treatment of books as literature, their relation to aesthetic or moral principles which reviewers sought to inculcate in their audience (35).

[12]   Virginia Woolf, 'Middlebrow', *The Death of the Moth and Other Essays* (1947): 112–19. See also Leonard Woolf's defence of the highbrow against attacks in the press, *Hunting the Highbrow* and Joan Shelley Rubin's discussion of Woolf's piece on the middlebrow (ibid.: xiii) as well as Cuddy-Keane's contextualization of this essay, '"Middlebrow" (1932) and its Cultural Inter-texts' (ibid.: 22–34). Nicola Humble's *Feminine Middlebrow* (2001) and Claire Hanson's *Hysterical Fictions and the Woman's Novel in the Twentieth Century* (2000) are enlightening on this subject, as are Alison Light's *Forever England* (1991) and Marion Shaw's 'The Making of a Middle-brow Success: Winifred Holtby's *South Riding*' (1998).

[13]   Here are some of Orwell's views on Penguins and the brows: 'In my capacity as reader I applaud the Penguin Books; in my capacity as writer I pronounce them anathema ... if other publishers follow suit, the result may be a flood of cheap reprints which will cripple the lending libraries (the novelist's foster-mother) and check the output of new novels. (*New English Weekly*, 5 March 1936, *Collected Essays*, 1968, Vol. 1: 167); 'And lending libraries and very cheap books, such as the Penguins, popularise the habit of reading and probably have a levelling effect on literary taste' ('The English People', *Collected Essays*, 1968, Vol. III: 23); 'One phenomenon of the war has been the enormous sale of Penguin Books, Pelican Books and other cheap editions, most of which would have been regarded by the general public as impossibly highbrow a few years back' (*The War Broadcasts* excerpted in Steve Hare, ed., *Penguin Portrait*, 1995: 102).

[14]   Robert Graves and Alan Hodge, *The Long Week-End* (1941): 42.

[15]   As Graves and Hodge note, 'Edgar Wallace was by far the best-known and most widely read low-brow writer, and a successful dramatist too ... During the last six years of his life – he died in 1932 – twenty-eight of his novels were published and it was a joke to ask at a bookstall for the "midday Wallace"' (*The Long Week-End*: 137).

[16]   The other nine were André Maurois, *Ariel*; Dorothy Sayers, *The Bellona Club*; Compton Mackenzie, *Carnival*; Ernest Hemingway, *Farewell to Arms*; Mary Webb, *Gone to Earth*; Susan Ertz, *Madame Claire*; Agatha Christie, *The Mysterious Affair at Styles*; Eric Linklater, *Poet's Pub*; Beverley Nichols, *Twenty-five*.

[17]   From 1 November 2003, Design Museum, London, <http://www.designmuseum.org>.

[18]   Modernist architects, like Wells Coates, who built the Lawn Road Flats, looked to technology, modern transport and functionalism; their designs were influenced by the clean, simple, strong lines, the decks and funnels of ocean vessels.

[19]   Charlotte Robinson, 'A Brief Portrait of a Publisher – Jonathan Cape – Part I', <http://www.ibooknet.co.uk/archive/news_june03.htm>.

[20]   The Young Papers show, however, that Young was at work on *Chatterton Square* as early as 1941.

[21]   E-mail correspondence to Chiara Briganti, 6 March 2000. We thank Carmen Callil for permission to quote her helpful comments on E.H. Young.

94   *Domestic Modernism, the Interwar Novel, and E.H. Young*

22   For a thoughtful discussion of the figure of the wounded soldier, see Trudi Tate, *Modernism, History and the First World War* (1998), ch. 4.

23   The writer of the paper on E.H. Young was a Rosemary Winslow. In a well-researched essay presented on 15 November she describes the success of *William*, the 'ever-increasing group of admirers on both sides of the Atlantic' (1), then outlines Young's publishing history, summarizes reviews of the novels and offers her reading of the five novels Young had published to date, including *Miss Mole*.

24   *The Misses Mallett, Miss Mole* (1984); *Jenny Wren, The Curate's Wife* (1985); *Chatterton Square* (1987); *William* (1988); *Celia* (1990); *The Vicar's Daughter* (1992).

25   Callil, see n. 21.

26   <http://www.gutenberg.org/etext/8131>.

27   The problematic assignation of Young's literary status is reflected in her idiosyncratic presence in literary dictionaries and histories. While D.L. Kirkpatrick does not include her in *Contemporary Novelists* (1976), the *Longman Companion to Twentieth Century Literature*, ed. A.C. Ward (1975), briefly refers to her as the 'author of distinguished novels in a plain style about plain people' (589). Whereas James Vinson in *20th-Century Fiction* (1983) does not mention her, Peter Parker in *The Reader's Companion to the Twentieth-Century Novel* (1994) chooses *Miss Mole* for the year 1930, praising it as a text that offers us 'one of fiction s most remarkable and difficult heroines, disquieting in her blend of "frankness and slyness", always exhilarating, often discomforting, tremendously attractive but even less knowable than most human beings. The novel … was a worthy winner of the 1930 J.T.B. memorial prize' (153). Parker also notes that Young's work 'has been undergoing a revival of interest in recent years since Virago began to reprint her novels' (153). However, Young *is* included in a number of reference works on women: Virginia Blain, Patricia Clements and Isobel Grundy, eds, *The Feminist Companion to Literature in English* (1990), pp. 1199–1200; Lorna Sage, ed., *The Cambridge Guide to Women's Writing in English* (1999), p. 686. She appears in Helen Reid and Lorna Brierly's history of Bristol's female past, *Go Home and Do the Washing: Three Hundred Years of Pioneering Bristol Women* (2001), and also has an excellent substantial entry, written by Stella Deen, in the 2004 edition of the *Dictionary of National Biography* published by the Oxford University Press. In the volume of the *Dictionary of Literary Biography* dedicated to 'British Novelists Between the War' (1998), the editor George M. Johnson presents lesser-known writers like Enid Bagnold, Elizabeth Goudge, Georgette Heyer, Nancy Mitford and D.E. Stevenson. Although he does not include some of the novelists we discuss here (Young, Delafield, Robertson, Gibbons), Johnson mentions that with 'the retreat in the postwar years from heroism on a large scale, another type of fiction, centering on domestic life, came into prominence', which focused on 'marriage, child rearing, relations with servants, and the house itself as a symbol of security'. He points out how in Brett Young's country-house novel, *White Ladies* (1935) and in several of D.E. Stevenson's novels, the house is the central character and 'embodies emotional and spiritual strength' (xxii–xxiv). There is also an entry on Young in Sandra Kemp, Charlotte Mitchell, David Trotter, eds, *Edwardian Fiction* (1997), p. 427.

Chapter 5

The Turn to Domestic Modernism

> A human being, to her, was a continuous wonder, a group of human beings made a drama
> of which she was half creator, half spectator, and she was baffled to know how people
> amused themselves without this entertainment which never palled and never ended.
>
> *Miss Mole*: 173

Here, Young has Hannah Mole self-consciously echo Jane Austen's famous dictum that '3 or 4 Families in a Country Village is the very thing to work on', and thus both inscribes herself in a specific tradition and writes her own poetic manifesto.[1] With her two most popular novels, *William* and *Miss Mole*, Young turns her attention to the specific domestic sphere of two Bristol bourgeois homes and fastens her mocking, yet empathetic, gaze upon the dynamics of family. Interrogating the meaning of home and 'the Good', she mulls over alternative domesticities and proposes subtle adjustments to the domestic order. She gently ridicules hypocrisy, pretension and convention, evading the descent into melodrama and sentimentality that mars her earlier works. The symbolic (rather than heavily descriptive) representations of houses, domestic interiors and objects signal her turn to domestic modernism.

Both novels are unusual in that in *William* we observe the father rather than the mother figure embodying an idea of home, which strives for the nurturance and well-being of its inhabitants; while with her wit, self-confidence and sexual experience, Hannah Mole is an antidote to the stereotype of the superfluous, repressed and abject spinster, subject of many contemporary articles, novels, plays and invectives. Nevertheless, and with every good intention, William and Hannah seek to control their domestic spheres and to manipulate the lives of others; they are, so to speak, authors of their own little worlds, personas of Young herself in performing the art of living on a small scale. Thoughtful and self-reflective, William and Hannah are deeply preoccupied with their inner selves and fiercely protective of personal privacy; yet they cannot long avoid the messiness of personal relationships.

Pater Familias

William is focused on the deliberately small compass of an ordinary family: William Nesbitt, a former sea captain who has built a successful business as the owner of a fleet of local boats, his wife Kate, his adult children Dora, Mabel, Lydia, Walter and Janet, with the members of their respective families remaining in the wings. Of William's early adventurous life at sea we are told nothing, his seafaring adventures now replaced by the leisurely walk from home to office.

96   *Domestic Modernism, the Interwar Novel, and E.H. Young*

The novel centres on the ship-owner's domestic difficulties, triggered by Lydia's marital indiscretion. Lydia, William's favourite child, is the embodiment of the romance which eludes him in his life and marriage; he is the only one of the family for whom her desertion of her husband for another man 'would have no sense of loss or shame' (122); for, although to everybody else she may be a rather plain, if striking woman, he sees 'how she loved beauty and tried to reach it even through ugliness' (122). In a sense, the novel represents William's (and Young's) education into the appreciation of the complexities of ordinary life. As Young learns to appreciate the value of the ordinary, William will have to learn to see that which nobody else can – the beauty of Lydia's gesture, the more muted grace of his younger daughter Janet and he will have to accommodate his wife Kate's staunch worship at the shrine of respectability.

Here, too, Young begins her practice of dialogue as a guerrilla tactic; so, for instance, although the narrator slyly comments that William kept nothing from his wife except the meaning of his words, when her youngest daughter Janet cryptically refers to an 'antidote', Kate quietly decides to look up the exact meaning of the word (92). The epistemic modality 'of course', which 'appears to offer common ground ... [but] is actually an appropriation of the listener's discourse' (Giltrow: 227), is frequently used by Kate to impose her presuppositions about conformity, behaviour and morality upon her family: '"Yes, he has been for a holiday on Dartmoor alone. Janet met him, but of course", Mrs. Nesbitt was fond of those two words, "of course Lydia told me he was there. I thought she might have told you too"' (113).[2] Although Lydia appears to be a modern character, her unconventionality and her modernist house, so emphatically different from the comforting Victorian ambience of the paternal house, remain external accoutrements that do little more than make her an unconvincing version of the modern woman of so many novels of the period; they do not succeed in dispelling the somewhat archaic flavour of her character which in its single-minded intensity recalls the Theresas and Helens of Young's early fiction [3] If *William*, as one reviewer noted at the time, 'carries its modernity with a beautiful ease', it is not because the portrait of a modern woman dominates it but because of its interest in behaviour and in the contact of differing outlooks (review of *William*, *Spectator*, 30 May 1925: 896).

Comments such as this alert us to the fact that the very notion of modernity is a historical, fluid construct and its range of possibilities richer than what is granted by a telescopic view of literature. Such a range may very well include oblique participation in the debate surrounding the meaning of domesticity, which acquired considerable proportions during the interwar years. As the reviewer in *The New Republic* noticed, this novel reverses the pattern of treatment reserved for 'the father in the family novel who usually shows his admirable qualities to the world outside: within the family circle, he is usually either a cipher or a tyrant' (anon., *The New Republic*, 9 September 1925: 78). Indeed, the 'undomestic' father is a fixture of the domestic novel, whether he be ineffectual and flirtatious like Bruce in Ada Leverson's *The Little Ottleys*, who feels 'cramped in [his] surroundings' (104) and dramatically explains his elopement

The Turn to Domestic Modernism   97

as an alternative to death: 'If I'm to keep sane, if I'm not to commit suicide, I must give up this domestic life' (540); or driven by a misguided desire for the exotic, like Gerald Challis in Stella Gibbons's *Westwood, or the Gentle Powers*, who is unable 'to notice exquisite ordinary objects under his nose' (244); or seeking the bracing atmosphere of the army mess as a refuge from the 'slow contagion' of domesticity, like Colin in Betty Miller's *On the Side of the Angels* (1945: 223). In William Nesbitt, Young also presented a corrective to Wyndham Lewis's idea of the 'modern city man', who 'in his office ... is probably a very fine fellow – very alert', but in his 'villa in the suburbs' is reduced to 'an invalid bag of mediocre nerves, a silly child' (quoted in Reed 1996: 11). While William may be very alert and combative in his office, we know him at home only through domestic struggles that show his considerable acuity. The rare glimpses into his offices are significant in their omission of the particulars of the business life; instead, his workplace is invaded by his domestic life. When in *William*, Young represents a father and husband's perspective on family and home, she interprets male subjectivity through her feminine gaze and offers a revisioning of the *pater familias* as a private, rather than a public, figure by lending him her own acute sight and sympathy, which will allow him to read his children with greater acuity and accept his wife with deeper understanding.

'That Campaign Inscrutable/of the Interior' (Emily Dickinson 1188: 830)

The novel opens with William stepping 'out of the old, gabled house in which he carried on his business' (5). His gaze moves from a view of his own steamboats, to the meadows mounting to the horizon and 'the ordered confusion of river, docks, factories, ships and little bridges; while to his right, dizzily high up, there swung the famous suspension bridge of Radstowe' (5). This is a definitive farewell to Young's fascination for the hills and the moors and a harbinger of the celebration of provincial city life, a sea-city palpitating with the life of the docks. Only the slight roll in William's gait betrays the sailor who at sea had written romantic verses for his wife. The romance that inspired them lurks as a hidden treasure in his heart and is to be found now 'in the old houses beyond the shops, in the wide green with its elms newly-dressed for spring, in the hoot of a steamer in the river ... and there was romance, streaked with irony, in the narrow road where his own low, white house, sheltered by a sweep of garden, showed its wide front behind the trees' (7). This house is 'not only a home but a shrine for memories' (8), in particular the memory of his daughter Lydia, the only one of his children to have left Radstowe and yet the one who is always in his thoughts. With its 'thick carpets, warming to the eye as well as to the feet', this white-panelled house is a far cry from Lydia's modern minimalist home, 'with its drab floor coverings and sober Persian rugs, its elegant, severe furniture' (24) where Mrs. Nesbitt feels chilled. Lydia's exchange of the heavy mahogany furniture representing Victorian oppressiveness for slim-legged tables and chairs, the bareness of the rooms relieved only by a still life of flowers amassed in a bowl, marks Lydia as a non-conformist, a

98   *Domestic Modernism, the Interwar Novel, and E.H. Young*

woman who would share the contempt of Lettice Cooper's Delia for 'cretonnes and pouffes' and a preference for 'white walls, clear, pale rooms full of light' (11);[4] Lydia would heartily agree with Delia that 'furniture goes with ways of living' and that her parents' generation 'cluttered up their rooms and their lives with things that weren't any use' (119). But if in Delia the distaste for clutter bespeaks a benign utilitarianism, in Lydia's case it is a foreshadowing of a more radical dismissal of Victorian morality as her parents unconsciously understand and of a preference for the provocative challenge to anything safe and predictable, characteristic of the bohemians of the 1920s and 1930s. Thus, Lydia seems to exemplify artistic London – 'parties, theatres, people in and out' (15), modernity and the sexual and domestic rebel. There is, however, a hint of satire in Young's depiction of bohemian London. Although bohemianism could be as claustrophobic in its performance of ritual as the Victorian drawing-room, it nevertheless offered women a taste of liberty and a salutary alternative to the inflexible rules of propriety. Thus, in E.M. Delafield s *Three Marriages* (1939), Violet, a young society woman, after visiting an art student in her flat, begrudgingly admits that there is a life beyond mahogany and antimacassars. While she had expected squalor and shabbiness, the room with its large window, unframed drawings, books, green and white striped curtains and sparse furniture 'all painted green and white … was nice – for those who cared to lead the Bohemian life' (241).

As Nicola Humble has persuasively argued, in almost every middlebrow novel from the 1920s to the 1950s, 'the modernity of certain women is encoded in terms of their use of colour in decoration'. Such modernity 'is principally carried in the description of the room's isolated spots of glowing colour' (144). To Humble's examples, Jennifer in Rosamond Lehmann's *Dusty Answer* and Florence in Margaret Kennedy's *The Constant Nymph*, we would add Muriel Hammond's bid for freedom from the suffocating hold of her native village, as figured in the description of the room that she arranges for Delia Vaughan and herself in Holtby's *The Crowded Street* (1924): 'roses in rough blue vases; dark bookshelves ranged against the plain buff walls, space, space everywhere and a complete absence of irritating decoration – surely the room meant the materialization of her dreams?' (271). In Rosamond Lehmann's *The Echoing Grove* (1953), Dinah's contempt for conventional morality is apparent to her sister Madeleine in the décor of her room, vaguely reminiscent of Bloomsbury:

> deep settee, brown with lemon-coloured cushions, brilliant red curtains, Khelim rugs, a dresser covered with painted bowls, plates, jugs – foreign-looking, cheap but attractive, one huge round glass lamp on a low table strewn with portfolios, art books, magazines: material, doubtless, for intimate cultural evenings, Dinah teaching him all about Picasso, Matisse, Renoir, Greek and Persian art, before they went to bed. Place of treachery and passion, broken in upon, exposed, sealed up, vacated ….Reassembled again. (76, Lehmann's ellipsis)

Equally, it is Lydia's surroundings that first alert Mrs. Nesbitt that there may be trouble brewing in her daughter's life. In response to William's observation that the house expresses Lydia, she is quick to answer sharply: 'I should be sorry to think my

The Turn to Domestic Modernism   99

daughter was like that – practically, well, practically undressed' (24). Lydia's domestic 'undress' is indicative of modernity's antipathy to ornament and decoration that is reflected not only in modernist public monuments but also in domestic architecture, interior decoration and literary expression.

The novel invites us to concur with Mrs. Nesbitt in establishing reciprocity between home and character for every home in this narrative is an index to the personality of its inhabitants, the Nesbitt parents and children. The lacklustre, 'inglorious' quality of drab Mabel's life is mirrored in the utilitarianism of her scrupulously neat modern villa in which everything – from the tablecloths, chair covers and curtains of a 'useful shade of green' is 'warranted not to fade and [is made] of a material likely to last for years' (25) – and everybody, including a bony servant who looks as if she would stand no nonsense, concurs to make the business of living an unending struggle against dirt and wear. If Mabel's life and surroundings bespeak dreariness, in Richard's childless marriage on the other hand we are invited to scent trouble for the flat he inhabits with Violet, full as it is of knickknacks, 'combined with the excessive powdering of Violet's face, vaguely suggested impropriety' (25). Dora's pseudo-Gothic castle, instead, feels like a second home to Mrs. Nesbitt, for it seems an embodiment of the solidity of Dora's marriage, just as her own home seems the embodiment of the solidity of her marriage. In the bohemian atmosphere of Lydia's home, with its deficiency of curtains, commodious armchairs and thick carpets, Mrs. Nesbitt rightly senses 'uncertainty and danger' (69), while Dora's 'castle' welcomes her with its comforting coziness: 'it had the soft hangings, the pretty, tender colours, the deep arm-chairs that Mrs. Nesbitt loved: it was what she called a home' (25). Ensconced in comforting surroundings with a stolid, if meanly irritable, husband and five robust children, Dora seems destined to proceed uneventfully to comfortable middle age. But although Mrs. Nesbitt, unable to bear the 'sudden dark glimpse into a life which had seemed all brightness' (113), is determined to attribute Dora's paleness and weariness and her uncharacteristic advocacy of 'one holiday a year without your family' to a struggle with 'dreadful drains' (113), William (and we, through him) knows that Dora's difficulties cannot be solved by a plumber. William's education depends on his ability to dislocate the carefully established reciprocity of home and character, to discover, for instance, a kind soul behind the excessive powdering of Violet's face and to defamiliarize the home, to rearrange, as it were, its furniture as well as its inhabitants and the reader in a different pattern.

Halfway through the novel, noticing in a kind of 'domestic fallacy' a new stillness and chill in his house, William feels 'like an exile returning, after a long time, to a place which was once a home' (149). However, this estrangement which makes tangible his estrangement from Kate, has been pre-announced in a muted way in the very first line of the novel with William stepping 'out of the old, gabled house in which he carried on his business' (5) and whose gables repeat the quizzical lift of his eyebrows (33). This is the first example of many steppings out and steppings in that William and other characters will have to go through before they will be able to rearrange the furniture in their own house. Even though William is ostensibly the sage man 'without a single

100   *Domestic Modernism, the Interwar Novel, and E.H. Young*

trace of the whimsical, eccentric, wistful, Peteresque touch' (*New York Literary Review*, 29 August 1925: 2), there is indeed more of Mr. Bennet in William than is good for him; his education is education away from irony and into sympathy and also away from the allure of the romantic into an understanding of the beauty and grace of the ordinary, of the extraordinary behind the superficially humdrum. If Kate must learn to shed her prejudices and relent her obduracy, William, like Young, may need to shed his own romanticism. He had reflected complacently that

> It's a charming relationship for a man with a satisfactory daughter. Now a mother can't feel romantic about a daughter ... A father is more detached, more of a stranger, and where there's strangeness there's excitement. I'm glad I'm not a mother. There's too domestic a flavour about that – aired underclothes and plenty to eat! And a daughter is always a woman and a mystery. (159–60)

Now he must overcome the temptation to invest the relationships with his daughters with the romanticism that he misses in his marriage.

Paradoxically, Lydia, the wayward child whose challenge to Victorian morality constitutes the thrust of the narrative, is the one character (aside from Mabel, who is sacrificed to comedic unidimensionality) that remains fixedly framed, the only one who may justify John Bayley's judgement of the '*passé*' ('Introduction': v) quality of the novel. In a letter to her father, written shortly after she has left Oliver and moved in with Henry, Lydia imagines herself as a 'deserted' heroine, acting her part in a melodrama and embodies the house as an objective correlative of her anomalous position: 'we just stealthily crept and the house looked stealthy too and rather cunning. It seemed to wink at me as though it had known all the time that Henry would bring me here' (151). She then describes her lover's home in revealing detail; its square sitting rooms, square bedrooms, square bathroom, dingy wallpaper, gloomy oil paintings and, in particular, the family portraits hanging everywhere, combine to create an atmosphere of unrelieved oppression:

> I believe [Henry's mother's] ghost walks in these square rooms with the high windows – you can't see out of them properly unless you stand up – and the heavy furniture she bought when she was young. You can't imagine anything more unlike me, but I don't feel I can alter anything, not even the plush frames. (152)

While in Ivy Compton-Burnett's *A House and its Head*, the shifting of the portrait of the recently deceased Mrs. Edgeworth is emblematic of the struggle for power and position within the household, Lydia must resign herself to live with an old photograph of Henry's mother watching disapprovingly 'over her long nose' (152). Lydia's final decision to remain with Henry, exchanging a safe life for an uncertain one, appears the ultimate 'modern' choice. However, the description of the house somehow dispels the atmosphere of modernity and bohemianism that Young had associated with Lydia's character. And she, not Dora, appears at the end immured in a not so pseudo-Gothic

The Turn to Domestic Modernism 101

castle where 'the hall is narrow and dark and the walls seem to tell you, gently but firml , that they mean to squash you flat (153).

In this novel, Young has inverted the conventional focus of the domestic novel by placing the father and husband at its centre, a *pater familias* who is as preoccupied by parental obligations and the vicissitudes of marriage as the customary heroine. For Kate, the meaning of home is comfort, soft armchairs, familiarity, the illusion of family solidarity; for William, it implies the achievement of a dream, the layering of memories and the romance of family; while for Lydia, the modern London house mirrors her would-be bohemian self and the dark Gothic house in the country, brooded over by gloomy ancestors, oddly represents her struggle to be, as her mother finally concedes, 'good'.

Within the home, another contest is quietly waged as Young puts accepted notions of masculinity under scrutiny. By making William, a busy man of commerce, romantic, solicitous and invincibly domestic, she counters Orwell's fears of the 'snare of domesticity' (Plain: 41). She redefines male subjectivity, an effort that she will go on to pursue in her following novels, thus revealing a continuous concern with the examination of prescriptive masculinity and femininity that also preoccupied many of her contemporary fellow women writers. As Stella Deen aptly notes, 'Young's vision of a new domesticity rechannels that masculine heroism into domestic and private enterprises' (2003).[5] In presenting an extensive view of William from the interior, Young positions us with him, slightly on the outside, as in this passage where he contemplates Lydia's difficulties and his own anxieties: 'He had tried to readjust his vision of her … He could not clarify his own confusion … and he saw her subdued, less swift, almost trapped in that dark little house muffled in creepers, Brussels carpets and heavy furniture, quietly writing a letter by the light of a single candle' (155). In her next novel, *Miss Mole*, in which she combines her own brand of domesticity and modernism, Young portrays an equally complex focalizer and adept manipulator of households, albeit one in a marginal position, almost diametrically opposed to that of the master of the house.

Keeping House: Out of the Boarding House

> Lies were a form of imagination and a protection for the privacy of her thoughts and, in a life lived in houses which were not her own and where she was never safe from intrusion, it was necessary to have this retreat. (*Miss Mole*: 100)

In *Miss Mole*, the heroine Hannah Mole, an impoverished spinster with a surprising secret and a delightfully sharp tongue, takes up a position as housekeeper in the home of a nonconformist minister, where she proceeds to manage his troubled household in her own nonconformist manner. Entering the novel, and house, from her perspective rather than from that of the master or mistress or children of the household, we are drawn into the arena of alternative domesticities. Hannah Mole, with no apparent home of her own, in her role as keeper of houses of and for others, attempts to make

102 *Domestic Modernism, the Interwar Novel, and E.H. Young*

herself *at* home. In the trope of the competent housekeeper, we recognize an imposing figure of authority who commands the keys to the house and mediates between the patriarchal *habitus* and the secret reaches of the domestic household; we encounter this figure in Mrs. Fairfax from *Jane Eyre* and in the more sinister Mrs. Danvers in Daphne Du Maurier's *Rebecca*; but whereas the housekeeper in those novels remains a secondary figure, here Miss Mole rises above class, gender and indigence to control house and novel.

If *William* complicated the notion of separate spheres from a male perspective by centring on the domestic struggles of a business man, the choice of a protagonist such as Hannah Mole in *Miss Mole* gave Young the opportunity to explore the identification of femininity with forms of interiority, which has been identified as one of the markers of women's fiction between the wars. Such identification had, of course, had a long gestation throughout the nineteenth century; it is indeed due to Emily Dickinson that we owe the richest exploration of interiority through spatial metaphors and, in particular, through the association of interiority with the house. As Diana Fuss has persuasively argued, although much of the critical commentary on Dickinson's poetry is vitiated by the unexamined association of retreat into the house with entombment and incarceration (1998: 1–4), for Dickinson 'interiority was not only a matter of physical enclosure. Interiority was a complicated conceptual problem' (4). Following Emily Dickinson's prescription, Young and other domestic novelists challenged the notion of the domestic world as incarceration and exposed it to the same scrutiny as the public world; the domestic interior became the ideal site within which to locate an 'insatiable interest in men and women' (*Celia*: 90).

Certainly in *Miss Mole* Young perfected her medium. By further reducing the number of characters and the scope of their lives and refusing to lend her heroine the illusion of a romantic past, Young made the self-imposed limitations of her practice more stringent than in *William*. In this novel, attention is unremittingly kept on an ordinary life whose narrow perimeter is immediately rendered in the description of the stuffy room in which Hannah Mole sits with her employer Mrs. Widdows (perhaps a pun on the many widows of whom she has been a companion) at the opening of the novel: 'a large fire blazed and crackled, the canary made sad, subdued movements in its cage, Mrs. Widdows' corsets creaked regularly, her large knees almost touched Hannah's own, for the two women sat near each other to share the lamplight' (8). However, though for most of the novel Miss Mole may do nothing more than go quietly about her homely chores, she is no subdued canary and through a bit of sly scheming she finds a way out of Mrs. Widdows's stuffy room: she hides a much-needed reel of silk in her pocket and, under the pretence of walking to the shops, gains a temporary escape. She is well aware that she will have to pay a price for her brief adventure (only a foray into the teashop): she will be dismissed and will have to seek a new situation. In this act of defiance, Miss Mole speaks for the many paid companions in literature, the heirs of Jane Eyre and Agnes Grey, hovering between the servant and the gentlewoman, whose situation had not greatly changed since the nineteenth century. When Miss Burke in Compton-Burnett's *Mother and Son* (1955) quips 'companions

The Turn to Domestic Modernism

are solitary and penniless. Have you no knowledge of life or literature?' (112), her words resonate with those of the cook in Emma Worboise's *Married Life* (1872): she has 'no one to speak to, and nothing to think on but the better days as are gone and the worser days is coming' (24).[6] And it is with Hannah Mole's new situation and her struggles to restore order and harmony in the home of the Reverend Corder, 'a muscular Christian' whose 'capacity for coercion and constraints are prefigured in his name' (Parker: 152), that the story develops.

Out of the Pink Cottage

Young's fascination with the figure of the single, genteel woman in reduced circumstances whose life has drifted from employer to employer can be traced back to 'Lena Maude', the tale she published in 1925 in *Time and Tide*. In this slight, melancholy sketch of a woman's brief night of excitement from an evening at the theatre and the encounter with a burglar, Young had done little more than write in the tradition of spinster fiction. Despite her brief rebellion, the end of the story sees Lena Maude once again immured in her cold room knowing, as Hannah Mole knows after failing to return promptly to her duties, that next day she will be 'sacked' for not having bolted the door. There is more than a hint of Hannah Mole in Lena Maude: both are past their youth, have no beauty, no money, no friends and have spent their lives in musty houses as hard-driven companions of disagreeable employers. Indeed, early in the novel Hannah Mole reflecting on her journey to her new employer's house, shares this vision of herself as being part of an army of women forming a very melancholy procession, women 'who went from house to house behind their boxes, a sad multitude of women with carefully pleasant faces, hiding their ailments, lowering their ages and thankfully accepting less than they earned' (51).

But whereas Lena Maude has 'no accomplishments beyond the capacity for obeying orders and bearing slights' (775), and her encounter with the burglar, however graciously he may treat her, is no harbinger of freedom and romance, we soon learn that Hannah Mole has other resources and that indeed has had, if not romance, an affair. Her strength is her vibrant imagination and her own awareness of it. She may have few possessions, but she will always be able to view ordinary things like the lights of Radstowe 'as camp-fires, and herself as an adventuress' (90). The development of the character of Hannah Mole points to two central motifs in Young's aesthetics – the art of everyday living and the imaginative lie.

It was not only the middle-aged woman of reduced means who held a fascination for Young. In the tellingly entitled story, 'An Artist', which she had published in *Time and Tide* in 1924, she created the character of a 15-year-old nursemaid who escapes 'the horror of hard facts' (61) and the memory of the orphan home in which she was raised in a newly-discovered ability to reinvent her own past for her charges. In these new stories, instead of villains and seduced helpless young women, there is the nursemaid herself, living happily and glamorously in a house of her own creation.

104   *Domestic Modernism, the Interwar Novel, and E.H. Young*

Like the nursemaid, but a good deal more self-conscious and witty, Hannah Mole is a *raconteuse* fascinated by words who can make up stories at will and move beyond the cultural bounds that obstruct her physical mobility, thus eschewing awkwardness and pity. When the youngest of her charges, Ruth, after having ignored her in the street out of embarrassment for her eccentric appearance in an old ulster, remorsefully inquires where she had been, her vivid description of trees blazing like torches in the fog makes the girl wish that 'Moley' would never stop talking, for she says 'things differently, in Ruth's experience, from other people and in a different voice' (96).

Such talent provides Hannah Mole not only with a much-needed tool to deter the discovery of her illicit past through the creation of a fictional double (Deen 2001: 361) and to soothe Ruth's loneliness and appease the other daughter Ethel's stormy moods; but, more importantly, it gives her the power to turn herself from character into author: in one of the stories she tells Ruth, Hannah Mole herself goes through an adventure identical to that of Lena Maude, but it is a story that she admits to be the fruit of her own imagination. No mere recipient of another's imagination, Hannah Mole thus rescues herself from the role of victim to become the maker of her own life, an artist:

> she was a magician, changing ships into leviathans with some tiny adjustment of her brain, and, in addition, she had a freedom such as, surely, no one else in Radstowe could claim, for she was in possession of herself and did not set too great a value on it. (119)

As unscrupulous as any gifted writer about the truth, Miss Mole dismisses it as a limiting and an embarrassing convention, dull and often awkward, 'a relative good … to be adulterated and adapted, like a drug, to the constitution of each individual' (27). In her quiet, but determined, endorsement of imposture, lies are both a form of imagination and a protection for the privacy of her thoughts – an indispensable retreat 'in a life lived in houses which were not her own and where she was never safe from intrusion' (100). 'Getting the sack' will not free Lena Maude from her life of servitude; another house, if not Mrs. Davis', will 'receive her into its clutch' (775) and she will be forever part of that sad multitude of women moving from house to house in melancholy procession. (It is out of the contrast between just such a procession of shabby and desperate spinsters and Miss Pettigrew's romantic, ebullient 'day' that Winifred Watson creates the bittersweet comedy of *Miss Pettigrew Lives for a Day* (1938).) Miss Mole may indeed be occasionally forced to join this procession, but she is capable of walking alone, liberated and enriched by her imagination.

Into the Minister's Home

Hannah Mole's imagination and human sympathy – her irony and passionate love for beauty and even more significantly, her unsuspected power 'to drag it from the hidden

The Turn to Domestic Modernism 105

places' (44) – describe the qualities essential to the artist. She is not any artist, though; rather, like her author, she is a domestic artist. Miss Mole's sallow complexion and nondescript features may well encourage other characters and the reader to dismiss her as a resigned middle-aged spinster, but Young is quick to remind us that what may appear to some 'as the resignation of middle-age was the capacity to make drama out of humdrum things' (74). To a woman like Hannah Mole, who is 'thrilled by the sight of strangers and by the emanation of their personalities' (173), the Corders's household provides a society that albeit commonplace is 'a miniature of all societies, with the same intrigues within and the same threatenings of danger from outside' (74).

The daughter of a man 'as little given to eccentricity as one of his turnips' (24), Hannah Mole turns her lowly class status into a form of freedom, thus becoming an example of that 'paradox of power and marginality, of enormous strength within narrow limits' that is Martha Vicinus's description of the single woman (9). And indeed, although Miss Mole shares the *angst* of nomadic existence that characterized the period, this rootlessness, which is associated with a lack of class status, gives her logistic mobility. Respectability makes her cousin Lilla, equipped with the suitably yoking hyphenated surname, Spencer-Smith, a hostage to snobbishness, trapped in a replica Elizabethan manor house where the knocker is too gleaming, the tiles too red and the chrysanthemums are rigidly arranged in tiers on the porch; Miss Mole's view from the margins, instead, allows her to regard people on their way home from work not solely with envy, 'but with the cynical reflection that some of those homes might be comparable to that of Mrs. Widdows – stuffy and unkind' (8) – or to the boarding house where a young man has attempted suicide, 'holding tragedy maliciously streaked with humour' (8). So we do not really believe that she regrets not having married a farmer and born him robust children, or that she would have considered this 'good, hard life … worthier of an active human being than this trailing from house to house, a dependent on the whims and tempers of other people and a victim of her own' (181). She knows perfectly well that no one in the Corders's house has ever given her 'a thought detached from some personal connection' (88), but is also quick to see that this 'lack of interest … had its advantages' (88). And precisely because of her lack of attractive physical characteristics, she can be an occasional *flâneuse* of a provincial town; her very shabbiness, lack of beauty and outmoded clothes protect her with a cloak of invisibility under which she can traverse the city (and the narrative) with the freedom to exercise her intellect and her aesthetic taste; for 'no one who saw through that cloak would have suspected her power for transmuting what was common into what was rare and, in that occupation, keeping anxious thoughts at bay' (10).

In a realignment of the pairs of interior/exterior, private/public analogous to that detected by Diana Fuss in Emily Dickinson (4), Miss Mole, who at home is as much under surveillance as any other member of the Corder household, finds much-needed privacy in the streets. She revels in those rare moments when she can saunter around Radstowe, taking in the 'city's facility for happily mixing the incongruous' (10) and finding her chief delight in 'the mingling of the familiar and the unknown' (89), remarks that, not fortuitously, echo Young's own special talent. It is with her eyes that

106 *Domestic Modernism, the Interwar Novel, and E.H. Young*

we scrutinize the houses of Radstowe and read them, noting the old school building, with its walled garden and 'wrought iron gate for visitors and mistresses and, at the back, a door for everybody else' (26) which spell age-old divisions; we notice the tendency of the houses in Radstowe to grow shabby; we imagine their still-present desire to give 'the impression that nothing unusual or indecorous can happen within their walls' (44). But even though nothing ever happens in these houses, to Miss Mole they remain cultural artefacts that signify; she continues to be curious about them and spends a good deal of time peering into rooms from which she is excluded. On more than one occasion, she peeps into Mr. Blenkinsop's large sitting room in the boarding house where she took brief refuge and where he sits cozily surrounded by his mother's mahogany and cushioned by her legacy, whereas Hannah, 'threatened by her past, had to wander the streets' (126).

The reader is positioned to peep into Hannah Mole's thoughts and recognize her artistry; more than the previous characters in Young's novels, she reveals herself through free indirect discourse; her biting observations, while rendered through the mediation of a narrator, are evidently her own words and expressions: 'He was not the man to sit in a room with the door open, and before he came back, there would be time she thought, for a peep … In the unlikely possibility of Mr. Blenkinsop's having a past he need not be afraid of it' (126). The irony which is Hannah's aesthetic achievement, and which is of a more cutting and risible variety than Delafield's provincial lady's self-deprecating and self-narrated humour, also ensures the reader's complicity. And yet the reader is not privy to all of Hannah's thoughts and a secret is calculatingly withheld.

Hannah Mole is not given to wander over moors and hills (she is rather a 'specialist in roofs') and her mission is not the search for truth. The only slight reference to Young's early pastoral idealism occupies no more than a brief moment, when Hannah, in Platonic mode, reflects on the beauty of the shadow of leaves reflected on the pavement and, wondering why 'the reflected object should always seem more beautiful than the original', draws a comparison with her own lack of attractiveness, so different from the image 'she chose to project for her own pleasure': 'not the thing itself, but its shadow' (9). But she nourishes no deep illusions about the value of shadows for 'in the one case when she had concentrated on the fine shadow presented to her, she had been mistaken' (9) and the war hero with whom she had a brief affair and to whom she 'rented' her little pink cottage had turned out to be a squalid squatter. Emblematic of illicit sexuality, this pink cottage, like the other deceptive sanctuaries in *A Corn of Wheat* or *The Misses Mallett*, harbours and represents sexual fears and anxieties. Miss Mole tries to repress the memory and the existence of this sexualized home, but like repressed fears and desires, its memory and presence return to haunt her and to effect an ironic dénouement; the pink cottage in the countryside lingers in the background, harbouring a dangerous sexual secret and serving as the medium of misunderstanding and romantic exchange, a *domus ex machina*.

With no interest in pursuing higher Platonic truths, Hannah Mole draws pleasure when she is allowed entrance from refashioning homes. Her first glimpse of the

The Turn to Domestic Modernism

Corders's house offers scant promising material; it does not take her long to conclude that the architect who designed it was no artist; and this is not solely a matter of aesthetics, for the house next door, although equally unattractive to the eye, looks infinitely more habitable. As she might have suspected from her long experience of living in strangers' houses, the much-dreaded faint smell of cooking is there and although she is spared the green serge cover on the table, she must resign herself to the presence of the unavoidable 'rusty fern' (64).

As the figures of Woolf's Mrs. Ramsay, E.M. Forster's Mrs. Wilcox, Betty Miller's Honor (*On the Side of the Angels*) and the late Mrs. Corder poignantly suggest, the house is not only the mother's dominion, but is also embodied as mother; and when she dies the 'house itself seems to die as well' (Garber: 59). It will be up to Miss Mole to revive the Corders's house. She does this by weaving stories that, as those of Sherahazade, 'don't finish (222). She does not have a free hand, she cannot change the ugly furniture and she soon finds out that the Corders are unlikely characters for the drama she would like to conceive, but she can introduce 'friendliness and humour and gaiety' into it; she can 'get some sort of beauty into the house' (67); she can keep chaos at bay and, with her capacity to lend life to humdrum things, contribute to the psychosexual drama of the house, pay homage to the deceased mother and protect her children from suffering from the contact with a coarse mind.

However, although Miss Mole and Young experience, imagine and critique a variety of alternate domesticities – paid companion, housekeeper, extramarital affair in a pink cottage, boarding house life, the comfortable bourgeois home of the Spencer-Smiths – Miss Mole ends up in an unexpected marital relationship. In the unfolding of this surprise romance, the pink cottage serves as the medium of felicitous denouement.

The End of the Novel of Love: Her Own Home

> Miss Mole was not curious about him; it was the house she was concerned with, and if she could put her hand inside its door, she would know, at once, whether she could be happy in it. (46)

We know from the very beginning of the novel that Miss Mole holds no excessive respect for truth; but we can be sure that although she does not have any scruples about cheating her employer of two pennies and lying about her past, she has no desire to lie to herself. And the reader would do well to ignore the titillation of romance and believe that it is the house, and not Mr. Corder, that Hannah Mole is interested in. Although Miss Mole, like Rose Mallett, succumbs to the marriage plot in an Austenian resolution, Young writes beyond the conventional marriage plot ending. In fact, even more emphatically than in *William*, where romance, albeit from the margins, continues to play a role in the plot, in this novel love no longer acts as an organizing principle. Diana Wallace reads Miss Mole as a subversion of the 'second wife novel' through the setting up of 'what appears to be a classic Jane Eyre plot where the housekeeper,

108   *Domestic Modernism, the Interwar Novel, and E.H. Young*

Miss Mole, will marry her widowed rector employer, but then marrying her to the delightfully unromantic Blenkinsop' (2000: 41). This reading, however, places undue emphasis on the romance element – it is not there that energy is invested.

Young, we assume, would agree with Vivian Gornick that love is no longer sufficient as the narrative impetus of the novel: 'what is required for the making of a self is the deliberate pursuit of consciousness. Knowing *this* to be the larger truth – in literature as in life – now comes as something of an anticlimax' (162, Gornick's italics). As she embarks upon marriage with the laconic and sketchy Mr. Blenkinsop, Hannah Mole sees 'something whimsical and unlikely in their love' (288), while middle-aged Rose Mallett's final thought as she casts off her romantic notions of love and marries her flawed childhood sweetheart is an 'appreciation of the joke' (256). Miss Mole, rather like Young, tends towards irreverence on the subject of marriage and is chastised by her proper cousin Lilla, 'Don't be vulgar, Hannah. I think jokes about marriage are in the very worst taste' (16). Indeed, the later novels, *The Curate's Wife*, *Celia* and *Chatterton Square*, following the trend of the domestic novel to investigate matrimony and family life, evade the predictable quest for love ending in conventional closures and scrutinize instead the marriage state with complete lack of sentimentality.

Young's most illuminating insight is not the disturbing exploration of married sadness, but rather the sense that love has ceased to be a sufficient shaping force for the development of the self and the narrative of the novel. As she envisions it, the self is forged by relationships that extend well beyond the romance and is mirrored in the rooms and domestic interiors of houses. In Young's later novels, the outline of the self emerges forcefully from a movement of recoil at the prescriptive limits of marriage and from the complex web of relationships and nuanced feelings and liberties nurtured within the domestic sphere.

Notes

[1]   'Letter 100. To Anna Austen', 9 September 1814 in R.W. Chapman, ed., *Jane Austen's Letters* (1979): 401.

[2]   'At one level it [of course] says, "You know *x* – this is knowledge we share". But at another level it says, "*Behave* as if you know *x*". The compelling signal registers the speaker's perception of potential resistance and dominates or disarms that resistance, imposing constraints on the listener to profit the speaker' (Giltrow: 227).

[3]   With her swift thin figure and little ardent head (8), Lydia resembles Margo Metroland in Evelyn Waugh's *Decline and Fall*, Stella Gibbons's Flora Poste in *Cold Comfort Farm*, Tuppence in Agatha Christie's Tommy and Tuppence series, Hervey Russell in Storm Jameson's 'Mirror in Darkness' trilogy, or Cecilia in Bowen's *To the North*.

[4]   See Mark Wigley's engaging discussion of the identitfication of modern architecture – and modernism – with the whiteness of surfaces (2001: xiv) and his explanation of Le Corbusier's influence in promoting white surfaces in *White Walls, Designer Dresses: The Fashioning of Modern Architecture* (2001). Le Corbusier in *L'art décorative d'aujourd'hui*

The Turn to Domestic Modernism

(1925) argued that 'modern architecture can only be modern inasmuch as it is white' and that 'the whole moral, ethical, functional, and even technical superiority of architecture is seen to hang on the whiteness of its surfaces' (2001: xvi). In his biography of Somerset Maugham, Jeffrey Meyers quotes Cecil Beaton's description of Maugham's wife, Syrie's interior decoration:

> Syrie caught the 'no color' virus and spread the disease around the world ... [She] bleached, pickled or scraped every piece of furniture in sight. White sheepskin rugs were strewn on the eggshell-surfaced floors, huge white sofas ... white vases against a white wall. Mayfair drawing rooms looked like albino stage sets (88–9).

[5] See also Stella Deen's discussion of domestic modernity in *William* (2003).

[6] See Katharine Leaf West's *Chapter of Governesses: A Study of the Governess in English Fiction, 1800–1949* (1949), which is dedicated to her governess, Florence Homer Mole – 'Moley'! We suspect that there may be a family connection between Katharine West and Young's sister, Gladys, who had married Algernon West, thus accounting for Young's use of the names, Miss Mole and Moley.

Chapter 6

Vicarages and Lodging-houses

> If you come to a Vicarage, you ought to be prepared to find a Vicar.
>
> Agatha Christie, *The Murder at the Vicarage*: 10

> If I had a little capital, I'd start a boarding-house, for what they call single gentlemen, myself, and I'd look after you like a mother, Mr. Blenkinsop.
>
> *Miss Mole*: 141

With their public face and communal disposition, the vicarage and the boarding house inflected by the English idea of home and, in turn, inflicting this idea of home upon its inhabitants, are common, often comic, alternative models of domesticity. The heads of these hybrid households, the vicar and the landlady, too, are familiar, stock, textualized figures in English literature, variously farcical, nosy, rigidly authoritarian, kindly and inept. The vicarage, adjacent to but separate from the public and sacred space of the church and the boarding house, usually a former grand private house, mirror the English propensity to consider house and home as a detached dwelling. Through these 'homes', Young, like so many of her compatriots, considers domestic reconfigurations with relish, finding in them the occasion to explore a microcosm of society, expose social mores and exercise her ironic touch.

A Door Ajar

> It would not be becoming were I to travestie a sermon, or even to repeat the language of it in the pages of a novel. (Trollope, *Barchester Towers*: 49)

> Domestic fiction resounds with the clink of teaspoons and the accents of the curate. (Stevenson, 'A Gossip on Romance')[1]

In *The Vicar's Daughter* (1928), *Jenny Wren* (1932) and its sequel *The Curate's Wife* (1934), Young portrays the anatomy of marriage and the precarious bonds between mothers and daughters and sisters within these peculiar domestic settings. Just before World War I, and between the wars, the English village, rural cottage and vicarage represented compelling images and stereotypes of home, nation and the *beau ideal* (Davidoff et al. 1976: 144). A spate of domestic and detective novels set in vicarages appeared during this period, including Elizabeth von Arnim's *The Pastor's Wife* (1914), May Sinclair's *The Three Sisters* (1914) and *The Rector of Wyck* (1925), F.M. Mayor's *The Rector's Daughter* (1924), Ivy Compton-Burnett's *Pastors and Masters* (1925),

112   *Domestic Modernism, the Interwar Novel, and E.H. Young*

George Orwell's *A Clergyman's Daughter* (1935), Agatha Christie's *The Murder at the Vicarage* (1930), Joan Coggin's recently reprinted *Who Killed the Curate?* (1944) and G.K. Chesterton's Father Brown stories. From Oliver Goldsmith's *Vicar of Wakefield* (1766) to Margaret Oliphant's *Chronicles of Carlingford* (1862–66) and Anthony Trollope's Barchester series in the 1860s to Barbara Pym's post-World War II fiction, the vicarage novel comprises a sub-genre of the domestic novel, proffering a small, close-knit community with ample opportunity for the observation of human foibles and interactions. Novelists were evidently inspired to examine how the ritualized 'texts' of the domestic spaces of church, manse, and village or parish 'organized social relations' (Dorothy Smith: 279).

And how predictable the scenarios of vicarage novels are – celibate curates pursued by doting spinsters and widows in competition over knitted socks and flower arrangements and suffering from 'one of those old-maid-sweet-on-the-parson complexes' (Holtby, 1931: 190), in tandem with the power politics and hierarchical battles of church officials and parish women. Behind the vicarage door, we find many a vicar cowering under the protective wing of an unmarried sister or motherly housekeeper, fending off amorous approaches, mounting fêtes in alliance with the local squire or lady clad in good tweeds to repair the church roof or tower, and undoubtedly boring his parishioners with overly-long sermons filled with obscure literary allusions. As the sly narrator of *Barchester Towers* comments: 'there is, perhaps, no greater hardship at present inflicted on mankind in civilized and free countries, than the necessity of listening to sermons' (52). We wonder, then, what possessed Young, who as Henderson wryly noted, had never been to a revival meeting or the inside of a 'home as that presided over by the successful preacher Robert Corder' ('*E.H. Young*, her Muse, her Method & her Message': 7), to situate three domestic dramas in clerical settings (*The Vicar's Daughter, Miss Mole, The Curate's Wife*)? Certainly Young, in the vein of Oliver Goldsmith, Jane Austen, Anthony Trollope, Agatha Christie, and Barbara Pym, recognized the vicarage's potential as fertile ground for the unfolding of a human comedy.

An uneasy hybrid of private and public, profane and sacred space, the vicarage mediates between the individual and the community. Opening its inner private home space to the public, the vicarage imposes ecclesiastical values onto the outer community, but it is, at the same time, pregnable to its alien values. Although its inhabitants act as agents of surveillance over the community, because of the public face of the vicarage they themselves are also continually under surveillance. In *The Curate's Wife*, the officious Mrs. Doubleday energetically and maliciously engages in coercion, domination and surveillance under the guise of preserving Christian values, and seizes the authority normally assumed by the vicar. Dahlia (*The Curate's Wife*) and Margaret Stack (*The Vicar's Daughter*), like Judith's dead mother in *A Corn of Wheat* or the deceased Mrs. Corder in *Miss Mole*, do not hesitate to criticize religious doctrines and rituals and mock their husbands' professions. As Margaret Stack muses: 'to act the part of the parson's wife, however, was too extreme an instance [of marital adaptation]. She did not feel like a parson's wife' (1928: 82); and Cecil Sproat 'hardly

Vicarages and Lodging-houses

knew how to deal with Dahlia's attitude towards his calling', which seemed 'to have a slightly comic element for her' (1934: 14). Adopting an architectural metaphor, the narrator in *The Curate's Wife* observes that Dahlia sees in the narrow windows and the steeple much that is repulsive to her in her husband's religion and revolts against 'the cramped windows and thin loftiness of the spire' (165). Young's worldly and ironic view of the Church roused one fan, a Mrs. Mallett, to protest that 'Really, there are no Mr. and Mrs. Doubleday in these days if there ever were in Trollope's time' (Letter to Young, 11 November 1934, Young Papers). Mrs. Mallett may have been right; however, as Craig and Cadogan point out, by the 1930s in England, 'the mild vicar', together with 'the brisk nurse, the adenoidal kitchenmaid, the effusive spinster, the gruff colonel, the pampered actress and the reliable doctor' had become a stock character of farce, romance, and melodrama. The appearance of these instantly recognizable figures, 'seems to rule out moral or psychological ambiguity … this merely adds to the reader's enjoyment when one of them is decisively unmasked' (162).

It is possible that by offering her characters, particularly her women, the opportunity to engage in animated and irreverent exchanges about the Church, Young found a convenient vehicle with which to contrast conventional morality with true goodness, beauty, and intelligence. By mocking self-righteous and humourless clerics like Robert Corder and Maurice Roper (even their names are telling), and by affectionately depicting the intellectual, unworldly Edward Stack who was 'more interested in the theory of religion than in the practice of it' (1928: 28) and the lazy but kindly Mr. Doubleday, she could expose the hypocrisy and hollow practices of religious leaders and the institution of the church. We, along with Mrs. Doubleday, the Reverend Corder and Maurice Roper, must learn to distinguish between morality and teleology and respect true goodness and rightness. In the vicarage drawing-room or study, a deceptively comfortable site for serious philosophical discussions, Margaret, elaborating on the apparent 'hasty sins' of John Blunt and her husband, Edward, ponders cause and effect:

> the problem of good and evil, in intention and in result, could not be settled until the end of time, for, as the cause of sin might lie in some good intention generations back, so what seemed evil might be productive of future good. There was nothing to be done with the past or the future except what seemed good in the present, and even that was doubtful. (241)

An anomaly among the later Bristol novels, *The Vicar's Daughter* – originally titled 'The Blunts'[2] – takes place in a rather unappealing seaside town, Old and New Framling. Young's manuscript notebooks suggest that she had intended to write a more sensational novel than the overstrained comedy of errors, secrets and misunderstandings she ultimately published. These earlier plans are outlined on a few sheets as 'accident suicide murder by James, murder by Edward; verdict is an open one' (Young Papers). There are also unfinished dramatizations of 'The Blunts'. Although other Young novels revolve around misunderstandings and sexual secrets, *The Vicar's*

114 *Domestic Modernism, the Interwar Novel, and E.H. Young*

Daughter seems to waver erratically between Gothic romance and drawing room comedy and mystery, and between fiction and drama. Without a doubt, this novel, with its unities of place (two houses, study, drawing room, garden, the street), character and time (the action takes place over a couple of days), and its theatrical dialogue has a staged, drawing room quality. What indeed could be more theatrical than Margaret's reflection that 'as Maurice had once seen her standing by the drawing room window, like a character in a play, at the rising of the curtain, she saw this room, the dinner-table with its pretty china and bright glass and silver as the setting of a scene in a comedy' (258)? However, because Young's manuscripts and the records of the BBC Written Archives indicate that she dramatized two of her novels (*Miss Mole* and *William*) primarily for BBC radio productions, it is difficult to determine whether this one originated as a play or whether it was specifically revised in dramatic form for the BBC. As mentioned earlier, we surmise that Henderson is referring to this novel in his appreciation, '*E.H. Young*, her Muse, her Method & her Message', when he comments that criticism by Edward Garnett, Jonathan Cape's celebrated reader, occasioned the rewriting of an unnamed book (4). We speculate whether Garnett's advice was sound and whether this odd and awkwardly reconfigured novel, dominated by voyeurism, would have been more powerful as the originally intended tale of murder.

Like *The Curate's Wife* and *Chatterton Square*, this is a story of what goes on behind and between the façades of two neighbouring houses. In the Vicarage live Margaret and Edward Stack and their daughter, Hilary. Their cousin, the ungainly Reverend Maurice Roper, given to ominous references to the 'Hand of God', is staying on for a visit after having replaced Edward during the latter's holiday. Imagining that the Blunts' housekeeper, Caroline Mather, is Edward's illegitimate daughter, he alternately relishes and frets over this secret, which he gradually and pruriently reveals to Margaret. Roper has been in love with Margaret for many years. His bitter musings on the good fortune of his cousin, his jealousy of Edward's popularity and natural vigour and his censure of the laxity of Edward's faith extend to the size and comforts of the vicarage, 'too fine a house and too large a garden for a country vicar' (12) and Margaret's decorating strategies in her tasteful choice of colours. In his censorious eyes such attentiveness to aesthetic matters, 'had occupied the thought which should have been given to other things' (12). Her spacious house, 'of a period antagonistic to all his feelings ... shocked him as Margaret had often done; it was, in fact, like the woman herself and it gave him the same uneasiness, compounded of pleasure and distrust' (12).

Margaret, who is compared to Jane Austen's Emma (*New Statesman*, 20 October 1928: 52) and who regards 'the management of one man and one child ... hardly enough to occupy an intelligent woman' (85), relieves her boredom by attempting to solve 'the immediate problem which ... created and ignored by him [Edward], lay in the narrow space between the Blunts' house and her own' (84) in order to preserve Edward and Hilary from scandal. Margaret worries that her 'presumptuousness will be the undoing of us all' (171) and at the close of the novel, she admits that 'for this comedy of errors she could only blame herself, but all her emotions found their vent

Vicarages and Lodging-houses 115

in laughter and she was laughing when she let herself into the house and saw Maurice sitting, crumpled, in his chair, keeping his unnecessary watch' (286).

Margaret's predilection for arranging rooms and furniture replicates her penchant for arranging the lives around her; she is the first of Young's middle-aged domestic artists, and through her control of the home seeks to create an atmosphere of well being and express a conscious aesthetic. In his review of this novel in *The Canadian Forum*, Gilbert Norwood caught the essence of Young's art of fiction when he observed that Margaret Stack is a 'magnificent practitioner in the most difficult and most necessary of all arts – living successfully with other people' (288). Her art receives greater emphasis through the contrast between the vicarage and the Blunts' house across the road where live James and John Blunt and their young housekeeper, Caroline Mather, oppressed by the ghosts of the Blunts' harsh father and long-suffering mother. This house, in which 'there had been no laughter' (116), harbours dark family secrets; James the younger brother is disturbed and unstable, John, the older, in love with Caroline, is a thief, having destroyed his father's will and kept the money intended for the church:

> The Blunts' house had the face of a tired old man, patient under the prospect of more fatigues, but the Vicarage kept its air of possessing a superiority for which it took no credit but which could never be denied, like a person of good lineage who, honestly believing he is unconscious of it, contrives to impress other men with its importance and his own differences from themselves. (184)

Given this Gothic-tinged portrait of the Blunts, one can see why Stella Gibbons mocked the strong, silent, brooding male with her portrayal of the Starkadder men in *Cold Comfort Farm*.

Inexorably, the dark secrets of these two embodied and personified houses are entangled and 'the people on both sides of the road were involved in each other's business' (80). The Blunt brothers fear that their old servant, Sarah Scutt, will reveal the truth about the destroyed will to Edward; Margaret fears that the Blunts will expose Caroline as Edward's illegitimate daughter; and John fears that Caroline will reject him as a thief. That which has been repressed and concealed returns to haunt the increasingly uncanny household and begins to afflict the neighbouring house. By means of the contrast between the two households, one darkened and immured by fear and tragedy, the other comfortable and carefully controlled, Young explores the relationship of physical space and ideas of home and family. By situating themselves voyeuristically at a window or on staircases, doorsteps and crumbling bridges, the characters try to determine their own positions in relation to these intertwined secrets and to each other. The staircase carries the characters and the narrative from communal spaces and conversations (drawing room, dining room) up to the privacy of bedrooms and self-reflection; as Bachelard notes, 'we always *go up* the attic stairs, which are steeper and more primitive. For they bear the mark of ascension to a more tranquil solitude' (26).

116   *Domestic Modernism, the Interwar Novel, and E.H. Young*

The literal 'crossing' the road from one house to the other and the confrontation with closed doors and shuttered windows are also metaphorical attempts to penetrate secrets and hidden selves: 'she [Margaret] could see the Blunts' windows, like blind eyes, and the Blunts' door: even the knocker so assiduously polished by Caroline was visible but, as she watched, it slowly disappeared and wondering when she would wake from this nightmare, she realized that some one was opening the door' (272). Setting the Vicarage up as a prime site of surveillance, Young continually shifts focalization from character to character, in particular from Maurice to Hilary to Margaret, who watch each other as intently as they observe the Blunts across the road: 'Margaret stood at the study window and gazed at the opposite house, dark, lifeless, grilled by rain, it took on a malignant aspect' (234). She creates a kind of Jamesian 'house of fiction' with figures standing at symbolic windows, watching the show of life with their highly individual visions (James: 46). Through the reiteration of increasingly anthropomorphized houses, rooms and windows, and of the observer at the window, Young accentuates the view from the interior, as this outward gazing also reveals each character's inner self and personality.

Georg Simmel claimed that the door 'displays a complex difference of intention between entering and exiting' and distinguished it from the window, which, 'directed almost exclusively from inside to outside … is there for looking out, not for looking in'. Because of this 'one-sided direction', the window has 'only a part of the deeper and more fundamental significance of the door' (68). And although looking through a window is not entirely an asymmetrical experience, since the reader, who is positioned alongside the observers, is given glimpses back into their inner lives, it is the opening of a door that is the decisive and connecting act: 'Mentally, she [Margaret] had crossed the road so many times during the last few days that there was relief in taking her body with her' (241–2).[3]

In the final chapter, which is titled 'The Door Ajar', we learn that Caroline is too young to be Edward's daughter and that she will marry John; sordid secrets are untangled, and for some characters, at least, the symbolic door opens: 'She [Margaret] had a moment of intense humility in which, as though a door was opened, she had a glimpse of mysterious things made plain, but John Blunt changed from one foot to the other and the door was gently shut' (286). For Young, as for Emily Dickinson, the 'door ajar' suggests possibility, choice, 'an entire cosmos of the Half-open' (Bachelard: 222). And so the novel concludes with this exchange between Margaret and Edward:

> 'God?' he said, wondering at that name on her lips. 'I thought you always pretended to know nothing about Him.'
> 'Yes,' She remembered that moment – in the street – when the door had opened. 'But sometimes He leaves the door ajar,' she said. (288)

Homesickness

> It is thus that the domestic world does not cease to operate on our passibility to writing, right up to the disaster of the houses ... Thought cannot want its house. But the house haunts it.' (Lyotard, '*Domus* and the Megalopolis': 277)

> Now what would that poor old Mr. Padsoe have said, could he have seen his child trying to keep a lodging house? She is quite mad. I shall speak to the Vicar. She should be put away; it is not safe for us all. (Stella Gibbons, *Bassett*: 154)

Like *The Vicar's Daughter*, *Jenny Wren* is structured around the symbolic of houses and home, but unlike the earlier novel, it highlights homesickness, homelessness and the yearning for home and belonging. Beneath the novel's light and amusing tone lurks the pervasive sadness of those who have no home (Miss Morrison), those who are deprived of the home to which they belong (Louisa Rendall, Edwin Cummings) and those who long for an ideal home and family (Jenny).

Jenny Wren, in line with several of the Bristol novels, opens with a narratorial panorama of a 'sloping, one-sided street called Beulah Mount' (5) in Upper Radstowe that maps out in painstaking detail the physical and symbolic topography of the neighbourhood:

> no two houses are alike. Some of them are flat-fronted, a few are bow-windowed and some have flimsy, roofed balconies outside the first-floor windows, and these, even when they are in need of painting, give an effect of diminished but persistent gaiety to a terrace built in an age of leisure and of privilege. Differing in breadth, in height, in the shape of chimney-pots and the colour of roofs, in the size and number of the front steps ... the houses, standing shoulder to shoulder, like a row of eager but well-behaved spectators, are united in an air of personal dignity, unmoved by changes of fortune, and in the proud possession of the finest view in Upper Radstowe. (5)

The exploration of the possibilities and constraints of the national domestic ideology of urban housing that structures and animates Young's later domestic novels is already apparent in the symbolic valences of the once elegant eighteenth-century crescent row, which, like many Victorian terraces, conformed to the new ideals of social and spatial privacy and segregation.[4]

Shifting her gaze from this row of houses, the heterodiegetic narrator sweeps over a terrain familiar to readers of Young – down the steep slopes of Upper Radstowe to the busy docks, then over to the dramatic Avon Gorge and its cliffs and the suspension bridge that once again 'spans the gulf'(5) between the pastoral and the urban. Gradually, the narrator closes in upon one specific house: 15 Beulah Mount, a 'benign old house', which becomes the 'centre of a tiny storm' (306) created out of the relationships and domestic lives of a small group of people, a 'small knot of personalities in No. 15 Beulah Mount ... attached by slender filaments to the households on either side' (120). As Jos Boys notes in her discussion of the

118   *Domestic Modernism, the Interwar Novel, and E.H. Young*

relationships between architecture and gender, 'while architecture does not "reflect" society, and is only partially shaped by our continuing and contested struggles for identity, the buildings and cities we inhabit remain deeply implicated in shaping our everyday experiences' (217). This is certainly true of *Jenny Wren*, where Young sets up houses as tools not only for the analysis of the human soul, but also of human relations within an intricately described web of everyday experiences. Throughout the novel we find anthropomorphized and embodied houses exerting their agency upon the characters who inhabit them by sheltering, protecting and observing their inhabitants: 'the windows of her home ... seemed to look at her [Jenny] rather anxiously ... all it could do was to watch her with this anxiety and with entreaty' (175–6).

The narrator then further narrows her focus to the heroine, Jenny Rendall, the 'Jenny Wren' of the title, who takes up her role as the novel's prime focalizer. Jenny is located in 'her favourite post' (112) by the 'protruding' bow window gazing at the busy scene below: 'she knelt down in front of the window ... In the affairs of their [the flanking houses's] occupants, she took the exaggerated interest of an exile watching the activities of her proper world, and of an imaginative person who, awaiting romance in her own life, must make it out of the lives of other people' (10–11). Thus Young develops her network of domestic signifiers and signals to the reader the marked correspondence between house and fiction and between the window and the 'eye' of the novel, Jenny. As Henry James notes in his metaphoric house of fiction: 'the spreading field, the human scene is the "choice of subject"; the pierced aperture, either broad or balconied or slit-like and low-browed, is the "literary form"; but they are ... as nothing without the posted presence of the watcher ... the consciousness of the artist' (46). Through Jenny's gaze and voyeuristic position at the window, that liminal space posed between the domestic interior and the external public world and, concomitantly, between inner consciousness and the world of experience, Young allows us the opportunity to assume shifting subject positions in which we simultaneously observe Jenny and participate in her gaze.

Brooding and self-absorbed, Jenny may not be the 'kind of young woman most novelists would pick for their heroine' (W.E.H., 25 February 1933, *Boston Evening Transcript*: 1), but in creating this complex and narcissistic young woman, Young adds her characteristic depth and surprise to the domestic novel genre. In her narcissism and romantic ideas of love, which are quickly dispelled by the reality of class distinctions and later in *The Curate's Wife* by gross male sexuality, Jenny recalls Beryl Fairfield in Mansfield's 'At the Bay', who also gazes out of her window at the night dreaming of romance, only to be by appalled by Harry Kember's rough embrace and 'bright, blind, terrifying smile' when a 'lover' does materialize (314). In her posture as romantic and introspective heroine, Jenny will dream and wait in vain by this window for her idealized lover, Cyril Merriman, to come riding up on horseback. In contrast, her sister Dahlia, a more matter-of-fact heroine who ventures forth to attend church activities for the practical purpose of meeting neighbours and potential boarders, is associated with the public and perilous doorstep: 'It did not occur to her that though the doorstep was for her a place of safety, it might be dangerous, when she occupied it, for other

Vicarages and Lodging-houses 119

people, dangerous, for instance, to Mr. Sproat, who went by, carrying a letter to the pillar-box and returned with swiftness, fearful that the figure, half-seen as he passed, would have disappeared' (130). We eventually learn that Jenny and her sister, Dahlia, are the daughters of Louisa Rendall, an attractive countrywoman, widow of Sidney Rendall, a gentleman, who recently sold White Farm on the other side of the bridge and bought the house at 15 Beulah Mount, which she plans to operate as a lodging-house with the assistance of her well-bred and well-educated daughters.

Though taking in lodgers was a way of 'providing a livelihood for widows or other women left without support' with 'the convenience and respectability of being able to earn income within the four walls of the house', by the nineteenth-century, 'lodging and boarding began to carry moral opprobrium. On the part of both lodger and householder, it came to be considered a necessary evil and a sign of the loss of genteel status' (Davidoff 1979: 83, 89, 68). Boarding houses encountered in the novels of Jean Rhys, Laura Talbot and Stella Gibbons tend to represent the decline of great houses and the upper classes and an increasingly urban, mobile society; they shelter figures from the margins of society – single, impoverished and genteel, who must work for a living and live 'in digs'.[5]

Unusually for the genre of lodging-house novels and stories, *Jenny Wren* focuses on the owners, *their* sense of homelessness and the transitory, *their* lack of privacy and *their* constrained lives rather than on the situation of the lodger. Here, as in Gibbons' *Bassett*, the reader, who is positioned amidst the everyday routines of a boarding-house and alongside the women who perform them, is accorded a realistic view from the interior.[6] This shift in focus indicates a turn towards the critical, but sympathetic, investigation and validation of women's domestic lives, their perspective on domestic space and the performance of the everyday that marked the domestic novel of the interwar years. Like the private houses that dominate Young's other novels, the Rendalls' lodging-house is also a representative material form of English domestic and national culture, ideology and practice; lodging-house life is ritualized and regulated to conform to middle-class respectability and customs. Young's intimate and inside view of lodging-house domestic life serves – as does her entry into the lives and spaces of her fictional houses – to mirror and reveal the inner subjective states of her characters. In this presentation of lodging-houses and lodgers, the demonization of these homes during the Victorian period as sites of disease, promiscuity, poverty and its attendant vices and of haunting, ghosts and revenance has been transformed into a site of quiet middle-class desperation.

When Young's narrator observes that 'the fierce pride of [Jenny's] eighteen years rebelled against the social stigma of keeping lodgings' (9), she shows us how the phenomenon of the lodging-house exacerbates the class divisions and the discourse of class which dominate this novel and *The Curate's Wife*; for though this lodging-house is intended as a fresh start for the Rendall women, 'living in lodgings … with its sharing of part of someone else's house, was a sign that the family could no longer be kept private and implied a loss of caste' (Davidoff 1979: 68). In *Bassett*, middle-aged spinsters Miss Padsoe and Miss Baker are spared the sexual implications associated

120   *Domestic Modernism, the Interwar Novel, and E.H. Young*

with the lodging-house's status as a hybrid of public and private space, wavering uneasily between middle-class respectability and the sexually risqué. The three Rendall women, however, are uncomfortably conscious of that stigma since 'spatial proximity', in the eyes of the community, is associated with 'sexual promiscuity and improper behaviours' (Sharon Marcus: 104–105). Moreover, despite, or because of, shared sitting rooms, beds, bedrooms and the lack of privacy, there is much proximity, but little intimacy, between Louisa and her daughters and between the two sisters, highlighted through many poignant moments of missed opportunities to communicate and confide; while, in keeping with the sexual implications of boarding houses, the enforced intimacy produces a relationship between Jenny and the young male boarder, Edwin.

As Young's focus on the owners shifts the perspective from the impoverished and lonely inhabitants who shelter behind the façades of many fictional lodging-houses, so Louisa, Jenny and Dahlia comically foil the stereotypes of the nosy landlady and the adenoidal, grumpy and overworked maids which are a fixture in the novels of writers of the period from Jean Rhys to Agatha Christie. Concerned with the comfort and well-being of their lodgers, the Rendalls unusually try to create a home out of the lodging-house experience. At the same time, the customary rituals and practices of the domestic everyday, from dusting to serving meals, evolve into covert media of communication and opportunities for romantic encounters. For, as a transitory home where lodgers come and go and where space is communal and privacy scarce, the lodging-house, more than the family home, offers a dramatic site for intrigue and romance.

The lodging-house highlights Jenny and Dahlia's transient and hybrid situation and anomalous class; offspring of a country peasant mother and of an upper-middle-class father, they belong nowhere. They are no longer at home in their childhood home, White Farm, now possessed by their mother's lover, Thomas Grimshaw, nor are they at home in the faded gentility of Beulah Mount and its parochial parish church. Louisa's 'sin', her affair with Grimshaw, shadows her and her two daughters throughout the two novels, jeopardizing their marriage prospects: the girls are spied on by neighbours in Beulah Mount, by their former neighbours and by Grimshaw. Despite its genteel and elegant history of 'the ladies in hooped skirts and the gentlemen in brocaded waistcoats who had taken the waters at the wells ... and made Beulah Mount gay with their wit and elegance' (6), the lodging-house is defiled by the economic realities of housekeeping, marketing, making ends meet, the scrimping and saving and exchanging of money. In the Victorian era, 'the demonology of boarding' implicated lodgings as 'thoroughly antidomestic, both because it typified the city (which ... was opposed to the home) and because the imagery of dirt and contagion contradicted the domestic ideal's emphasis on cleanliness and order' (Sharon Marcus: 104–5). Thus, for several of Young's heroines (Miss Mole, Henrietta Mallett and the Rendalls), the sign of improvement in their fortunes is the move from a lodging-house to a private home.

The absurdity and intricacy of English class divisions have been a favourite target of many domestic novelists. In Rose Macaulay's *Keeping Up Appearances* (1928),

Vicarages and Lodging-houses

the heroine recognizes that becoming conversant in the idioms obtaining to different classes 'was like knowing intimately two languages' (49): she remembers the familiar phrases she would hear as in her childhood she shuttled 'to and fro between her mother's house and her aunt's: … Have some more, come again; had enough, done very well; napkins, serviettes; woman, lady; man, gentleman, or fellow; jam, preserve; cos*ume, cos*tume; of 'n, of*ten*' (48–9). In *A Pin to See the Peepshow*, Julia regrets that although as the daughter of 'a clerk in a House and estate Agency' she is better off 'than being Mary Barnes, whose father was a small draper in the Chiswick High Road', she is not as well situated as 'Edith Darling, whose father was Something-in-the-City, or Anne Ackroyd, who was a doctor's daughter' (9). Later, she sees her incompatibility with her husband exacerbated by the fact that while as a shopgirl she 'could be anybody's friend … a manager in a branch of gentleman's outfitter's' could not possibly be 'an officer and a gentleman' (Jesse: 160). By the end of the novel, however, F. Tennyson Jesse's indictment of the English class system acquires a grimmer tone, as the novel makes clear that Julia's destiny has been sealed by her belonging to the wrong social class:

> In the class above hers the idea of divorce would not have shocked, and a private income would even have allowed her and Carr to live together without divorce, and no one would have been unduly outraged. Had their walk in life been the lowest, had they been tramps or part of the floating population of the docks down London River, they could have set up in one room together, and no one thought twice about it, as long as the husband wasn't a big strong man who made a row and tried to do them in. (391)[7]

Although in *Jenny Wren* the characters' class assignation has no tragic consequences, Young's sympathetic presentation of Dahlia's and Jenny's social predicament is as minutely and as painstakingly detailed as Tennyson Jesse's, exposing 'a social structure so rigid, so confining and ultimately so absurd, that it distorts and twists people's lives, spawning hypocrisy, inhumanity and unhappiness' (S. Beauman 1985b: viii).

Repeatedly, Young returns to Louisa Rendall's peasant origins and seems to alternate between scorn for Louisa's speech, her lack of education and her unrefined appearance, and admiration for her beauty, honesty and sensuality. In her unsympathetic portrait of Sidney Rendall as a cold and desiccated aesthete who disdained the woman he once passionately desired, Young harshly condemns class hypocrisy. In sharp contrast to Louisa's natural sensuality and generosity, the neighbouring landlady, the spinster Miss Jewel, twisted by sexual fear, repression and jealousy, obsessively spies on the Rendalls. While Jenny is allowed to observe the world avidly from her bow window, Miss Jewel's surveillance, like her warped personality that despises and punishes the sensual, is curtailed, literally so as the window in her basement kitchen only offers a partial view of the Rendalls' house. Her austere lodging-house, where she had 'scraped and pinched for years' (283), contrasts with the comfort, warmth and wholesome food of 15 Beulah Mount. The vehemence with which the narrator observes that the ironically named Miss Jewel 'had an insane hatred of physical fulfillment or its promise' (272) suggests a personal

122   *Domestic Modernism, the Interwar Novel, and E.H. Young*

resonance for Young concerning her own unusual sexual arrangements and the public scrutiny she must have dreaded.

Young has set out the dilemma of the art of living for her two young heroines and, as V.S. Pritchett remarks in his review in the *New Statesman and Nation*, although Jenny is 'hardly vital enough' to hold the book together, she is also 'shown to be an artist in her own life' ('New Novels', 26 November 1932: 660–62). Dahlia accepts the proposal of the curate Mr. Sproat, Miss Jewel's lodger; in a fit of maternal self-sacrifice Louisa marries Thomas Grimshaw; and, in opposition to the expected romance ending, Jenny's romantic fling with the snobbish and weak Cyril Merriman ends. Desperately seeking a home, Jenny departs with her lodger and suitor, Edwin Cummings, to his domestic idyll (as fabricated by Jenny) in a second-hand *furniture* shop in a Somersetshire town to become part of another family's domestic arrangement.[8] In their behaviour, and choice of lovers, the sensible Dahlia and the romantic Jenny obviously echo another pair of sisters, Elinor and Marianne in Austen's *Sense and Sensibility*. Young, perhaps even more than Austen, writes beyond the ending to present her heroines' marriages as practical solutions to personal dilemmas that will sorely try their passion for the art of living. Jenny's fate remains unresolved at the end of *Jenny Wren*, for we do not know how she will settle into her new home or what turn her relationship with Edwin will take.

Neither Dahlia nor Jenny can conceive of an art of living beyond the domestic. The pattern we noticed in *The Misses Mallett* and *The Vicar's Daughter* recurs here as, once again, Young retreats from the plots available to the New Woman into more traditional endings for her heroines. Young's narrator observes that the spinster, Miss Morrison, who briefly lodges with the Rendalls, 'had been born into a generation that had learnt to walk and to think freely, but she did not belong to it' (155). In contrast, despite their constrained lives, Dahlia and Jenny feel at liberty to walk the streets and The Green in Upper Radstowe, and Jenny frequently crosses the suspension bridge into the countryside where, in an appropriately pastoral setting, she clandestinely meets Cyril Merriman.

The lodging-house at 15 Beulah Mount dominates as setting and symbol and narrative frame for the novel, but other houses are equally evocative of their owners and their dreams and provide a fulcrum for action and a network of domestic signifiers. White Farm, the former home of the Rendalls purchased by Thomas Grimshaw, is a vaguely pastoral, but not nostalgic, idyll whose memory is contaminated for Dahlia and Jenny by the coldness between their parents and by the closed doors and whisperings that hint of Louisa's 'sin'. Cyril Merriman's home, Merriman House, a 'long, low house with the colour of wisteria fainting against the red brick of the old walls' (22) near White Farm across the bridge, is occupied by unworthy, *nouveau riche* inhabitants. It, however, serves as the vehicle by which Edwin Cummings woos Jenny: 'the house was taking shape in his mind as an excuse for crossing the bridge with her' (64).

Furniture, domestic interiors and household objects, like the houses that contain them, are animated and Young's narrator, and Jenny as focalizer, readily endow

Vicarages and Lodging-houses

'inanimate things with human attributes' (70). In Edwin Cummings' eyes Jenny is a 'piece of cherished furniture' that 'belonged to the best period in mahogany' (53). Sidney Rendall's walnut bureau with its little ivory knobs, an object representing taste, class and lineage in the transitory declassé space of a lodging-house, links Jenny to a more 'respectable past' and assumes a fetishistic value for her tenuous relationship with Edwin. A duster serves as a *domus ex machina* for romance when Dahlia purposefully drops it from the window to attract Mr. Sproat's attention. And it is through Jenny's interaction with, or viewing of, domestic objects that Young most successfully enters into her consciousness as in: 'Jenny looked at the bed and the boots and the bath with a sort of anger and she thought they represented in their shabbiness and neglect the lot to which her father had left his children ... they *would age until their faces were crumpled like the boots*' (70–71: our italics). This correspondence between the material domestic and consciousness is characteristic of Young's writing from *William* onwards; nevertheless, unlike the more adventurous Woolf, Mansfield, or even Compton-Burnett, Young relies on an interfering and interpreting narrator who dispels the power of the snippets of free indirect discourse and Jenny's own voice, which is indicated by the italics above. Thus the moralizing narrator intervenes to comment adversely upon Jenny: '... and, she [Jenny] thought complacently, *ignorant of what time and disappointments could do to pretty faces*, there was no reason why they should be ugly when they were old' (71: our italics).

The bow window at which Jenny so often stands and watches becomes the site of a voyeuristic spectacle that brings about the novel's first dénouement; Mary Dakin's fiancé, Mr. Allsop, who temporarily lodges with the Rendalls, kisses Dahlia at her instigation. Since the curtain, that signifier of the protective barrier between inside and outside, has not been drawn, this public kiss is observed by Mr. Sproat, Miss Jewel and Sarah, Louisa's interfering sister. Contrary to the malicious intentions of Miss Jewel and Sarah, the 'kiss' has unexpected consequences for Dahlia by provoking Mr. Sproat's marriage proposal. And while this kiss is no more welcome than the kiss Beryl receives from Harry Kember in Mansfield's story, or Dorothy from her mentor, 'fattish, oldish' Mr. Warburton, whose 'thick male body', 'harsh odour of maleness', 'furry thighs of satyrs' fills her with fear and aversion (Orwell 1935: 283), it has a nicely ironic outcome.

A second dénouement occurs during another spectacle, a rare public outing undertaken by the key protagonists to the Zoological Gardens to see *Twelfth Night*, which, with its siblings, romantic entanglements and misunderstandings, pointedly reflects the plot of the novel. Through the mechanism of the play, Young's narrator creates a multilayered spectacle, drawing the reader into observing the characters as they, in turn, watch the play and interact with each other. Modelling a dramatic mode, the novel's characters themselves then engage in events and conversations that precipitate crucial incidents and bring the novel to an open-ended closure: Louisa's marriage, Jenny's departure from Upper Radstowe and the end of the Rendall family's experiment with lodging-houses, a kind of 'disaster of the houses' (Lyotard: 277). As the reviewer in the *Times Literary Supplement* astutely noted, in this novel Young

124   *Domestic Modernism, the Interwar Novel, and E.H. Young*

speaks the 'language of the everyday,' but in her mouth 'the words take subtle alien meanings' (1 December 1932: 920). As a result of the apparently unsuccessful outcome of this experiment with a different model of home, the three Rendall women retreat to more conventional domestic arrangements, Louisa to the pastoral idyll of White Farm, Jenny to what she imagines as a more traditional and amiable family home and Dahlia to married life in a clerical living.

Marriage as a Career

> I feel as if we ought to be doing marvellous, heroic, splendid things and all we really do is to wash up the dishes. (*The Curate's Wife*: 235)

> Even so small a thing as the choice of a house in some other part of Upper Radstowe would have completely changed their circumstances. (295)

Appearing in 1934, two years after *Jenny Wren*, *The Curate's Wife* shifts attention from the lives of young girls in flower who 'hadn't half enough to do' and 'so, of course,... had to fall in love' (142) – perhaps an echo of Austen's *Persuasion* – to an unremitting scrutiny of the marriage state. This sequel turns from Jenny to Dahlia, newly married, charming and unruly. As Dahlia remarks to her husband, the curate Cecil Sproat, 'both Jenny and I ... are rather like what our grandmothers must have been. We just get married ... It was the right career for them; with us it's a sort of accident ... It's so easy to forget that marriage can be a career, too' (333). This novel, along with Young's *The Vicar's Daughter* and the later *Celia* and *Chatterton Square*, belongs to that genre of domestic novel that remorselessly dissects married and family life in the vein of Virginia Woolf's *To the Lighthouse*, E.M. Delafield's *Diary of a Provincial Lady*, Jan Struther's *Mrs. Miniver* and Elizabeth Cambridge's *Hostages to Fortune*, or in the more mordant tone of the fiction of Rosamond Lehmann, Elizabeth Bowen, Rose Macaulay and Ivy Compton-Burnett. It also shrewdly observes the difficulties inherent in the marriage of an older curate to a younger, beautiful and apparently frivolous woman who arouses strong physical passion in him; this September–May union is also an issue probed in Christie's *The Murder at the Vicarage* and Coggin's *Who Killed the Curate?*, albeit tongue in cheek.

With its possessive form and impersonal nomenclature, *The Curate's Wife*, the title which replaced the original *Dahlia*, more accurately reflects the conflicted subject position of Dahlia, who must negotiate her role as a public and exposed figure, her desire for autonomy and Cecil's compulsion to possess her physically and morally.[9] In the novel's delineation of this couple's painful education into the realities of married life, we are spared neither quarrels, sexual withholding, nor naked desire. Indeed, the reader is placed in the frustrating position of an eavesdropper, privy to both points of view, yet incapable of arresting the couple's deteriorating relations. Referring repeatedly to the anonymous 'examiners' who judge her, Dahlia, like the newlywed clergymen's wives Charlotte in Jane Austen's *Pride and Prejudice* and

Vicarages and Lodging-houses   125

Ingeborg in Elizabeth von Arnim's *The Pastor's Wife*, struggles to find her place in marriage through the trope of her new house and home. As she ponders the meaning of love and sexual attraction, Dahlia admits she 'depended more than she knew on his [Cecil's] regard for her. It was like a home not greatly valued when things went well outside but waiting for her in case of need and, slowly, some of her objections to using it permanently were being removed' (261).

As in *Miss Mole* and *The Vicar's Daughter*, the endeavour to abide by principled adherence to the Good and to Truth is set against the background of church and parish, where petty ambitions, narrow-minded morality and moral laziness prevail. Through sharp and witty dialogic exchanges, Young ironically exposes hypocrisy and moral failure. Once again setting in play two contrasting households and two marriages – the curate's and the vicar's – Young presents the newlywed Sproats and the elderly Doubledays, briefly encountered in *Jenny Wren*, who have long ceased to have any affection for each other. Through closely examining and interposing all four participants' inner consciousnesses, Young astutely reveals the compromises, evasions and power struggles within marriage. In addition, Jenny, who flees from Somersetshire to the Sproat household, and Reginald, the Doubleday's son who arrives home from Africa, begin a romance and complicate the relations between the two households. Although in his review of this novel Graham Greene warns that Young is 'not an experimenter' and is a 'writer on the margin of contemporary literature' (*Spectator*, 7 September 1934: 336), *The Curate's Wife* is a complexly structured novel with effective shifting focalization, mordant dialogues and convincing introspection. While some of the narrative summaries seem unnecessarily lengthy, there is undeniable power in the portrait of Dahlia's struggles with her conscience. For example, in the following passage, the narrator allows Dahlia's own words to express her characteristically muddled and endearing blend of shrewdness and childishness: 'she could not contemplate a future in which he [Cecil] was entirely absent; *he need not be very near, but he had to be there, when she wanted him*' (291: our italics).

Young begins boldly with the newly-married couple waking in bed and already engaged in those small deceptions that ease married life. Their first exchange, revolving around the noisy cistern in the attic, has dropped us abruptly into the commonplaces of the Sproats' daily life. A similar ignoble domestic plumbing detail later crops up in the famous opening of Virginia Woolf's *Between the Acts*: 'It was a summer's night and they were talking, in the big room with the windows open to the garden about the cesspool' (7). Unglamourously essential, the cistern becomes a crucial domestic space in the novel, occasioning romantic encounters between Dahlia and the object of her unfulfilled romantic desires, Simon Tothill, and between Jenny and Reginald Doubleday. The everyday offers a lexicon of domesticity that subtly performs an ontological function: against the backdrop of distempering walls and sorting boxes, the characters converse, quarrel and think about morality, love, charity, sin and Christianity. Here again the home narrates the novel. Domestic chores occasion conversation and reflection. Listening to the domestic activities of Jenny and Dahlia, 'the rattling of crockery, the turning on and off of water' (206), Cecil broods over their

126   *Domestic Modernism, the Interwar Novel, and E.H. Young*

easy companionship and his own estrangement from Dahlia. Throughout the novel, Young reveals Dahlia quietly performing 'marvellous, heroic, splendid things' in a quotidian, minute way through small kindnesses, dignified behaviour and courageous resistance to Mrs. Doubleday's bullying. In these ways, Young strives to validate the heroism of the everyday and creates a new style of heroine.

As in her other later novels, decoration, furniture and ornaments here assume a symbolic value as objects through which the characters communicate and reveal themselves. Mild, hen-pecked and passive, Mr. Doubleday triumphs, at last, over his domineering wife and shifts the domestic balance of power by suggesting that the new green chair she has purchased for her adored Reginald's room clashes with the new carpet. Continuing the grammar of the home, Young relays Mrs. Doubleday's fear that she has lost ground to her husband for whom she feels only contempt through the simile, 'she felt like a stranger in her own house' (117). (We may add that Young grants Mr. Doubleday a further triumph by allowing him to reappear, wifeless, in her last novel, where, still irrepressibly curious and chatty, he holds the passers-by 'to the ransom of a little talk' (*Chatterton Square*: 50).) Jenny's courtship with Reginald, like her earlier relationship with Edwin Cummings, is mediated and facilitated by hunting for antiques through the shops of Upper Radstowe. And it is ironic that Mrs. Doubleday, who objected to both Jenny and Dahlia because of their mother's 'adultery' and working-class origins, 'was glad … of his [Reginald's] interest in antiques … She could not be jealous of tallboys and sofa tables' (267). Jenny's tenuous relation with Edwin Cummings and his family is terminated symbolically through his return of her father's elegant walnut bureau. As Jenny remarks to Dahlia, Edwin had said 'ages ago, he wouldn't have it without me, so you see, this is a way of saying he doesn't want me any more' (202).

Edwin's house *cum* furniture shop, which had been idealized as a site of belonging, is eerily transformed into the *unheimlich*. Dahlia imagines Jenny 'standing forlorn in the midst of furniture which was second-hand much more often than it was antique' (54); old Mr. Cummings, with his straggly beard and crooked lips, shuffles around the house at night and wanders into Jenny's room, where the door has no lock. His kiss, which Jenny represses by protesting that it was repulsive but harmless, drives her home to Upper Radstowe. When Dahlia comes to her at night, a traumatized Jenny wakes in fear with a whimpering cry (149).

Finely balanced between the two houses – the vicarage and the curate's home – the novel enacts the reciprocity of home and character. With the Sproats caught in the throes of decorating and furnishing their newly-rented house, the process of interior decoration and negotiation mirrors the arrangements and interior decoration of their marriage. Their home, which had 'its place in the medley of houses round The Green', literally embodies their personalities and marital situation – old-fashioned, in bad repair and uninhabited for a long time:

> Its face was morose, its figure ungainly, its arrangement was inconvenient and its stairs were many: a low rent, a narrow unkempt garden at the back and an individuality of its

Vicarages and Lodging-houses   127

own were its attractions for Dahlia, who had a contriving mind and preferred grappling with this oddity in houses to enduring the draughts of a bright little labour-saving villa without a single cupboard. (14)

And so, too, Dahlia undertakes to mould her tall, ungainly, sombre husband whose hair hangs too long at the back. This odd house's individuality reflects Dahlia's scepticism about her husband's profession and her rejection of his rigid morality; to Dahlia 'morals are conventions' (175) and people who use the word sin, which she dislikes, 'sound so holy' (176). Thus, she rejects Cecil's condemnation of a young woman's illegitimate pregnancy and 'his campaign against sexual transgressions in the parish' (92) and without his knowledge quietly and efficiently finds a home in the countryside for the girl, Ivy. Young's intense representation of Cecil's horror of marital infidelity, sex outside the law and the church, and the narrator's interjection that illicit love 'might have dignity and beauty' and 'that the outfacing of convention, even in a moment of passion, could have an astringent, purifying bitterness' (24), surely echoes Young's own personal anguish and experience. And yet, through alternating focalization between husband and wife, Cecil emerges as the most psychologically developed of Young's clerics.

The Doubledays' home is the domain and embodiment of Mrs. Doubleday; comfortable and conventional, in an abrupt shift of perspective it turns uncanny. When Reginald looks around 'his mother's conception of what a drawing-room should be', he sees a grey carpet with a pink floral design, a cornice with ornamental plaster in corresponding pink, gilt frames around pictures of herbaceous borders, waterfall and sunsets behind trees, and chairs covered in rosy damask. Suddenly, Reginald perceives the room and home as uncanny: 'The room had the obviousness of unimaginative sanity; as a surrounding for his mother at this moment, it had that effect of nightmare which is produced by ordinary things in conjunction with the extraordinary' (199).

Initially portrayed as a selfish, egotistical, manipulative woman – an object of Dahlia, Jenny and Cecil's mockery and disdain, with her gaunt figure, tall hat, funny feet and snobbish attitudes – Mrs. Doubleday, a version of Trollope's infamous Mrs. Proudie, poses a malicious threat to the already fragile harmony of the Sproat household. However, as her son and her husband wrest themselves from her control and Dahlia and Jenny achieve victories in the battle of words, she is subtly transformed into a figure of pathos and abjection. As Mr. Doubleday, who has affinities with Mr. Proudie, sorrowfully comments to his wife, 'You haven't a kind heart, Flora. And if we are not kind-hearted at our age, we're in a sad case, a sad case' (320). Both Cecil and Dahlia recognize, to their consternation, that the loveless marriage of the Doubledays, in which there is no genuine communication, no physical passion and in which one partner repeatedly capitulates to the other, constitutes a warning: the Sproats could transmute into the Doubledays. On the other hand, in a final and ironic contrast to the clerical households, Young invests Louisa Grimshaw and the Grimshaw farm with the *beau ideal* of rural harmony: 'inside the house there was the smell of stored sunshine' (79), and Louisa, for whom 'perhaps the conditions of her life were

128 *Domestic Modernism, the Interwar Novel, and E.H. Young*

more important than the actual personality of her husband ... looked like the human expression of the house and the farm and all their scents and sounds' (80).

More complex in its orchestration of characters and events and dialogue and in its engagement with the art of living through an anatomy of married life than *Jenny Wren*, *The Curate's Wife* is also more playfully intertextual. In his review, 'A Writer of Sense and Sensibility' in the *Saturday Review of Literature*, Basil Davenport not surprisingly compares Young with Jane Austen, noting that 'she has the most delicate perception of all the currents of thought and feeling in her chosen section of suburban society, the tiny social distinctions and the intricate human relationships ... she comprehends how great are the trifling tragedies of everyday life' (17 November 1934: 291). Young deliberately nods towards Jane Austen at several points: Dahlia, like Emma who stoops to tie her bootlace so that her friend, Harriet Smith can meet the eligible vicar, fiddles with her shoelace at the vicarage gate in order to observe Reginald Doubleday's arrival. In a 'quotation' from *Persuasion*, Cecil, appearing to be 'absorbed in parochial matters', eavesdrops on the two sisters who are writing a letter to their former headmistress and discussing how to announce Dahlia's marriage, thereby offering a covert gloss on the Sproat marriage.

> ' "Dear Miss Headley, I don't think I ever told you I am married ..." '
> 'She'll send you a piece of Italian pottery'.
> 'I must risk that, "Married, and now I'm living here with Cecil Sproat".'
> ' "Because" ', Jenny commented, ' "I found I could not bear my husband".'
> 'Yes, it does sound like that,' Dahlia said slowly. (210)

Austen offers the opportunity for another clever ironic moment: when Mrs. Doubleday warns Jenny against marrying Reginald, Jenny smiles and exclaims, 'I knew someone else had said these things, nearly these things. It was Lady Catherine de Burgh' (317). Mrs. Doubleday is taken aback: 'These girls were claiming important friends and relatives all over the country' (317). Mr. Doubleday, who occasionally neglects the detective novels he indulges in secretly in his study and turns 'with some relief to a literature which had some of its delight for him in the knowledge that his wife would not understand it if she tried to read it' (330), gently cautions Mrs. Doubleday not to introduce Lady de Burgh into her conversation as a 'valuable acquaintance' (330). Through this amusing exchange, he reveals his affinity with Mr. Bennet and reduces Flora Doubleday to a silly and ineffectual Mrs. Bennet.

By means of grim, but unsentimental, vignettes of working-class youth, unwed mothers, patronizing charitable Christmas dinners and donations of clothing during the Depression, Young, more deeply than in her other novels, engages with the hardships of the working class and their ambivalent relation to a church that seeks to control their physical and moral well being. She offers a wider span of social realism and class division than, for example, in her portrait of Louisa Rendall in *Jenny Wren* or her depiction of Miss Mole's poverty, loneliness and desperation. By skillfully and subtly inserting Ivy's illegitimate pregnancy into the ideological and marital struggles of the Sproats, and by portraying the curate determinedly bicycling

Vicarages and Lodging-houses 129

with his undernourished youth group in the countryside without authorial comment or judgment, Young effectively offers the reader a matter-of-fact view across class divisions and into the suffering of the Depression years.

Along with E.M. Delafield, we wish that Young had continued the story of Dahlia and Jenny, but as another war loomed closer, her attention turned to darker explorations of alternative domesticities and of 'peace with honour' in marriage as well as on the international scene.

Notes

[1] Quoted in Glenda Norquay, ed., *R.L. Stevenson on Fiction* (1999): 57.

[2] Other titles listed in the ms. are 'This is the New Leaf' or 'The House in [?] Hawthorn Road'.

[3] And Bachelard on doors: 'How concrete ... everything becomes in the world of the spirit when an object, a mere door, can give images of hesitation, temptation, desire, security, welcome and respect ... is he who opens a door and he who closes it the same being? ... And then, onto what, toward what, do doors open? Do they open for the world of men, or for the world of solitude?' (224)

[4] Victorian developers 'gated and locked formerly communal gardens in squares, set terraced house far back from the road, and used architectural treatments that rendered the individual houses within a row more distinct ... individual gables and pillared porches ... iron railings ... recessed doors ... and protruding bow windows ... that separated one house from another' (S. Marcus: 97).

[5] Mary Cadogan and Patricia Craig note how 'Dorothy Richardson's novels underline the association of feminine independence with a squalid, boarding-house type of existence' (21) in *Women and Children First: The Fiction of Two World Wars* (1978).

[6] In Stella Gibbons's *Bassett*, Miss Padsoe, 'an Edwardian achievement' (148), agonizes over her decision to turn her family home, The Tower, into a lodging-house. Though slightly 'barmy' and ineffectual, she is not blind to the fact that such step will inevitably signify a 'loss of genteel status' (Davidoff: 68). Her neighbours are harsher in their judgment, regarding her action not only as inappropriate to her class, but as 'an insidious invasion of the privacy and dignity' (154–5). Left to her own devices, Miss Padsoe would hardly succeed. But thanks to the businesslike and feisty Miss Baker, who looks disgracefully 'like an under-housemaid' (78) not only does the boarding house refurbish Miss Padsoe's income, but of the three homes in the novel – the Cattons', full of noise and arguing, and the Shellings', cold with the self-love and egotism of its inhabitants – The Tower alone, with its front door wide open and ringing with the laughter of the lodgers, 'looks most flourishing' (307).

[7] This argument is borne out by a commentator of the period: 'For the majority of working people, divorce no more exists as a way out of matrimonial difficulties than champagne as a morning pick-me up', S. Reynolds, R. Woolley and T. Woolley, *Seems So!* (1911): 247. Quoted in Henry Pellin, *Popular Politics and Society in Late Victorian Britain* (1968): 66.

[8] We recall Judith in *A Corn of Wheat* disparaging the bourgeois and pragmatic desire for a 'house and its furniture' (6).

130 *Domestic Modernism, the Interwar Novel, and E.H. Young*

9   The title reflects a convention of domestic novels of the period (Young's own *The Vicar's Daughter* (1928), F.M. Mayor's *The Rector's Daughter* (1924) and *The Squire's Daughter* (1929) and George Orwell's *A Clergyman's Daughter* (1935)). In the case of Orwell, the possessive and the impersonal nature of the title indicates the complete evacuation of any sense of self in the young heroine, Dorothy. Tellingly, after suffering amnesia, a psychological reaction to her constrained and impoverished life, she wonders '*Who was She?*... she had not the dimmest notion of who she was ... She realized more clearly than before that her body existed and that it was her own . She now grasped that in order to identify herself she must examine her own body ...' (86–7).

Chapter 7

Modern Heroines of the Everyday

> The children, the house, the ordering of the meals, the servants, the making of a laundry list every Monday – in a word, the things of respectability – kept one respectable. In a flash of unavoidable clear-sightedness, that Laura would never repeat if she could avoid it, she admitted to herself that the average attributes only, of the average woman, were hers.
>
> (E.M. Delafield, *The Way Things Are* 1927: 336)

> '…Same old things day after day.'
>
> 'But they are never quite the same. Except, I'm afraid', she added, 'the things you get to eat …. People and the things that happen to them. To their minds. It's very interesting…'
>
> (*Celia*: 102)

As late as 1903, when planning *Leonora*, Arnold Bennett found that reviewers 'were staggered by my hardihood in offering a woman of forty as a subject of serious interest to the public' ('Preface' to the *Old Wives' Tale*: 32); three decades later, E.M. Delafield amused the readers of *Time and Tide* with the domestic struggles of a middle-aged woman, who according to Mary Borden was 'too intelligent not to rage at her niggling fate, but too sensible and too gallant to bemoan her lot' (Preface: xi), while Jan Struther turned the middle-aged housewife into a national icon with her fortnightly articles on Mrs. Miniver printed anonymously in *The Times* and published as a book in 1939. By making two middle-aged homemakers the protagonists of her last two novels, Young responds to Woolf's initiative with the characters of Mrs. Dalloway and Mrs. Ramsay and to the genre made popular by Jan Struther and Delafield, as well as later twentieth-century works by Elizabeth Taylor, Margaret Drabble, Elizabeth Jane Howard and Alice Thomas Ellis. By 1937, increasingly, interaction with, or viewing of, domestic objects, from beds to doll's houses, signaled key personal or interpersonal moments in Young's novels.

Celia Marston is married to a struggling architect, Gerald, and has two children and two linked secrets: the newspaper clipping of a dream house and an imagined romantic life with Richard, a war amputee, brother of her friend Pauline, with whom she has had a brief affair in the past.[1] But there is a reason why this work was originally entitled 'Middle-Age'; for although Celia for the most part occupies the place to which her author has entitled her, the anatomy of intimate married life (carrying on the process begun in *The Curate's Wife*) is not limited to the heroine's life, but includes those of her brother John and her sister May and their spouses, all struggling through mid-life crises.[2] While much attention is also given to parenting

132   *Domestic Modernism, the Interwar Novel, and E.H. Young*

and sibling relations, heterosexual love ceases to be the impulse of the narrative, and the family comes under scrutiny as a site of the constriction of individual freedom, but also of great amusement.

Young's shift from romantic individualism to an exploration of the fabric of human relationships becomes more marked as the choice of the focus on middle-aged characters leads her to investigate life's 'network of complications' (*Celia*: 167). Celia's heroism, along with that of other middle-aged heroines of the 1930s domestic novel, often derives from the repeated refrain of 'just going on'. Thus Catherine in *Hostages to Fortune,* who marries a struggling doctor, copes with a large old house in Oxfordshire and three children, and sticks her 'Wessex' novel away in a drawer, wonders at the end of the novel how 'she could explain that her life, so trivial, so humdrum in appearance, was a complicated and intensely interesting job'. Yet throughout she, too, announces resignedly: 'she would go on. She had always meant to go on' (165).[3] Delafield s Laura Temple, aside from managing the family on insufficient income, does a little writing to pay the bills ('It is really quite a new idea to me ... that my writing matters anything at all') (171)). In a more humorous tone from which anguish is not altogether absent, she, too, accepts that 'life continued to be uneventful, full of slight harassments, trivial satisfactions, and harmless, recurrent anxieties' (*The Way Things Are*: 69–70).

In *Chatterton Square,* the role of heroine, as played by Rosamund Fraser, is further deconstructed. After the breaking up of her marriage, Rosamund has returned to live with her five children and her childhood friend, Agnes Spanner, in the house in which she had grown up and lived with her father until the end of the war. Rather than being the pivot of the narrative, her failed marriage with Fergus and her romance with Piers Lindsay constitute no more than a background to the 'network of complications' with her family and neighbours – Bertha and Herbert Blackett – on the eve of World War II. Both Celia and Rosamund rebel at times against the demands of the family on the 'domesticated female' (Lehmann, *A Note in Music*: 52). Both, like the Provincial Lady, feel the need to have a rest from the 'incessant pressure of domestic cares' (*Diary of a Provincial Lady*: 110) or, like Norah in *A Note in Music* from 'this perpetual crumbling of the edges, this shredding out of one's personality upon minute obligations and responsibilities' (52). They break for freedom only to return to the home where freedom can then be experienced merely vicariously.

Life's Network of Complications: *Celia*

> There seems to be something wrong with houses tonight. (*Celia*: 179)

The narrative in *Celia* is set on a carefully circumscribed stage, located once again in the world of upwardly mobile middle-class families in Upper Radstowe. Celia's brother, John, has inherited 'the best draper's shop in the city' (21) from his chapel-going father, and under his guidance the business has flourished [4] He is married to

Modern Heroines of the Everyday 133

doll-like Julia with whom he has six children. Her sister May, characterized by Celia as ox- or cow-like, 'a stupid woman accidentally gifted with an unerring eye' (71), is the wife of Stephen Grey, a successful lawyer. It is Stephen's short-lived escape from domesticity and tryst with Hester, another sister – single and independent – who curiously never appears in the novel, yet is an absent presence that create a crisis in this small community. This crisis diverts Celia's (and the reader's) attention from her own marriage as it prompts her astute and amused investigation of the structure of the family and its effect on the individual, her covert manipulations and finall , her painful gradual self-realization. This novel is mainly focalized through Celia, with the result that since the reader is positioned to view the domestic scene from her perspective, the reader, in tandem with Celia, must learn through the course of the novel to 'read' domestic spaces and relationships more perceptively and generously. Threading its way through the novel is the power struggle between the women and between husbands and wives over who controls the domestic space.[5]

We are told in the very first page of the novel that Celia is 'deeply thankful for middle-age' (64). She trusts that her capacities for love and gaiety are 'unchipped, unfrayed' (55) and her uneventful life has not dulled her ability to respond to the tiniest variations in her daily routine; when everything else fails, 'there's a different dream every night' (280). Moreover, far from believing that she has reached the age at which 'nothing could matter very much', Celia is convinced that people of her generation, after the years of personal uneventfulness since the end of the war, 'were aware of some yeasty element working in them … and she thought it might be well for human beings of a certain age to experience some healthy emotional fires (105–106). Mrs. Miniver's novel-diary, too, opens with a celebration of middle age as Mrs. Miniver, settling down again at home after the 'irrelevant interlude' of the holidays, basks in the 'various beauty' of autumn. The crispness of the trees, 'brindled by the first few nights of frost', prompts a comparison with her life and like Celia, she realizes that she is enjoying her 40s so much more than her 30s because of the 'difference between … the heaviness of late summer and the sparks of early autumn, between the ending of an old phase and the beginning of a fresh one' (1–2). However, in sharp contrast to the opening of *Mrs. Miniver*, Young's novel begins with Celia (who is never Mrs. Marston, as Mrs. Miniver is never simply Carolyn) literally struggling to step out of the frame as she stands on a wooden stool to look out of a high-set window, a position she will metaphorically maintain almost until the conclusion of the novel.

For the blessings of middle age are not unmixed. While its sparks enliven without ruffling the serenity of Mrs. Miniver's life, Celia painfully feels that the emotions of her youth, having never been properly released, 'warred with her age, her experience and the humour she could always turn upon herself' (371). For Mrs. Miniver, the joys of marriage are found in the 'nightly turning out of the day's pocketful of memories', which gives one 'almost a double life' (203). In Celia's marriage there is no pocketful of shared memories; Celia and Gerald's relationship can at best be described, as she herself perceives, as 'unwilling on her part, unsatisfied on his' (244). Mrs. Miniver enjoys the sight of her husband coming out dishevelled from a bath and feels thankful

134 *Domestic Modernism, the Interwar Novel, and E.H. Young*

that 'Clem's good looks were wearing well' (4), whereas it is with a clinical eye, barely mitigated by pity, that Celia observes Gerald's thickening figure, suggestive of 'a permanent state of warmth and woollen underclothes, without any charm for the eye to make mental differences much more negligible and physical contact more endurable' (187).

It is not only her marriage that Celia questions, for though she realizes that the perfect unit is composed of both parents and their children, 'when she looked for it among her acquaintances, she did not find it. The tie was too close and it was knotted with the conventions that had grown round it. The happiest home she had known was one with no parents in it ... the best marriage in her experience was that of Pauline with her Reginald where there were no children in the house' (86–7). In contrast, Mrs. Miniver views her room 'laced with an invisible network of affectionate understanding' (47) and unlike Celia, who gazes beyond the window frame, Mrs. Miniver, a woman perfectly happy with her lot, is half afraid to step outside the frame of her normal life in case she finds she can not get back in again (3). Struther's prose is studded with the pronoun 'they', which underlies the commonality of interests and activities the family and nation happily share, whether it be hunting or fireworks on Guy Fawkes' Night. In *Celia*, 'they' never makes an appearance and there is little relief from the 'devastating intimacy' of marriage (Struther: 94). As Celia's niece, Susan, puts it, 'a family isn't several separate persons. It's a lot of – of dismembered people. Somebody has your head and another one has your hands and you have bits of all the others fastened on to you' (181). This sense of stifling intimacy is palpable in the Marstons' cramped flat, which at times seems to Celia 'to be full of people and to have no place where she could be free of interruption' (99) and in which she 'had to teach herself with difficulty that the mind need not be bounded by walls' (17). While the heroine of Young's first novel had dismissed the house as 'so many bricks and nails and tiles, so much mortar and wood, where bodies might be sheltered and seated' (*A Corn of Wheat*: 6), Celia animates her domestic spaces as a form of agency. As Jean Baudrillard has pointed out, the 'arrangement of furniture offers a faithful image of the familial and social structures of a [traditional] period' (309). His argument that the dining room/bedroom combination, centred around a monumental sideboard or bed in the middle of the room that closes off space, is the foundation of the patriarchal bourgeois interior (309, 310), resonates with Celia's own hostile reaction to the 'baronial oak', the sideboard drawer that 'would not run easily' in the dining-room or the 'barbaric bed' and 'heavily carved furniture of Gerald's choosing' in the bedroom (*Celia*: 35, 50, 17).

In Celia's flat we experience what Susan Sidlauskas has described as the sense of 'disorientation and discomfort' that characterizes the destabilized relationship between ground and figure in the domestic interiors of many modern painters from Sargent to Whistler and Vuillard. Sislauskas' comment on how the oversized furniture in Vuillard's *Mother and Sister of the Artist* exaggerates the narrowness of the space and adds to the 'all-over sense of constriction' (73) aptly describes Celia's bedroom, where, unnerved by Gerald's snoring, she feels as crowded by his hovering bulk as by

Modern Heroines of the Everyday

the massive carved furniture that he has brought from his paternal home, 'the wardrobe like some large animal' (101), the 'barbaric bed'. (No massive double bed, barbaric or otherwise, inconveniences Mrs. Miniver; a description of the gathering of the children in the parents' bedroom delicately hints that Mrs. Miniver and Clem have chosen twin beds.) There could be no clearer example of Baudrillard's patriarchal interior, traditional, bourgeois and hierarchical in which the 'primary function of furniture and objects ... is to personify human relationships' (309). And, without a doubt, these domestic spaces and furniture shape and inflect personal relationships.

But it is not only Celia who feels oppressed in her own flat. John's capacious house has 'plenty of rooms, but no room' (166); in it John feels more and more 'like an intruder' (264) – 'in none of these rooms, behind none of these doors, could he find a place which was all his own' (263) – as he comes to the discomforting realization that, though ideally marriage implies sympathy, 'practically and by its very nature, it allowed, as no other did, of fierce antipathy and verbal cruelty, as though one form of passion caused and let loose the others and then, after a time, submerged them' (263). In his marriage with the placid May, Stephen encounters neither antipathy nor verbal cruelty, 'none of the sharp retorts and wearisome complaints usually incident to marriage'; yet even 'the creaking of the newspapers as she [May] turned it and the sight of the sheets scattered on the floo ' (127) become a further incentive to test 'the limits of his vagrancy' (248).

Tasteful Houses, Dream Houses, Doll's Houses and the Domestic Interior

An indifferent housewife who prefers the contemplation of the March sky streaked by clouds 'like white-clad ladies of infinite leisure' (9) to the tidying of drawers, Celia, like Elizabeth Taylor's Julia in *At Mrs. Lippincote's*, Beth the writer in Taylor's *A View from the Harbour*, or Isa in Woolf's *Between the Acts* is a 'domestic rebel' (Humble: 113). 'Absent-minded in her housekeeping and unimaginative about food' (20), Celia, however, admires her housekeeper Miss Riggs's passion for order and spotlessness. Celia may be flippant about her sister May's decorating talent, which extends to her daughter Priscilla (a spoilt child, but lovely, for 'May simply can't make an aesthetic mistake' (43)) but, applying her own decorating strategies, the narrator travels between Celia's flat and her sister May's big cream-coloured house and forces Celia to acknowledge with perplexed admiration May's skill in creating an air of peace and comfort by 'the choice of colours and shapes and the disposal of her possessions' (71). For, unlike Celia, May is in control of her domestic space; she chooses and arranges the objects not only in her own home but also in Stephen's office. This foreshadows the end of the novel when Celia, who had assumed she was the one skilled in arranging domestic relations, realizes that May has created a warm, comfortable and charming home life. May is rescued from banality and even stupidity by her unwitting participation in that modernist undertaking that was the construction of the housewife-as-artist, engaged in home decorating as 'a mode of

136   *Domestic Modernism, the Interwar Novel, and E.H. Young*

personal expression and a means of creating an aesthetically-pleasing, but also a comfortable and intimate space for the family's domestic life' (Tiersten: 21).

Though it is mainly in Celia's and her siblings' houses that we enter embodied domestic interiors, we also reside temporarily with Celia in her mother-in-law Mrs. Marston's grim and tidy little lowbrow house with no view except the neighbour's tin bath hanging on the wall and briefly catch a glimpse of her wealthy friend Pauline Carey's luxurious home and gardens. Pauline's fast car, restless, hurried travelling, glamorous clothes and flights to Paris to shop (Figure 9).[6] contrast with Celia's placidity, dowdiness and domesticity; the modern, urbane Careys, like Cecilia and Emmeline in Bowen's *To the North*, are continually on the move and Celia's encounters with them occur primarily in their cars.

Woven in among these lived houses are two somewhat heavy-handed and symbolic houses: Susan's miniature doll's house and Celia's newspaper clipping of a Georgian dream house. Susan's doll's house embodies Susan and Celia's secret, locked away self (significantly, Celia believes that in Susan her former lover Richard may 'see a reincarnation of herself' (371)). In a perhaps unnecessary intervention, the narrator explains: 'this doll's house, as Celia had soon come to understand, was not a toy. It was a little world Susan was going to create … it was a world … which could not get beyond control … and there were no wilful human beings in it to upset her plans' (49–50). Consistent with Bachelard's discussion of the house in miniature, as a false object that possesses 'a true psychological objectivity' (148), Susan is 'like her own doll's house: people could look at it through the windows, but she still kept the key' (96–7).[7]

Similarly, Celia's 'miniature' Georgian house, embodying her secret self and her fantasy life, is a Bachelardian dream house, unattainable, idealized, a clipping stored in an envelope proprietarily labelled 'My house' (19). This perfect house shelters the possibility of attaining 'personal perfection' (18); it symbolizes her idealized relationship with Richard who 'would put on his spectacles, consider it gravely and say, 'Yes' (19). Celia has 'a sick longing for that house', a nostalgia, literally 'home sickness', for the freedom of a premarital past, the war years and a desired solitude. She does not go as far as letting slip in conversation, like the Provincial Lady, that 'the most wonderful thing in the world must be a childless widow' (256), but she admits to herself that 'she wanted no one else in the house', not even her children, 'except for visits' (18). At the end of the novel, when Gerald has produced his drawings of a building for a client, not original but sober and solid (395), which bears an uncanny resemblance to Celia's Georgian house, Celia feels 'something had happened to [her] house. The dreams had gone out of it' (411). In translating a dream into a built form and observing that 'our tastes are very much alike' (292), Gerald has shattered Celia's imagined inner world. Deciding that it had lost its value for her (293), Celia tears her picture into pieces. As her gesture indicates, 'it is better to live in a state of impermanence than in one of finality (Bachelard: 61).

Throughout the novel Celia represents her marriage, and Gerald, by means of architectural metaphors. Gerald is ruthlessly compared to Reginald Carey, the husband of Celia's friend Pauline. Courteous, reserved Reginald Carey, is a successful architect

Figure 9   'Paris Frocks by Air', *The Wonder Book of Aircraft for Boys and Girls*, ed. Harry Golding, London: Ward, Lock & Co., 1920: 31.

138   *Domestic Modernism, the Interwar Novel, and E.H. Young*

whose fine-grained skin and small, well-placed lines at the corners of his eyes and mouth seem 'to match and to account for his fastidious choice of material for his buildings and the economy, without affected severity, of their design' (233). In contrast, Gerald's involvement in the practice that one of the characters in Lettice Cooper's *The New House* sourly condemns as the building of 'nasty little jerry-built houses' (95) and Elizabeth Cambridge tags as 'a series of bungaloid blemishes' (223), does nothing to atone for his 'plump and domestic' appearance. Celia's reflection that she had 'little faith in the material firmness of the material foundations on which Gerald's houses rose' (23) and that 'while he kissed her eyelids, she thought she was justified in her mental reservations about the sad results of all his conscientious labour' (52–3) are also a commentary on her feelings about their marriage, his aesthetic sense and her own sexual revulsion. It is through the instrument of a house that Celia receives several shocks concerning Gerald: her discovery that Gerald is designing a home for a woman client which resembles her Georgian dream house, that he has wisely safeguarded her small inheritance and quietly cherished his dead sister. Moreover, he has kept these secret from her and she has been wilfully misreading him. The effect of these narrative shocks on the reader is to make her/him aware that the interior view is not necessary the accurate view.

Celia's conservative modernism expresses itself in her resistance to Gerald's suggestion that they live in one of his 'hideous little villas' (Celia's words 19), where there would be 'plenty of fresh air … a bit of garden … big windows … no sloping ceilings' and which have 'no ornaments' and would be 'labour-saving' (51). However, although Celia likes plain and simple things, in keeping with Bachelard's penchant for home-inspired reveries and Baudrillard's disdain for the secularization and impoverishment of traditional good taste promoted by modern interior design (Baudrillard: 310), her 'dream house' is 'a Georgian country house of character' (18). When Miss Riggs, the housekeeper, notes that there is no call nowadays for a cabinet maker 'designing his own work, inlaying it with ebony and satinwood', Celia exclaims:

> Oh … must everything be sacrificed to speed? The cabinet makers, all the lovely leisurely things. The art of conversation went long ago … then words themselves will go because they won't be heard above the roaring of machinery … Just gibbering, grimacing apes, that's what we shall be, hurling bombs at each other instead of coco-nuts. (298)

It is Pauline Carey, with her clothes, hair, makeup and mobility – her big yellow car, her plane trips to Paris to shop – who represents the new, modern, independent woman, unencumbered by domesticity; however, as Young gradually reveals, Pauline is tormented by her mentally handicapped child and speed and movement are her forms of escape and distraction.

Modern Heroines of the Everyday

Aesthetics and the Domestic Everyday

> Even the lowest, intrinsically ugly phenomenon can be dissolved into contexts of color and form, feeling and experience which provide it with significance. (Simmel: 69)

Exemplifying Young's own literary practice, Celia tunes her eye and ear to the 'daily round' and 'some little thing [that] was always happening' (105); here she finds fertile ground for dreams, reflections and amusement [8]

> The art of living, the only one Celia tried to practise, was as exacting as any other: it might be that it was the most exacting, for no concessions could be made to the artist whose skill was in doing without them, and Celia's worst failures happened in that bedroom crowded with the heavy, carved furniture of Gerald's choice. (16–17)

Celia, with her vivid imaginary inner life, house-consciousness and ironic self-reflexivit , appreciates that 'the artist in living has no medium except life itself' (17). Her skills, talents and failures echo those of the writer, of Young herself. Celia's artistry is on a minor scale; her pleasures emanate from the everyday, domestic ritual and the drab and from her capacity for irony, which she is always ready to turn against herself. As noted earlier, in Young's fiction there are no writers, but in each of her novels, she may be detected behind one of the characters: Miss Mole's efforts to restore harmony in the Corders' household; Dahlia's 'instinctively artistic performance' (*The Curate's Wife*: 33) in dealing with early married life; Rhoda's sure taste in garden design; Rosamund's honesty in human relationships ('she was too much of an artist in her own line, to be anything but simple and frank' (*Chatterton Square*: 106)), as well as her sartorial skills ('It's important to make everything as beautiful as one can' (177)), and Miss Spanner's pleasure in concocting fictions out of 'the immediate human scene' (*Chatterton Square*: 30). Thus, when Celia supposes 'without regret, that she revealed her limitations in the simple pleasure she found in the sight of familiar places and people' (105), we can assume that through her, Young is assessing her own novelistic art. Later in the novel, Celia reflects that although hers seemed a very narrow world, 'these simple tasks gave her mind space to roam in, far more space than was possible to a woman who was doing important public business' (282). In this reflection may lie the explanation of Young's shift away from the independent young women in *A Corn of Wheat* to the wives and mothers of the later novels. After 1928 she may have shared the sense, indeed common to many, that with the Equal Franchise Act the battle for women had been won. Thus, while her first novels responded to the suffragette movement, by the 1920s and 1930s she had imbibed some of the ideas of the New Feminists who were focusing less on equal opportunities for women and more on domesticity, motherhood and attempting to improve women's lot in the home; and who were supremely interested in placing as much value on feminine as on masculine modes and realms of experience.

140 *Domestic Modernism, the Interwar Novel, and E.H. Young*

'Stories Can Occur When One Looks Out as Well as In'[9]

Young highlights Celia's artistry in living by means of specific domestic spatial metaphors. In his comparison of architecture and literature, Philippe Hamon notes how literary texts specify different locations as sites of language performance; the bedroom as site for intimate disclosures, the threshold and hallway for ritualized greetings and the poet's attic for writing and dreaming (48).[10] As the characters come and go, mostly up and down the stairs to and from Celia's small, crowded flat, relationships between parents and children, siblings, husbands and wives become muddled amid spying (overseeing, overhearing) and conjecture over supposedly illicit behaviour. Each location is carefully drawn, its symbolic valences subtly suggested. The attic flat, with its continuous hot water, is concurrently Celia's refuge and her prison.[11] A hybrid of the functional modern present and the gracious traditional past, this house on an elegant terrace was converted into flats by Gerald. Looking metaphorically back upon her past and her romance with Richard and looking literally into the converted house and her present, Celia mounts the staircase, 'resenting, as she always did, the mutilation of the nobly curving staircase', a vile example of modernization and functionalism. The violence of Celia's reflections – 'he [Gerald] had been constrained to rob each landing of enough space to make a separate entrance and now the stairs crawled upwards like something wounded ... more money for the family and a little less beauty in the world' (33) – implies her resentment of Gerald's muddling up of her interior, her dreams and her nostalgic idea of home. Celia, however, does concede that 'there were no servants now, living in the underground vaults, no legs aching with going up and down these stairs' (33).

The sitting room, Celia's intimate space and a symbolic equivalent of her body and psyche, contains only a bureau, her books, her little rocking chair and the view from the window. The bureau's drawers lodge, on the one hand the 'accumulations of an indifferent housewife' (11), and on the other an archive of memories – a 'secret psychological life' (Bachelard: 70). In the bathroom, a shared private space, the bathtub with its hot steamy water and dirty ring left by Jimmy, hints at Celia's childrearing practices – no rules in the house, no obligations for the children to help with housecleaning. Bending over the tub, Celia murmurs, 'what a muddle and mess!' (48), which Jimmy assumes to be a comment on his bathing habits. Celia, however, is thinking in domestic metaphors about her relationship with Gerald, which was 'very much like her relationship with the little flat, but infinitely harder' (47). Undeniably, as Stella Deen points out, houses and architecture constitute a form of symbolic conversation (2000: 25).

Celia also engages in the tactics of verbal irony and conversation with double entendres to prick the self-delusions and pretensions of others, a favourite target being Julia. One of the wittiest moments occurs at Mrs. Marston's funeral when Julia tells Celia gently, 'You mustn't grieve. She is much happier where she is' and Celia refrains 'from thanking Julia for this assurance and asking for more detailed information' (403).

Modern Heroines of the Everyday   141

The grammar of the house furnishes Young and Celia as focalizer with the means by which to read and interpret social arrangements and interactions and to elaborate inner processes and subjective states: the house or the flat narrates the novel. Thus, Chapter XI opens with the reader following Celia into her interior space as she climbs up the dim, cool staircase (85); however, Young also effectively foregrounds the everyday when she begins Chapter X with a banal, yet poignant, detail – 'he [Stephen] had eaten a great deal of her butter' (78). This leads into an account of Celia's need to economize, a meditation on food and a commentary on Stephen's background, childhood home and character. One is reminded of Lefebvre's famous claim that the most menial events participate both in the individual life and in a complex social network. Unpacking the simple action of a woman buying a pound of sugar 'will disclose a tangle of reasons and causes, of essences and "spheres": the woman's life, her biography, her job, her family, her class, her budget, her eating habits, how she uses money, her opinions and her ideas, the state of the market, etc.' (1991: 57).

While key and lock represent private inner space, concealment and reticence, the door suggests the boundary between self and other and the equivocation of entry and departure. As Simmel observed, the door represents how 'separating and connecting are only two sides of precisely the same act' (67). Locked or closing doors are continually associated with Celia and Susan's desire for inner privacy. Celia shuts the door against outside criticism. Mrs. Marston obstinately sits outside the door to Celia's house munching gingerbread, then mounts the stairs and hovers outside the flat door, seeking the entry into Celia's social space that her very behaviour precludes (Figure 10). When Celia does admit Mrs. Marston into her flat, she ushers her away from the sitting room, sparing this cherished space 'the faint smell of camphor, the disapproval and suspicion' (35) and reinforcing 'the symbolic and emotional – indeed transformative – power of rooms' (Birdwell-Pheasant: 18). The narrator observes that Jimmy 'seemed to have opened a door giving on to underground, twisting passages and, though she [Susan] had known they existed, he had opened the door on the wrong day, when her Aunt Julia had already been fumbling at the handle' (179–80); to Jimmy the door signifies 'the temptation to open up the ultimate depths of being, and the desire to conquer all reticent beings'. The originary image of the door ajar, 'one of the primal images of the Cosmos' (Bachelard: 222) which we encountered in *The Vicar's Daughter*, recurs here when Celia recollects how her mother, in her last days, seemed to be uncharacteristically open to intimate confidences, leaving the door ajar for anyone who might enter (57).

Celia's carefully constructed domestic space, where there are no rules for the children, where she fends off Gerald's love with politeness and concealed revulsion and which she controls by ushering unwanted guests away from her sitting room into the 'baronial' dining room, is also the site of her reveries of her Georgian house, her fairy tale romance with Richard and her life as adventure, spectacle and artistic display. Who will come up the stairs next? What will she see, opening wide her veiled and drowsy eyes? What confidences and secrets will she hear, she who lives in the passive

Figure 10　　Celia's House, Royal York Crescent, Clifton. Photo by Kathy Mezei.

Modern Heroines of the Everyday

143

voice? And what amusement will she derive from the conversations and actions of her extended family and friends? Slowly, Celia undergoes an initiation and reviews and re-inhabits her domestic space and her inner self.

After all,

> her whole life ... was spent in opening and shutting that door, in hearing other people opening and shutting it, in watching people go down the stairs and hearing them come up, and lately the atmosphere of the home she made had been invaded by emotions from outside and they would not go. They hung about her sitting-room and disturbed the dreams she had housed there, threatening their beauty and their truth. (344)

In keeping with Young's emphasis on the look, Young focuses on characters' eyes and their ability to 'see clearly'. Stephen, whose 'eyes with their queer obliqueness ... actually made him see straighter than other people' (76), disappoints Celia with his confidences about his abortive affair with her sister, Hester; Reginald Carey, who unlike Gerald, 'made lovely buildings' and was 'incapable of any mixture of styles which would offend a critical eye' (237), also disappoints her with his outpouring of resentments against his wife's unmaternal behaviour (237). In contrast, Gerald, whose eyes are clear, 'might see more than she knew ... might even, she feared, see his own houses clearly' (190). The image of uncouth masculinity that Celia had constructed of Gerald shatters as he reveals himself to be honest, domesticated, a good father, devoted brother and an adept architect; he is no William, but nor is he Robert, the Provincial Lady's husband, who grunts and retreats behind the *The Times*. As Gerald tells Celia (and the reader): 'The mistake you've made with me ... has been thinking I'm much stupider than I am' (412).

When Mrs. Marston falls ill, Celia moves into her small, narrow house, with its sacred and rigidly arranged possessions, to tend to her. Removed from her home, relishing this other, if unattractive, space and difficult situation (Mrs. Marston dies), Celia turns her gaze upon herself. Observing her own reflectio in Mrs. Marston's window, she wryly confesses to Catherine, 'I've never seen myself any more clearly than I do now, in that window, through a glass darkly. Eyes overstrained, perhaps ... with looking for things that were never there' (380).

In contrast to the opening passage, where Celia gazes from inside her flat upon the outer world, close to the end of the novel Celia returns to her home around midnight and standing outside the house sees the dining room window illuminated (Gerald is completing his design for the commissioned house) and a locked outer door 'shut for the night, and she had no key' (372). Unlike the Provincial Lady, who, returning home, is struck 'as often before by immense accumulation of domestic disasters that always await one after any absence' (7), Celia suddenly realizes that her family has thrived and established a new intimacy during her temporary absence. On another day she returns to the empty flat to find everything in order, her sitting room spotless but neglected and forlorn. 'The one room she had really made her own seemed to agree with her that his former occupant had gone for ever' (394), while the dining

144 *Domestic Modernism, the Interwar Novel, and E.H. Young*

room 'had come into its own' with Gerald's architectural plans. Indeed, Gerald has taken over dining room, kitchen and cooking, and established an easy camaraderie with his children. The fear she experiences is akin to that voiced by Mrs. Miniver, that having stepped out of the frame of her life, 'one day she should find herself unable to get back' (*Mrs. Miniver*: 3).[12]

May's house, with its clean cream coat, the windows open, the front door wide open, too, and the gate into the garden ajar, now appears to her as 'a home ... and one could not destroy a home' (386). She also finds the front of Susan's doll's house open and 'the beautifully appointed little rooms ... at anybody's mercy' (387). Jimmy now has the key to the doll's house and is installing electric light and another one of Young's cisterns.[13] Like Gerald, who has built Celia's dream house, though not for her, Jimmy, with his practical bent, modernizes and invades Susan's 'house'; Celia and Susan thereafter appear to relinquish their secret selves along with their 'houses'.

Later, as she looks at Easterly church tower, 'very certain to-day of its knowledge of right and wrong', she acknowledges that 'she could see for such a very little way' and that 'in the course of an interesting journey, she had lost some of her luggage' (394).

The conclusion to Young's unpublished manuscript, 'On Window Curtains', 'yet why should not romance live even in drab-coloured surroundings and if the poet can turn the drabs to purples life is but so much the lovelier for him', could have been easily uttered by Celia; but these words would have been modulated by the realization that though nothing 'would have been more romantic, more satisfactory and more convenient than discovering in him [Gerald], at last, all she had always wanted' (374), this has not happened. All she can do is to go on, and that 'was not a bad thing to do' (414). After all, even Mrs. Miniver cannot avoid a note of wistfulness when, looking toward the window at the dark sky 'in its frame of cherry-pink chintz', she broods: 'Eternity framed in domesticity. Never mind. One had to frame it in something, to see it all' (48).

The novel ends with Gerald offering Celia her freedom; she chooses, however, to remain with him in the little attic flat. While earlier in the novel Celia and Susan seemed on the verge of proposing or enacting alternatives to the nuclear family and the family romance, both nevertheless accept, as did Dahlia in *The Curate's Wife*, the social contract of marriage and the rituals of domesticity with their attendant compromises and fraying of self.

Houses in Opposition: *Chatterton Square*

> I'm thinking what a nice staircase this is and how we've done nearly all the polishing of the rail ourselves. People's hands! Your great-grandfather's and your grandfather's and your mother's. (*Chatterton Square*: 88)

For Rosamund Fraser, what gives value to the house in Chatterton Square is the continuity it establishes between her familial past and present; her neighbour Mr.

Modern Heroines of the Everyday 145

Blackett, on the other hand, has recently moved into the square because of 'the atmosphere of an earlier and, as he thought, a more gracious day' (9). The Fraser household which, perhaps, 'felt so free because there was no father in it' (32), spills happily onto the balcony and on the sidewalk. On fine days, Rosamund will sit in her balcony to read or sew and neither she nor Agnes Spanner are opposed to being seen gathering around the greengrocer's trailer. Mr. Blackett's family is instead carefully sheltered from the outside. As Flora, the eldest daughter, reflects, their home is 'treated like a castle and everybody else like besiegers who must be repulsed' (31). Appropriately, Mrs. Blackett's drawing room is at the back of the house. It is, literally as well as symbolically, as sheltered and isolated as Mr. Blackett would wish his wife to be: Bertha 'was, or ought to be, as well content with her room as he was with his and she was the least curious of women' (10). Through careful use of focalization, Bertha Blackett is subtly, but unambiguously, introduced through her husband's perspective, her life neatly summarized in perfect accord with his imaginings of what a wife should be: 'she lived in a little world of her own with a home and a husband and three children to care for, and a peaceful, well-ordered world it was, good to come back to after a tiring day and these were troublous times' (10).

We smile at the way Mr. Blackett blunders through life, driven by egocentrism and self-importance – his mistaking Bertha's revulsion for modesty and love offered in 'a touchingly abiding way' (156) and appreciating her silence as 'another valuable quality' (54). We are also entertained by the war rhetoric of a man who deftly avoided fighting in the war in his view of a house without a father as an 'encampment … with no apparent male chieftain at the head of it' (10). Mr. Blackett's fancy that his little black beard, slim figure, well-cut clothes and jaunty hat give him the air of an elegant poet makes him a comical figure. Yet it is due to Young's skill at rendering the complexities of her characters that near the end of the novel, by shifting into his perspective, she induces a twinge of sympathy for this self-satisfied and self-deceiving man when we catch him feeling 'like some sad old dog who … must trundle home meekly to his kennel' (361).

Young's unconventional views are not limited to marriage and sexuality. If in Rosamund she creates a character who is capable of acknowledging the sexual bond that still ties her to her husband as well as her own shortcomings as a parent, through the character of Bertha Blackett she breaks what is arguably one of the most resilient taboos. For as we move closer to Bertha's perspective and increasingly see her family through her eyes, we learn not only of her sexual revulsion but also that the time spent in Florence represents for Bertha a repulsive nightmare that has forever tainted her relationship with her first born. Thus, while for Celia 'Catherine who was conceived in horrified reluctance was now a precious possession' (47), for Bertha 'Flora was stamped with the surprise and disgust and despair she had known as she trailed through the picture galleries of Florence on her honeymoon' (150).

146 *Domestic Modernism, the Interwar Novel, and E.H. Young*

'Rosamund ... Found Her Own Sex More Interesting'

> ... like many other women, [Rosamund] found her own sex more interesting. Their minds, being less direct, were more amusing to follow and the mind of a woman who had married Mr. Blackett, remained married to him and still seemed content, must either be nearly empty or else full of surprises. (*Chatterton Square* 175)

In Mr. Blackett's character Young created an uncharacteristically negative character. But this could not satisfy her. With her heroine Rosamund, Young did not only share unconventional views about marriage and divorce, the conviction that 'there was a monstrous moral tyranny in social and religious conditions which could penalize two mature people who chose to part' (80), but also interest in the 'less direct' minds of women. As noted earlier, heterosexual love is hardly the impetus of Young's narratives. And though Chatterton Square 'does not exclude heterosexual exchange as a moment of feminine pleasure', it articulates a discourse that 'does not revolve around the romantic paradigm as the founding topology of feminine discourse' (Radner 1995: 116, italics Radner's). Young's major accomplishment in this novel is that, though the attention is relentlessly and almost perversely focused on Mr. Blackett, the central relationship is the one between Rosamund and Agnes, while the novel's moral dilemma rests with Mrs. Blackett. For, as Bel Mooney has noted in her 'Afterword' to the novel, 'it is one thing to create a man who is a monster, and a downtrodden, unhappy wife; quite another to perceive the subtle collusion that is often at the core of such a desolate marriage' (374). What adds complexity to the character of Bertha Blackett is not simply her gradual rebellion, but the willingness to delve into her own darkness and recognize that if the two of them have lived in a mean little world, with her pandering to her husband's self-satisfaction for her own amusement, she has been the meaner of the two (268). Bertha, like Celia before her, must face the unpalatable truth that she has been reduced to drawing pleasure from the contempt she feels for her husband. Touched by the 'threads linking her family to the one across the road' and by Rosamund's 'sense of undiminished life' (151), she will cease to seek cover for her own cowardice in her husband's failings.

Bertha's longing for a husbandless life, which mirrors Celia's envy of her housekeeper's 'blessedly solitary bed', comes early in the novel. Watching the light in Rosamund's window, she broods: 'how pleasant ... to have a bedroom, even a bed, of one's own, to be able to toss and turn, to put on the light and read, to know there was a whole night in front of you in which to be alone' (36). Echoes of Virginia Woolf's famous dictum would not be lost on the reader; neither would the narrower horizon of Mrs. Blackett's aspirations and the allusions to a physical revulsion that will become explicit as the novel progresses.

Modern Heroines of the Everyday 147

Spinsters Makeover

> The sweetest of human ties was not for me, I could not be wife and mother ... I bowed my head in resignation to the Almighty will, saying from my most heart 'Thy will be done.' (Emma Worboise, *The Wife's Trials*: 14)

> women who want to get married, and can't, often turn very queer as they grow older. (E.M. Delafield, *Thank Heaven Fasting*: 155)

Perhaps one of the most innovative and subtle aspects of this novel, as in *Miss Mole*, is the creative revision and redemption of that icon of British literature, the spinster, privileged object of ridicule and invectives, whom F.M. Mayor, herself author of novels about single women, mockingly called the 'U.F.' (Unnecessary Female).[14] Male writers were particularly vitriolic about the U.F. Rudyard Kipling's title character in 'Mary Postgate' (1915) is a poignant example of a woman whose alleged sexual repression unleashes a horrific sadism. But William Platt's *The Passionate Spinster: A Psychological Novel* (1932) is perhaps the most extreme example of male sadistic fantasies roused by the spinster. Ostensibly dictated by clinical interest in the psychological effect of 'sexual starvation' on women, the novel harks back to a vision of woman as passive, static, waiting to be ravished by the aggressive male, 'an attacker, a creature of strong, urgent passions' (63). While 'a certain feminine instinct of chastity was ... needed to keep this male urgence from exceeding all bounds', Valerie, the protagonist, feels a yearning 'to be primitive, to feel claimed, to be raped, to be beaten and cowed, but ... to be a wife! ... She dreaded the ravisher, yet she awaited his onslaught' (62, 64). The conclusion of the novel is a proper rape scene. A 'burly German office ' enters the hospital from where all nurses have been evacuated except for Valerie (according to her superiors she is too unattractive to be in danger) and, 'enchanted by her resistance', throws himself on her, chanting: '"I have killed you, I who should have married you that we might together have raised such a brood of children as the world had never before seen!" ... And she, conscious as in a honey-sweet dream of these loving looks and wondrous words, she, the passionate virgin, felt death come to her as a lover, softly kissing her into sleep' (192). In *A Clergyman's Daughter*, Orwell has Dorothy's mentor, Mr. Warburton, lecture her for several pages on what her future will be like if she does not accept his proposal of marriage (280): 'you will sit through interminable church services ... All the while you will be fading, withering ... Do you know that type of bright – too bright – spinster who says "topping" and "ripping"... and she's such a good sport that she makes everyone feel a little unwell?' He warns her that after her father's death she will have to find herself a job, 'the sort of job that parsons' daughters get. A nursery governess ... or companion to some diseased hag ... Or ... English mistress in some grisly girls' school ... And all the time withering, drying up, growing more sour and more angular and more friendless' (281–3).[15]

Contrary to Warburton's predictions, the death of her parents, a couple who 'had

148   *Domestic Modernism, the Interwar Novel, and E.H. Young*

been eloquent on the sanctity and sufficiency of the home' (125), has freed Agnes Spanner from the tyranny of a smothering home. Significantl , the first thing she puts on the bonfire when 'the receipts and correspondence of two lifetimes had to be destroyed' (125) is the framed embroidery her mother had hung by her bed to welcome Miss Spanner on her return from one of her holidays, assuring her that 'home-keeping hearts were the happiest' (125). However, what has saved her from sharing the fate of the dependable family drudge, such as Emma Worboise's elderly spinster and her many successors, Orwell's Dorothy, F.M. Mayor's Henrietta Symons, Mary Jocelyn and May Sinclair's Harriett Frean, Lettice Cooper's Aunt Ellen and the 'pious maiden ladies in seaside boarding houses', or 'in stuffy boarding-houses in Bayswater and Bournemouth' who inhabit Holtby's *Poor Caroline* (1931: 29, 51), is not only the timely loss of her parents and the handsome legacy it left her. She owes her salvation to her 'innate independence' (106), human sympathy and a sensitivity to the beauty of words which was roused by her first glimpse of Rosamund as a teenager on her bicycle, a 'flying figure of 'beauty and freedom and happiness' (37). Her father having made 'short work' of her only suitor, she has never enjoyed 'the sweetest of human ties' and yet, like Harriet in Barbara Pym's *Some Tame Gazelle* (1950), who would not dream of exchanging a comfortable life of spinsterhood in a country parish 'which always had its pale curate to be cherished, for the unknown trials of matrimony' (124), she would not change places with Rosamund. Unlike the old maids reviled by the redoubtable Clifton Roderick Johnson in *Poor Caroline* ('Sex-starved. Sex-starved. Must use their energy somehow. Good works. Purity and social welfare. Nosing round to find nice juicy stories about child assault an' prostitutes. Rescue work. Anti-slavery. Feminism. Peace. Pshaw!' (113)), she does not feel the need to find compensation and gratification in good works. While Monica in Delafield s *Thank Heaven Fasting* reflects, 'a home, a husband, a recognised position as a married woman – an occupation. At last, she would have justified her existence' (287), Miss Spanner needs no husband to validate her existence. Nor is she going queer in the head, a fate that Monica's mother, like Warburton, predicts for all women who want to get married but cannot. Her keen imagination, which enables her 'to create exciting dramas' on crumbs of gossip from the charwoman and has allowed her to live a full life, is fed by literature.

Reading plays a large role in the feminine middlebrow novel, binding, as Nicola Humble has argued, 'the woman reader into a community of other readers through an almost cultish involvement with favourite books' (9). Keenly aware of the constraints of the domestic space inhabited by their heroines, domestic novelists fashion venues of escape for them (and for themselves) by making reading a highly symbolic act both as a key to characters as well as in the exchange of books, forays to the library and retreat to the privacy of bedrooms and gardens. The experience of reading presented in the domestic novel counters the conjecture in Mass-Observation that better-off women had less leisure for reading after World War I since the shortage of domestic help kept them occupied with housework ('Books and the Public', TC 20/4/G, 1942: 15).

As Virginia Woolf noted, Arnold Bennett has only to mention that in *Hilda Lessways* (1911) the title character is fond of reading *Maud* to suggest that 'she was

Modern Heroines of the Everyday 149

endowed with the power to feel intensely' ('Character in Fiction' 1924: 429). That Constance in *The Old Wives' Tale* (1908) will be perfectly happy with replicating her mother's placid life in Bursley is first intimated by her unquestioning acceptance of her mother's choice of reading material: Mrs. Baines 'never read anything except *The Sunday at Home* and Constance never read anything except *The Sunday at Home*' (136). Sophia, instead, displays a worrying taste for novel reading that contributes to the 'obscurely inimical' attitude with which Mrs. Baines regards the Free Library. In Dorothy Whipple's *High Wages*, Jane Carter is rescued from loneliness and despair by her friendship with Wilfrid Thompson, a clerk in the local Free Library, a friendship built on the exchange of books. In her next novel, *Greenbanks* (1932), Whipple suggests Rachel's modernity by showing her 'lying at full length on the couch reading with rapture a story by Katherine Mansfield (256). On the other hand, in E.M. Delafield's *Thank Heaven Fasting* (1932), not only the titles of Monica Ingram's books, but also her reading habits, are some of the few clues that establish the period of the story as some time before World War I: 'there was a set of Dickens, a set of Scott, a set of Ruskin, and several volumes of poetry ... She was allowed, now to read books from Mudie's in the drawing-room, provided that she asked her mother's leave first, as to each one' (26); while in *Diary of a Provincial Lady* the titles of the books the provincial lady reads (or avoids reading) constitute a running commentary on the literature of the period. Mary Jocelyn, in F.M. Mayor's *The Rector's Daughter* (1924), builds a bulwark against the influence of her father's formidable and censorious mind by surrounding herself with books of her own choosing, the 'rubbish she had bought at sales of work, all her children's books, her favourite Miss Yonge and Trollope, a large collection of Elizabethan dramatists and books of mediaeval mystics': 'She fell back on reading, and got the reputation of being "learned" ... She retired within herself, and fell in love instead with Mr. Rochester, Hamlet, and Dr. Johnson' (11, 14).[16]

Of all Young's novels, *Chatterton Square* highlights the figure of the female reader. In her cluttered bedroom, which to the child Rhoda seems to be both a library and a 'clean secondhand shop' (94), books have allowed Miss Spanner to make 'hundreds of friends, yes hundreds of them, good and bad and all interesting' (41) and to revel in love affairs with the characters of her favourite novels. The pleasure she draws from literature is contagious; as Rhoda realizes, while the books her father offers are always 'slightly tainted' by his edifying purpose, 'the same book from Miss Spanner must have a different and more wholesome flavou ' (94–5).

Agnes basks in Rosamund's beauty and in her affection for her, dreading that Fergus's decision to divorce his wife may lead her friend to remarry, for she believes that every free and reasonable man would want to secure Rosamund for himself (143). Rosamund herself, though often tempted to make Agnes over, rearrange her hair and put decent clothes on her, always comes to the conclusion that 'it would be a form of sacrilege to tamper with anything unique' (181). In spite of different tastes and experiences she believes that 'their detached yet close relationship' is what marriage 'ought to be like ... but it never could be. The bond was too obvious, the demands were inevitable, and the bond sometimes chafed and the demands were not satisfied (192).

150   *Domestic Modernism, the Interwar Novel, and E.H. Young*

She would never be free of her husband Fergus, for what had been the contentment of flesh and spirit between them 'though it might dwindle to a memory, remained a bond' (192). Indeed, one might argue that in Young's later novels, while love has ceased to be the teleology of the narrative, the narrative, like the home, is haunted by heterosexuality. Fergus, who after his gallant adventure has never readjusted to the humdrum of peace life, appears as a ghost in Rosamund's bedroom, a space from which the whole family has conspired to exorcise the menace of Rosamund's sexuality by turning it into a site of public encounters; this is where the children come every night with their troubles and where Agnes gathers together the threads of the day.

While the literature of the 1930s and 1940s abounds with figures of impoverished middle-aged spinsters, Miss Spanner's precursor is to be found in Ada Leverson's Anne Yeo rather than Emma Worboise's character. As 'Anne, wrapped in an extraordinary dressing-gown', very likely to have been made out of an old curtain from the reverend Yeo's library, her hair pulled up in a dismal knot, makes it a rule every evening to go in for a few minutes to see her friend Hyacinth 'and talk against everyone they had seen during the day' (*Love's Shadow*: 62), so Miss Spanner draws nourishment from her nightly conversations with Rosamund. Indeed, Young may have been inspired by Leverson, so similar is her characterization of Miss Spanner to that of Anne Yeo and so closely does the relationship of Hyacinth and Anne resemble that of Rosamund and Agnes. Although Miss Jewel in *Jenny Wren* is a bleak portrait of the sexually repressed and cruelly manipulative spinster who closely resembles the 'U.F.' depicted by Platt and Orwell, in Miss Mole, Miss Spanner and Celia's independent sister, Hester, Young transforms the stereotype of the superfluous spinster, or the single woman, in her attempts to poke holes in conventional ideas of home and marriage and to surprise and defamiliarize readers and their expectations.

Notes

[1]   For their insightful comments on the interaction between Celia and domestic space, we are grateful to Kathy Mezei's 2004 English 803 class, 'Modernity and the Everyday': Beverley Grey, Mathew Glezos, Steven Weber, Alison Mcdonald, Joanna Mansbridge, Erin Smith, Wendy Thompson, Sandra Walker and Bonnie Yourk.

[2]   In her notebook (20 May 1935) Young jotted the ages of her characters – Julia 43, Celia 45, etc. (Young Papers).

[3]   We thank Mathew Glezos for noting the recurrence of this phrase in *Celia*.

[4]   Amy Loveman's review in *The Saturday Review of Literature* 17:4 (19 February 1938): 330, is titled 'An Artist in Living'. Loveman begins with the statement: 'This is a novel of the type in which the English are particularly adept; the leisurely chronicle of family life in which action takes place entirely within the home'.

[5]   For this observation, we thank Wendy Thompson, unpublished paper 'Furniture and Rooms in E.H. Young's *Celia*' (2004).

[6]   We thank Gavin Stamp for the loan of this picture.

[7]   Stella Deen also discusses the relationship between privacy, doors and keys (2002:

Modern Heroines of the Everyday

100).

[8] See Stella Deen's exploration of privacy and domesticity in 'Dream Houses and Twisting Passages: Domestic Consciousness in E.H. Young's *Celia*' (2000).

[9] Tristram: 247.

[10] See Hamon's schematization of doors, windows, walls, mirrors and stained glass: 40–41.

[11] Judy Giles urges us not to underestimate the importance of the provision of hot and cold running water and its potential to 'transform women's daily lives at the same time as playing a crucial part in improved family health'. It also 'led to new ways of organizing domestic space' and 'bathrooms and indoor toilets enabled new forms of privacy' which shaped how people understood 'their bodies in relation to others' (2004: 20–21).

[12] See also Mary Westacott's cleverly constructed novel, *Absent in the Spring* (1944), in which a housewife's travel delays give her family a pleasant respite. Mary Westacott is a pseudonym for Agatha Christie.

[13] The cistern is the key to romance in *The Curate's Wife*; in *Celia*, Celia likens herself to a cistern (396).

[14] Rhonda Keith, 'Flora Macdonald Mayor', *Dictionary of Literary Biography* 36, 'British Novelists, 1890–1929: Modernists', ed. Thomas F. Staley: 169.

[15] W. Somerset Maugham's 1932 play, 'For Services Rendered', engages with the stereotypes of drawing room drama: a fatally ill mother who doles out tea at every crisis, a spinster daughter, hallucinating marriage proposals, an emasculated son, blinded by the war, for whom the spinster daughter finally refuses to give up her own life (*Modern Plays* 1967: 291–354).

[16] The symbolic valences of reading are ubiquitous in the interwar domestic novel and deserving of a study of their own. In Rose Macaulay's *Dangerous Ages* (1921), the literary tastes and attitudes about books of the characters are an index to their personality: thus, Grandmamma is presented as 'a cleverish old lady' through her appreciation of Checkov's letters, whereas her daughter Mrs. Hilary's prejudiced and prevaricating mind is first suggested by the narrator's comment that whether she had actually read a book or not, 'she knew beforehand what she would think of it if she had' (31). Kay Burns in G.C. Pain's *Surplus Women* is typical of the female reader discussed by Nicola Humble, for whom reading 'is a source of deep, sensual satisfactions, a self-indulgent pleasure, a means of escape as well as an affirmation of life choices' (47); indeed, reading in bed in the morning in the bedsit where she has moved after the death of her selfish and silly grandmother is Kay's first affirmation of a newly gained freedom. Julia, in F. Tennyson Jesse's *A Pin to See the Peepshow*, is also typical of Humble's middlebrow reader who 'responds to literature with a visceral immediacy' (Humble: 8). The romances she borrows from the circulating library provide an escape from the dreariness of 'Two Beresford', the house she shares with her dull parents; immersed in *The Forest Lovers*, she can settle down contentedly 'to being Isoult la Desirous, roaming the glades of sleep with Prosper' (Jesse: 45).

Chapter 8

England, My England

Ideas of Home and Englishness

> Family life ... as most of England still knew it, was a solid thing that could withstand heavy stresses. (Lettice Cooper, *The New House*: 46)

> England, my England! But which is *my* England? (D.H. Lawrence, *Lady Chatterley's Lover*: 156)

During the interwar years, the conjunction of the upsurge in nationalism, ideologies of nationhood and Englishness, persistent propaganda on behalf of the domestic sphere, mass housing projects, the dilemma of the woman at home and modernity conspired to foreground the house and to reify the reciprocity of house and novel. The domestic itself in a sense became the national; in particular, the 'home-centred feminine subjectivities of middle-class women were central to the construction of national identity' (Cohen: 86; Giles 2004: 12). Not surprisingly, the 'no-mans-land' areas of the First World War reinforced the soldiers' attachment 'to home as a source of identity, as illustrated by the imposition of a domestic topography onto the alien environment of the trenches' (Bird: 117).

In contrast to the French in Paris who were accustomed to apartment living, to be English was to live in a detached, single-family house with a garden. Indeed, as a character in Stella Gibbons's *The Bachelor* (1944) puts it:

> At least 90 per cent. of the British want a small house and a garden; a vote recently taken among men in the armed forces showed that that was what 95 to 98 per cent. wanted, and an inquiry made in Birmingham proved that 96.7 of the city's population wanted it too. If you ask almost any of them casually what they want from life, the answer's invariably the same – 'a nice little house and a bit of garden.' (142–3)

This view, which echoes Gerald's in *Celia*, is borne out by Mass-Observation's *Enquiry into People's Homes* (1943) report that the '"dream home" of the majority is still the small modern suburban house, preferably possessing all modern conveniences ... it should have a garden, and should be situated both near the open country and near the town' (226).[1]

In their study of Englishness, Judy Giles and Jim Middleton have noted how the housing policies that backed up the building of approximately 4,000 new houses between the wars 'enshrined beliefs about the ways in which domestic and private life was being reformulated to include the newly enfranchised citizens of a "modern"

154 *Domestic Modernism, the Interwar Novel, and E.H. Young*

England (women and men of the working classes) – those previously excluded from the ideals of English family life' (193–4). Implicit in the slogan 'Homes Fit for Heroes' was the idea that a return to the normality of established gender and familial roles would secure and restore stability in the wake of the upheavals of war. Adequate housing was seen by all political parties as a first step towards rearing a healthy citizenry and promoting 'national efficiency'. The idea of home was also linked to ideals of empire through the construction of England as 'the homeland', the motherland, the place of origin, safety and identity (193). A national housing policy was regarded as the key aspect of post-war social policy; it emphasized not only quantity but also quality in the houses constructed for the returning men and their families who would rebuild the nation (Burnett: 220).[2]

For early twentieth-century novelists, as a consequence, house and home were intimately connected with Englishness and cultural memory, whether satirically, as in Evelyn Waugh's Hetton Abbey in *Handful of Dust*, nostalgically in his *Brideshead Revisited*, critically in *Howards End*, where E.M. Forster views the ascendancy of the middle-class philistine with alarm, or ambivalently in Woolf's Pointz Hall in *Between the Acts*. Hetton Abbey is slyly approached through the perspective of a guide book as '*formerly one of the notable houses of the county ... entirely rebuilt in 1864 in the Gothic style and ... now devoid of interest ...*' (1951: 14, Waugh's italics), whereas Pointz Hall 'did not rank among the houses that are mentioned in guide books' (11). While Waugh ridicules cultural memory in this example of English Gothic, which like its owner, Tony Last, is the last of a kind, Woolf simultaneously celebrates and parodies Britain's rich heritage, while also demonstrating how present-day horrors – rape, war, bullying – are rooted in this past. Like many portraits of Edwardian houses, Baldry Court, the manicured estate of Rebecca West's *The Return of the Soldier* (1918), 'a *synecdoche* for Edwardian England ... the British Empire in Miniature' (Cohen: 67, 73), is tended by Jenny and Kitty as a shrine for the soldier of the title and a threatened bucolic idyll.

Upper and middle-class houses were 'cherished both for being repositories of, and for being more resilient than every day lives' and for being 'nostalgic signifiers (Moran: 610). Family homes, like Baldry Court and Pointz Hall or the Pargiters' house at Abercorn Terrace in London in Woolf's *The Years* (1937), were viewed by writers like West and Woolf with ambivalence for prolonging conservative values, encumbering a younger generation and, in particular, for being a recurring signifier of women's futile lives. Thus, for a number of women novelists and their characters, the reorganization of domestic life and conventions signalled new ways of living and relating (Giles 2004: 16). It is, of course, in *Cold Comfort Farm* that new ways of living are most dramatically enacted; Flora Poste's passion for re-organizing and modernizing the domestic space of the farm has startling consequences, with the son Seth becoming a movie idol and old Aunt Ada Doom flying off to Paris in a leather suit, although Flora herself succumbs to a conventional, if modern, marriage and cousin Judith Starkadder to madness. But in works not moved by satirical intent as well, architectural and domestic metaphors exhibit this concept of home, belonging

England, My England

and nation, while also standing as major fixed reference points for the 'structuring of reality' (Porteous: 386). The domestically modern Rosamund in *Chatterton Square* runs her old family home as she pleases, with no husband, and Celia resists the move to a modern villa with modern conveniences. The modern women in *The Years*, the sisters Maggie and Sara, have moved into a flat in an undesirable area of London, while their cousin Rose and niece Peggy live on their own, one a suffragette, the other a physician. Repeated references to a set of iconic domestic objects – the kettle that will not boil, the 'spotted walrus with a brush in its back that Martin had given his mother on her last birthday' (30) and Sara and Maggie's 'great Italian chair with the gilt claws that stood in the hall' (117), reminiscent of *their* dead mother – are touchstones of cultural memory, family traumas and, for the reader, of the passing years.

In *Celia*, where all the male characters had fought in World War I and marriages had issued from the peace, and in *Chatterton Square*, written during the period of 'appeasement', the house replicates the contentious rebuilding of society and the interrogation of Englishness in the interwar years. While Struther's *Mrs. Miniver* charmingly promotes the interwar cult of domesticity, Englishness, and the idea of home as the foundation of nation, Young's last two novels quietly expose its cracks and deficiencies. Through Celia's journey between houses and the contrapuntal narrative alternating between the two families living in Chatterton Square, as well as by means of her emphasis on the homosocial, and perhaps even homoerotic, relationship between Rosamund and Agnes, Young explores the unstable concept of what E. Arnot Robertson and Woolf (in her original title for *The Years*) called 'ordinary families', the meaning of home and the network of community.

Ideas of home and homeland are nowhere more intertwined than in *Chatterton Square*. As the focalization oscillates between the two houses and we trek back and forth between the Blackett and Fraser households, we are drawn into a vortex of personal, sexual and marital power politics that mimics the tense international situation of the late 1930s. In 'Portrait of a Londoner', one of six essays she wrote for *Good Housekeeping* in 1931, Woolf claims – not altogether jokingly – that for London to cease to be merely a spectacle and become a place where people actually live, its fragments must be ordered into a legible whole in Mrs. Crowe's drawing room.[3] The view that a bridge connects the private house with the world of public life, which Woolf stated more gravely seven years later in *Three Guineas* (32) and explored in her last two novels, *The Years* and *Between the Acts*, is mockingly enacted in Young's novel: public and private spaces are connected through the fi ure of Herbert Blackett, whose clinging to traditional forms of domesticity is equated with the retrogressive politics of appeasement.

Chatterton Square and the Politics of Appeasement

> I mean that 'er characters was no *use*! They was only just like people you run across any day. (Rudyard Kipling, 'The Janeites': 172)

156   *Domestic Modernism, the Interwar Novel, and E.H. Young*

> Never more in our lives, perhaps, have our homes meant more to us. (*Woman's Own*, 20 April 1949)[4]

Chatterton Square, the last of Young's novels, written between 1941 and 1945 but published only in 1947 at the height of reconstruction, is set in the crucial year of 1939, the end of a period of troubled and uncertain peace in a decade which had begun in economic crisis and had been seared by protest at home and war abroad and was facing the spectre of another world war. The Nazis had come to power in a country crushed first by the humiliating conditions set by the Treaty of Versailles, then by recession. By September, Italian troops were sailing for East Africa, the Italian delegation had walked out of the League of Nations and the Committee of Five had reached a deadlock. Young, as her lover Ralph Henderson noted, was deeply affected by the events and

> wrote nothing – except for two books for and about children – from Munich till the tide turned at Alamein. She just felt that she couldn't – the shame and degradation of what seemed to her to be a base surrender – simply froze her genius. She recovered just in time to write *Chatterton Square* – and then she died. ('*E.H. Young*, her Muse, her Method & her Message': 9)[5]

Young's sentiments, voiced by Rosamund Fraser and Agnes Spanner, were those of an increasing number of people who, despite the cataclysm of World War I, could not consider pacifism an acceptable alternative to the threat of Nazism.[6] And, as in *Between the Acts*, where the annual pageant and customary country weekend life at Pointz Hall are interrupted by planes flying overhead, the imminence of war in *Chatterton Square* is experienced through its effects on the everyday life of the Fraser household.

Though the initial reactions to Munich had appeared to be supportive of Chamberlain and sanctions were seen as a preferable alternative to being involved in war, the anger voiced by the *Daily Worker* – 'Neville Chamberlain returned smiling to Britain yesterday from the greatest betrayal of the century' – was soon shared in other quarters, most notably the Liberal Party, the most consistent and vocal in its criticism of appeasement:[7]

> We disagreed with the cold shouldering of Soviet Russia – the emphasizing of points of difference, the refusal to seek a basis of cooperation. We condemned the desertion of the League, the surrender to Italy on Abyssinia, the pusillanimous toleration of German and Italian armed intervention in Spain. We continually criticized the wholly inadequate effort for our own rearmament. From these causes came the impossible situation which this country found itself in at the time of the Munich conference. (Viscount Samuel, *Memoirs*: 275–6 quoted in Cameron: 50)

Furthermore, while a programme broadcast by the BBC in 1939 'was the only piece of broadcasting that gave a dissenting voice to appeasement' (Scannell and Cardiff: 101 quoted in Highmore 2002a: 108), a survey conducted by Mass-Observation and

England, My England 157

published in *Britain* exposed the discrepancy between media representation and *vox populi* (Highmore 2002a: 107). The Fraser household habitually listens with apprehension to evening radio broadcasts on the deteriorating situation and uniformly condemns Chamberlain's policy of appeasement, while Mr. Blackett avoids the radio and looks forward to a rosy future.

The sense of 'shame and degradation' to which Henderson alludes is palpable in *Chatterton Square*, the only one of Young's novels to be overtly inflected by political concerns. The question of appeasement does not remain in the background but, reflecting the emotion that charged the national debate on Munich, shapes characters and relationships. It also exposes a blind spot in feminist scholarship for, as Janet Montefiore has pointed out, feminist critics have tended to focus on 'gender equality and the politics of representation', thus failing 'to correct the ideological convention that men inhabit the public domain while women represent the home and/or sexuality' (20). Although solidly maintained within the boundaries of the home, Young's narrative is engaged in a continuous conversation with the public sphere, thus destabilizing 'essentialist theories that women are only passive war victims, war protesters, or complicit with the power of a masculinist war machine' (Lassner: 4). Rosamund Fraser, though the mother of two military-age sons, Agnes Spanner and Bertha Blackett, condemn appeasement and see no choice but war, backing up the view feminist scholars have been stressing for some time that women writers were far from endorsing peace with Hitler at all costs.[8]

For the characters in *Chatterton Square*, plagued by memories of World War I and now about to be plunged into the next one, the 'home' allows no complacency about the future. While the Fraser family chat amiably in their quiet room at the back of the house 'with birds singing in the bushes and a distant, homely sound of hammering from someone who was mending his fence, preserving his possessions, maintaining decency and order ... the threats in a land so very far away ... seemed like an old story of another age and not quite real' (22). However, Miss Spanner knows that shutting out 'the squabblings, the shoutings' (22) would be an act of cowardice. The Fraser boys, equipped with the higher awareness of a generation born during the war, are even denied the illusion that had sustained their father of entering into a gallant adventure. Yet, like Rosamund, Agnes Spanner, Piers Lindsay and, though less vocally, Bertha Blackett, they reciprocate the sentiment expressed by the narrator in Norman Denny's *Sweet Confusion*, a novel which shared the setting in 1939 and the publication year with *Chatterton Square*:

> Amid the hysterical plaudits of the House of Commons, the Prime Minister announced that he had been summoned to Munich. Off he went, and back he came, with a scrap of paper in his hand and a message of 'peace in our time'. It might, it appeared, be a somewhat uncomfortable peace for Czechoslovakia, which was called upon to undergo a major operation in the interests of the community at large; but peace it was to be; peace – peace ... The people heard the news and hoped for the best; but none the less they wondered, many of them finding it difficult to encounter one anoth 's eyes. (359)

158 *Domestic Modernism, the Interwar Novel, and E.H. Young*

Although the characters of Young's earlier works may wax lyrical over their love for the English countryside or take delight in roaming through the streets of Bristol, in *Chatterton Square* such love and delight are not only tinged by the threat of war but positively soiled by what is perceived as betrayal by the leaders of the country. Rosamund has never been abroad and yet has never doubted that despite the squalor of deserted works, no country could equal England for beauty and for the quality of its people, no meadows could compare to English meadows (173). But now, after Munich, taking a solitary walk to one of her favourite haunts in search of the 'comfort of the hill', Rosamund sees not the golds and yellows of autumn 'but a dishonourable tarnish creeping over them'. She imagines the whole of the country, the villages, the wide moors, the cathedrals, 'tarnished, blurred, and deadened' (346) and wonders if 'the good sound core' of her country, 'the land from which all derive their sense of identity and tradition' (Bracco: 69), has gone for ever (350).[9] In *Between the Acts*, Giles, heir to Pointz Hall, a not unsympathetic figure of iconic masculinity, is enraged by 'old fogies who sat and looked at views over coffee and cream when the whole of Europe – over there – was bristling – like …'. As the narrator points out, figures of speech are not Giles' forte; he can only come up with 'hedgehog' to complete his simile and, like Rosamund, projects his fears upon the place that he loves: 'at any moment guns would rake that land into furrows; planes splinter Bolney Minster into smithereens and blast the Folly'. For he too 'loved the view' (66–7).

We know that a first draft of *Chatterton Square* was completed on 21 March 1945.[10] Indeed, the sense of suspended time, with people still taking vacations (Flora and Mr. Blackett travelling to France, Rosamund's boys planning a hiking trip), as in *Sweet Confusion* and *Between the Acts*, evokes the climate of uncertainty as well as the view of the 1930s as 'the long weekend' (Graves and Hodge, *The Long Weekend* 1941). The 1930s appeared as a decade of rootlessness, affecting the perception of home, complicating its status as a site that allows for the anchoring of identity and 'continuous unfolding' of the self (Van Lennep quoted in Iris Marion Young: 150) and exposing it as a vulnerable, transitional space, susceptible to constant refashioning. Thus the repetition and routine of everyday life assumed urgency and desirability in order to stave off the fraying and dislocation of the self and the threat of the 'other'.

The Drama of the Doorstep

The impulse behind *Chatterton Square* resembles that which drove film makers such as John Grierson and Humphrey Jennings to insist on the importance of 'the drama of the doorstep': a desire 'to make a drama from the ordinary to set against the prevailing drama of the extraordinary' (*The Fortnightly Review*, August 1939 quoted in Forsyth Hardy: 18). Literally so, in a novel which, like *The Vicar's Daughter*, makes much of the space between houses and which accordingly shifts focalization from one interior view to another. Furthermore, in *Chatterton Square* Young seems to be guided by the same principle that drove the surveys conducted by Mass-Observation, 'the idea

England, My England

159

of juxtaposing the normal everyday pattern with the experience of the exceptional collective occasion' (Laing: 156) as she seeks out the ordinariness of extraordinary times by carefully juxtaposing the grand narrative of the impending war with actions that insist in bordering on the insignificant. As Henderson noted, 'there *are* no actions … only a lot of women talking … the really important and interesting actions are just those which take place within. Externally there is very little happening to the characters in these works ('*E.H. Young*, her Muse, her Method & her Message': 6). Similarly, Woolf depicts World War I in *The Years* by foregrounding dinner and conversation at Maggie's and Rennie's flat rather than by the bombing unleashed above or by descriptions of battles.

The accomplishment of *Chatterton Square* is in the reclamation of ordinary, habitual actions; even 'the tiresome and perpetual business of keeping people fed and clothed and clean' constitutes 'a merciful dispensation' and a bulwark against chaos. For 'the sufferer was upheld by … a willingness, even in rebellion, to accept unhappiness in the unconscious realization that it would drop in its place with all other experiences and enlighten or leaven them' (*Chatterton Square*: 81). Not only is the ordinary *vis-à-vis* the extraordinary that which ultimately insures continuity, but it is 'the very means by which history is actualized and made real' (Osborne: 190 quoted in Felski: 48). For Rosamund, life 'is made up of small matters, and if they were not important to us we'd be half dead and the big things wouldn't affect us either' (220). What Lefebvre regarded as 'the largely debilitating routines of everyday life' (Bennett and Watson: xiv) turns into a strategy of resistance and endurance. Indeed in this novel, like Woolf's *Between the Acts*, written under the pressure of time (caused by illness as well as the war), the repetitive nature of the everyday acquires a new poignancy in contrast with the linear dimension of monumental history.

Though refusing to condone an unthinking nostalgic longing for home, *Chatterton Square* affirms 'the symbolic richness and cultural complexity of 'home-making' (which is not just housework)' shown in the layering of things and spaces with meaning, value and memory, a materialization which 'does not fix identity but anchors it in a physical space that creates certain continuities between past and present' (Felski: 25).[11] Simple, everyday activities are invested with intense meaning. Thus Miss Spanner's graciously arranged placatory meal, while prompted by a desire to make amends to Rosamund, is also dictated by the increasing awareness shared by all the characters except for Mr. Blackett that there might be little time left for such displays of domestic artistry. When Miss Spanner takes pains with the supper table by carefully composing a still life of 'a bunch of pink roses and their leaves to match the salmon and raspberries, the peas and cucumber' (156), she is acting under the same impulse that has driven her to give money to the Fraser children for what might very well be their last holiday. Thus, rather than providing a means of enslavement to repetitive tasks of social reproduction and oblivion to catastrophe, perpetuating a view of the domestic sphere as cut off from the dynamic of history and change, the small quotidian actions of the Fraser family are in continuous dialogue with social change; rather than being opposed to transcendence, they are shown to be 'the means

160   *Domestic Modernism, the Interwar Novel, and E.H. Young*

of transcending one's historically limited existence', showing how through continuity and routine 'we organize the world, make sense of our environment and stave off the threat of chaos' (Felski: 20, 21).

Wounded Soldiers

The sustained critique of masculinity and prescriptive femininity Young is conducting in this novel is only apparently humorous. This is the darkest of Young's novels, not only because it is set in one of the darkest periods of Britain's recent history, but also because of the risks Young is willing to take in her portrayal of Mr. Blackett. Thus, if his unlimited capacity for self-delusion –'there were regions of his own mind which he did not care to explore with thoroughness' (53) – which prevents him from detecting the prurience behind his fastidiousness in sexual matters may be amusing, his smug assessment of Rosamund ('He liked to believe that, in any case of an absent husband, the woman must be to blame' (53)) is increasingly less so. If Mr. Blackett cannot be blamed for feeling thankful at only having daughters, the 'spiteful pleasure' he feels in detecting Rosamund's vulnerable spots 'in her two tall sons', is decidedly disturbing. In Young's economic prose, this man is subjected to a scrutiny that is almost sadistic, with each word carefully weighed and what is left unsaid reverberating loudly. (We had a foreshadowing of this perverse amusement in *Miss Mole*, when, along with Hannah Mole, we relished Reverend Corder's self-importance and egotism and Celia's perverse pleasure in opposing Gerald in her thoughts and through her guerrilla tactics of conversation, tone of voice and politeness.) Mr. Blackett's cherished vision of himself roaming the countryside of France clad 'in corduroy trousers and a coloured shirt, letting the Bohemian in him have proper play' is disturbed by the unwelcome associations of the word 'France'; because, unlike Fergus and Piers, who saw active service during World War I, Mr. Blackett had managed to land a job in the civil service and so France 'was a country which, unlike many of his generation, he did not know' (156). His insularity, expediency and bad faith are enhanced by his spiteful comments about Piers, Bertha's cousin, who has returned from the war lame and disfigured and for whom she had felt genuine love. In Mr. Blackett's uncharitable view, Piers' limp and 'his showy facial wound' (27) 'are not altogether a disadvantage. For one thing, they carry a comfortable pension with them and a disfigured face has extra compensations. It gives distinction to what it may have lacked before and assures its owner of admiration, solicitous and probably unwarranted admiration' (34).

Through the figure of Piers Lindsay and his contrast with Herbert Blackett whom, significantl , Rosamund finds 'feminine ... Not effeminate. Feminine. Very bad in a man, I think' (75), Young joins efforts with many of her contemporary women writers in re-examining masculinity. For, as Trudi Tate has argued, the body of the wounded soldier, 'a visual reminder of the war', 'carries a complex of meanings back into civilian society' (96). A figure of 'both fascination and dread', the wounded soldier who limps through the narratives of Ernest Hemingway, Storm Jameson, Winifred

England, My England

Holtby, Rebecca West, Rose Macaulay, Virginia Woolf, Naomi Mitchison, Young's *Miss Mole, Chatterton Square* and *Celia* to name only a few, and who embodies both a mutilated masculinity and 'a powerful social ideal of manhood', highlights and intensifies '[bodily, historical, and fantasmatic] differences *within* masculinity in this period' (Tate: 97, 96. Tate's italics). Celia's only harsh retort in the novel is prompted by her niece's mockery of the maimed Richard. When Prudence calls him 'a nice little man' and adds, 'he knits, Aunt Celia! He makes his own socks! Don't you think that's rather an effeminate thing to do?' (388), she responds with unwonted asperity: 'your generation seems to have no imagination. It doesn't seem to be conscious of its debts' (389). It is significant that of the three main male figures in *Chatterton Square* – Fergus, for whom war has been 'a gallant adventure' that has incapacitated him from returning to civilian life, Herbert Blackett, who has avoided war, and Piers – it is the latter that Rosamund will choose. Young's portrait of the Blackett marriage as she shifts focalization from Blackett to Bertha is unremitting and becomes harsher as the approaching war highlights Mr. Blackett's unsavoury political views. We experience Bertha welcoming Mr. Blackett's decision to take Flora to France as a respite from her 'barbaric bed' in an interior view that highlights the correspondence of the Blackett house and marriage:

> In nearly twenty years of marriage there had hardly been twenty nights passed by Mr. Blackett outside his home and now, with any good fortune, there might be at least twenty evenings … when she need not suffer the absurd indignity of clambering over his recumbent figure … and already there seemed to be more light and air in it [the house], as though the door had been opened into a bigger, freer world. (217)

A Herbertless house gives Bertha the modest freedom of reading her own newspaper and forming her own opinions. It should not come as a surprise that Mr. Blackett's newspaper is *The Times*, edited from 1922 to 1941 by Geoffrey Dawson, who 'without any knowledge of European history, still less of German history, without knowing one word of the language or having the slightest insight into the German mind … threw all his influence – which was immense – into undermining Versailles and doing the business of the Germans for them' (Rowse: 6). Bertha's 'extravagance' in buying a second newspaper, possibly *The Daily Herald*, like her visits to the Frasers' home to listen to the news on the radio, amounts to a declaration of independent thinking and a different political allegiance.

The Barbaric Home

> Home is a barbarous idea; the method of a rude age; home is isolation; therefore anti-social. What we want is community. (Benjamin Disraeli: *Sybil*)[12]

While it is doubtful that Young would have concurred with Disraeli's radical dismissal of home, in *Chatterton Square* she not only questioned 'the nostalgic longing for home

162   *Domestic Modernism, the Interwar Novel, and E.H. Young*

as a place of stable identities predicated on female self-sacrifice' (Felski: 25),[13] but also provided sufficient grounds for considering the vision of home to which Mr. Blackett clings a barbarous one and for revising her own conception of Englishness.

Mr. Blackett's narrow and socially exclusionary views are strongly reminiscent of the stereotyped image of the traditional home which, according to Nikos Papastergiadis, although in itself a myth nevertheless unsettles modernity. This home, like Colonel Pargiter's at Abercorn Terrace in *The Years* and Pointz Hall in *Between the Acts*, is 'locked into the frozen time of the past: bound to interchangeable customs; restricted to pure members; ruled by strict authoritarian figures'(quoted in Morley: 42). To this 'quiet kingdom' Blackett comes 'to be soothed' (313), finding solace in the books in his study (albeit carefully checking for 'disorder and dust' (264)) and warmth in the 'romantic sanctity' of the bedroom (314). His 'strong moral sense and views of propriety', reserved for the family, do not prevent him from condoning his own dallyings abroad, for he nurses an idea of himself as 'the essential artist, susceptible to all forms of beauty and restricted by no conventions' (263). So too Colonel Pargiter, bastion of Victorian values, returns home for tea after dallying with his mistress:

> The Colonel stood at the door and surveyed the group rather fiercel . His small blue eyes looked round them as if to find fault; at the moment there was no particular fault to find; but he was out of temper; they knew at once before he spoke that he was out of temper. (Woolf, *The Years*: 12)

Agnes Heller has pointed out that home is 'a firm position from which we "proceed": going home should mean: returning to that firm position which we know, to which we are accustomed, where we feel safe and where our emotional relationships are at the most intense.' Furthermore, one may very well say '"this is my home", but if others … do not co-sign the sentence, he will not be at home there. In a home, one needs to be accepted, welcomed, or, at least, tolerated' (quoted in Morley: 24). In the Fraser home, Miss Spanner, though occasionally tempted to assume the air of 'a consciously poor relation upheld by a sense of her moral value' (106), belongs; here, Rhoda too finds a more congenial community, whereas Mr. Blackett's declaration of belonging would find no co-signers. On his return from his French holiday, the humiliating and pointedly symbolic experience of finding himself keyless and locked out of the house that he had imagined eager to welcome him is both an ironic reference to his dread of the doorstep as a dangerous point of neighbourly invasion and a humorous foreshadowing of his later realization of loneliness and isolation, prompted by Bertha's outburst of anger. As Mr. Blackett wanders alone in the night:

> it seemed to him … that the world must be thronged with people who, for a while, might wander in the protective darkness of the night but, sooner or later, must go back to houses they hated, to houses where they were not wanted, because there was no other shelter for them, and he was one of them, like some sad old dog who had been beaten for a fault he did not know he had committed, but must trundle home meekly to his kennel. (361)

England, My England

163

To a larger extent than in her previous works, in *Chatterton Square* Young interrogates the idea of home and family, pushing further the significance of the drama of the doorstep, for indeed, much of what is being investigated through different and idiosyncratic configurations of home and family concerns who is left on the doorstep, who belongs in the family, what makes a family, what makes a home and what makes a nation. Young here questions the right to belong acquired through marriage and blood ties in juxtaposition with ideas of home and belonging that accommodate a Miss Spanner and pointedly exclude the patriarch. This novel is an important example of the project of interwar women writers, of their entry into modernity, 'a modernity which was felt and lived in the most interior and private of places' and their recasting of 'older forms of relationship and intimate behaviour' (Light: 10). In Woolf's *The Years* and *Between the Acts*, Lehmann's *Dusty Answer*, Mary Renault's *The Friendly Young Ladies* (1944), women live or travel together in obliquely described lesbian relationships. In Renault's novel, furthermore, Helen and 'Leo' make their home on a houseboat amidst a rough masculine world of boats, rivers and pubs, while Miss Latrobe, who stages the pageant in *Between the Acts*, shares her bed and purse with an actress in a house in the village.

In reference to postcolonial fiction, Bhabha has queried whether a novel can house unfree people and whether mimesis and techniques of realism are suitable to convey dispossession (446). Following Bhabha's line of inquiry, can we read Young's narrative technique of domestic realism, marked as it is by playful and multiple focalizations and the presentation of inner lives through the interaction with, or viewing of, domestic objects as an expression of her sense of belonging to a nation, a race, a people? Are not her odd angles of narration, interior views and wicked irony muted tactics of rebellion against the constraints and totalizing strategies of community and conformity upon the imaginative individual and the equivocal position of women as mothers, home makers and wives? Are the houses in *Chatterton Square* and *Celia* houses of appeasement, compromise and negotiation in relation to traditional heterosexual households with gestures towards alternative and 'modern' domesticities? For not only do the last two novels continue to strengthen the move away from individualism into a 'fabric of complications', but they also engage in the connection of home and homeland and display the current political and public sphere within the microcosm of the home.

Notes

[1] The enquiry also reported that in the task of 'rebuilding and rehabilitating Britain ... the voice of the people is never more clearly heard than when it is the voice of the creator of the home, the mother of children, the housewife, the woman in the kitchen' (iii).

[2] Beddoe notes that 'between the wars 1.1 million council houses were built and large housing estates on the outskirts of every town became new features of the landscape' (93). In her study, *Women, Identity and Private Life in Britain, 1900–50*, Judy Giles outlines how the link between home ownership and citizenship 'was the focus not only of policies directed at increasing house purchase, but also of municipal housing policy targeted at returning

164   *Domestic Modernism, the Interwar Novel, and E.H. Young*

servicemen and working-class men in regular employment. 'Homes Fit for Heroes' was a specifically gendered message, addressed to those returning from ... war, but it was also linked to the extension of the franchise in 1918 to all men over 21' (1995: 74).

3   Of the six essays Woolf wrote for *Good Housekeeping* in 1931, five were printed together in the 1970s and 1980s, but the sixth was lost and has only just been rediscovered and was published for the first time in *The Guardian*, 11 August 2004.

4   Cited in Jane Waller and Michael Vaughan-Rees, *The Role of Women's Magazines 1939–1945*, 1987, p. 34.

5   Young was not alone in experiencing an imaginative lull. As Elizabeth Bowen noted in 1942, those years 'rebuff[ed] the imagination as much by being fragmentary as by being violent. It is by dislocations, by recurrent checks to his desire for meaning, that the writer is most thrown out. The imagination cannot simply endure events; for it the passive role is impossible. Where it cannot dominate, it is put out of action.' (quoted in Rod Mengham, 'Broken Glass', 2001: 124–33, 125). And it is not surprising that she turned to books for children, for the frequency of childhood themes, with their appeal to infantile security, was a conspicuous trend of the war years (Mengham 2001b: 125).

6   See, for instance, Bertrand Russell: 'when, in 1940, England was threatened with invasion, I realized that, throughout the First War, I had never seriously envisaged the possibility of utter defeat. I found this possibility unbearable, and at last consciously and definitely decided that I must support what was necessary for victory in the Second War, however difficult victory might be to achieve, and however painful in its consequences' (*The Autobiography of Bertrand Russell, 1914–1944*, Vol. II, 1968: 191).

7   Cited in Roy Douglas, *In the Year of Munich*, 1977: 72; Ronald Cameron, *Appeasement and the Road to War*, 1991, p.52.

8   See especially Phyllis Lassner, *British Women Writers of World War II: Battlegrounds of Their Own* (1998). For writing by women during the second world war, see also Dorothy Sheridan, ed., *Wartime Women: A Mass-Observation Anthology 1937–1945* (1990); Jenny Hartley, ed., *Hearts Undefeated : Women's Writing of the Second World War* (1994); *Nella Last's War*, ed. Richard Broad and Suzie Fleming (1981); *Among You Taking Notes: The Wartime Diary of Naomi Mitchison, 1939–1945*, ed. Dorothy Sheridan (1986); Anne Boston, ed., *Wave Me Goodbye: Stories of the Second World War* (1994).

9   In his review of *Chatterton Square*, Woodcock, a pacifist, disagrees with Young's position over the Munich crisis and chastises her for casting the one person who opposes her views, Mr. Blackett, in a negative light; in so doing, Woodcock misses her subtle and skilled portrait of Blackett and her emphasis on the lives of women during this crisis.

10 The notebook containing the draft of *Chatterton Square* is dated 21 March 1945 (Young Papers).

11 Felski's advocation of the rethinking of feminist attitudes to house and home is based on Iris Marion Young's 'House and Home: Feminist Variations on a Theme', *Intersecting Voices: Dilemmas of Gender, Political Philosophy and Policy*, 1997, p. 153.

12 Quoted in Morley: 17.

13 Here, too, Rita Felski is basing her discussion on Iris Marion Young's 'House and Home': 153. Woolf's critique and analysis of the problems of women in the home and in the professions are more fully outlined in the essays she, in the end, omitted from *The Years* and which have been published as *The Pargiters*.

Conclusion

> Celia's was a narrow world, but what more was the greater world than a container of personalities and the pain and happiness they could bestow on their fellows? Here, in little, were most of the emotions, preoccupations and duties common to mankind – love, dislike, anxiety and doubt and the perpetual problem of right and wrong, the need to earn bread and eat it, to flavour it with humour and a little malice, to be temperate and forbearing, to keep the peace if it could be kept with honour. *Celia*: 225–6

In a quiet and unobtrusive way, through a lexicon of domesticity, Young explored alternatives to the Victorian family, the heterosexual couple and the small interwar nuclear family. She negotiated and nurtured a variety of independent feminine selves and subjectivities that surpassed the stereotypes of spinsters and the drabness of middle-aged housewives, to create plausible and complicated modern heroines of the everyday. Although she did not resort to the radical forms of interior monologue practiced by Woolf, Mansfield, Richardson or Stevie Smith, or the disruption of linearity and novelistic conventions advocated by Woolf and Richardson, she nevertheless developed a sophisticated 'synthetic impressionism' and a domestic modernism shared with many other interwar novelists.

With her attentiveness to looking, seeing and not seeing, and to views of houses, city streets and the countryside as well as of inner lives, often explored from unusual perspectives, Young is in line with Post-Impressionists like Cézanne who, in representing his experience of looking at objects, challenged conventional ideas of perspective in his still lifes. More mutely, but as scathingly as E.M. Delafield, Rosamond Lehmann and Stevie Smith, Young exposed the reality of marriage, so efficiently covered up by two-penny weeklies 'Fiction for the Married Woman' (Stevie Smith, *Novel on Yellow Paper*: 151), which Pompey Casmilus's chatty, quirky voice satirizes:

> It is all washing up and peeling potatoes, and there are several *kiddies*, and the furniture isn't paid for … already now so cheap and dull and gimrack, and not with the lovely deep rich olive green and brown and yellow sordidity of Sickert's London interiors, but oh so full of daylight that shows, oh how it shows and shows, and is so showing all the time. (151–2, Smith's italics)

But not all homemaking is housework (I.M. Young: 148), and the heroines of Young's later novels, Hannah Mole, Dahlia, Celia and Rosamund, attempt to find pleasure and meaning in daily banal tasks. Within the spaces of the domestic, they transmute their lives into works of art, mull over human interactions, and search out

166   *Domestic Modernism, the Interwar Novel, and E.H. Young*

the scattered and concealed parts of their selves. Although Georges Sand, echoing nineteenth-century ideologies concerning women and the domestic sphere, commented that 'woman will always be more of an artist ... in her life' while 'man will be more of an artist is in his work', Young, like other domestic novelists of the twentieth century, insisted on representing women's lives as works of art.[1]

And so Young impels us to question what it means to associate pleasure with the everyday and to acknowledge that this connection has to do with gender (see Langbauer: 3). What kind of pleasure is found in Young's world of narrow horizons and drabness; in other words, what in these novels rescues the quotidian from insignificance? One answer may lie in *Celia* where, through Celia herself, Young instructs her readers in what the middle-aged housewife describes as the 'art of living', the attainment of pleasure in lives ostensibly lived 'in the passive voice' (16, 91). This art and pleasure are experienced in a domestic space through a quietly iconoclastic exposé of lives inexorably bound by walls, and whose victories and accomplishments are inevitably on a small scale.

In her discussion of turn-of-the-century Paris, Lisa Tiersten recounts how journalists and decorative arts reformers claimed that home decorating provided women with new opportunities for artistic self-expression and a 'crucial role in defining a modern aesthetic for the bourgeois Republic' (18). She then suggests that the 'notion of an "art of everyday life" was as much a guide to chic for an emergent middle-class elite as it was a slogan of the avant-garde' (28), noting, however, that the housewife's aesthetic was limited 'to shopping for the home and arranging its objects' (30). Writers like Young lay claim to the domestic and everyday as aesthetic objects and to their home maker heroines as sensitive and creative beings, thus implying, and in some cases explicitly asserting, that those who serve the domestic are indeed artists in living.

By revalidating the home, domesticity, and the everyday, writers of the domestic novel have questioned and examined the ideological and cultural assumptions of their society. Like language, and any system of signs, the everyday can be read semiotically through an analysis of its location and function in culture and society. Domestic novelists are profoundly aware that the everyday supplies tactics through which to reveal the extraordinary in the ordinary. Celia's niece says to her, '"You look so sweet in that hat ... From a long way off it looks quite ordinary and then, when you get closer, you see how clever it really is. And that's what happens with you yourself"' (*Celia*: 393). Similarly, the tension and surprise of Mansfield s 'Bliss' revolve around how bliss transforms the everyday into the extraordinary for Bertha, although in the end an unexpected extraordinary spectacle dispels the order, ordinariness and bliss of her day and her life when she catches sight of her husband passionately kissing Pearl. By artfully positioning the reader alongside Bertha as she glances out of the drawing room door into the hall to witness Harry and Pearl embracing, Mansfield, through her view from the interior, enables her reader to 'see' not only the scene, but also into Bertha's inner self without narratorial intervention. Through such narrative strategies in which hallways, mirrors and doors play their role, the domestic interior,

Conclusion   167

as it is presented, entered and exited is not simply background but, more powerfully, an epistemology of the home, a Derridian possibility of thought belonging to the architectural moment, to desire, to creation.

The domestic modernism of interwar novels manifests itself in writers not only exploring the effect of the home but also integrating the figural, emblematic and structural expressions of domestic spaces, whether in the highly associative mode of Woolf's *To the Lighthouse* and Katherine Mansfield s 'At the Bay', or in the more realistic approach of Young's *Chatterton Square* and Lettice Cooper's *The New House*. This interweaving of the home as subtext and text devolves into an epistemology that is simultaneously a hermeneutics of cultural codes, inner consciousness and social relations, and a mode for reading novels and for re-evaluating the domestic novel genre. For as a letter to the editor of *The Guardian* in response to the furore over women writers, dullness, and domesticity retorted: 'Where are the art critics who would dare to describe the work of Vermeer and Jean-Baptiste Chardin as "disappointingly domestic?"' (L.S. Rudkin, *Review* 2 April 2005: 8)

As Young increasingly resorts to the home to narrate her novels, the domestic interior, the embodied home and household objects, from dusters to cisterns, perform as *domus ex machina* to expose and explore the sexual and power politics between men and women and between women, and to afford views of the interior. In Young's later novels, not only does home play 'a crucial role in people's definition of their self identity' (Després: 101), it also replicates in miniature national and capitalist ideologies and agendas. Amply demonstrated in the sexual and ideological 'war' in and between the two houses on Chatterton Square and in issues of class mobility and middle-class aspirations in *Celia*, the social geography of the house charts the course of relations between sexes and classes. In narrating the home and evoking domestic fallacy to reflect personal and social dilemmas, Young and other domestic novelists were encoding and interrogating the idea of nation and Englishness, just as England was struggling to rebuild itself in the face of the dissolution of its empire, the threat of spreading fascism and the challenges of modernity.

Yet as we have noted, Young, like Woolf, Mansfield, and Bowen, avoids unambiguous endorsement of the everyday while refusing to trivialize the everyday experience of women and men in her presentation of domesticity. Surely there exists a connection between Young's conflicted engagement with domesticity in her novels of the 1920s and 1930s and the appeal her works exerted on her readers – isolated, suburban lower-middle-class or upwardly mobile housewives, who comprised 'probably the most dedicated and consistent sector of the reading public' (McAleer: 87). Women trapped by domesticity and the propaganda surrounding the home in the interwar years could derive vicarious pleasure from the subtle verbal victories over their husbands by Dahlia in Young's *The Curate's Wife* or Mrs. Blackett in *Chatterton Square*. The superfluous spinster between the wars could identify with and achieve a certain catharsis through the tart-tongued diatribes of Young's Hannah Mole and Miss Spanner, with Miss Mole's unanticipated marriage and Miss Spanner's unconventional, congenial domestic arrangements. In conjunction with other domestic novelists, Young

168 *Domestic Modernism, the Interwar Novel, and E.H. Young*

questions the assumption of Elizabeth Wilson and some feminist critics 'that the desire for home is necessarily linked to the realm of tradition and opposed to self-definition and autonomy' (Johnson: 462), a question that characterizes domestic modernism.

With her wry and minute observations of married and domestic lives, Young has post-World War II heiresses in Barbara Pym, Elizabeth Taylor, Anita Brookner, Alice Thomas Ellis, Jane Gardam, Beryl Bainbridge, Margaret Drabble and Penelope Fitzgerald. Her validation of the everyday and the home has also resurfaced in the best-selling 'Aga sagas' of the 1980s and early 1990s by Joanna Trollope and her followers, and in the family sagas of Mary Wesley and Elizabeth Jane Howard (*The Cazalet Chronicle*).[2] The popularity of these novels, where frequently the house features as 'a major character ... which is manipulated by, and in turn manipulates, several successive generations of inhabitants', as J. Douglas Porteous notes, 'attests to the existence of ambivalent feelings about home' (387). Similarly, contemporary novels like Kazuo Ishiguro's *The Remains of the Day* (1989), Ian McEwan's *Atonement* (2001), Helen Humphreys's *The Lost Garden* (2002) and Andrea Levy's *Small Island* (2004), or films like James Ivory's highly acclaimed 1993 adaptation of *The Remains of the Day* and Robert Altman's *Gosford Park* (2001) revisit the domestic landscape once inhabited by the novels of Young, E.M. Delafield, Lettice Cooper, Stella Gibbons, Jan Struther, Elizabeth Bowen and Rosamond Lehmann.

Both films and fiction are manifestations of a revival of interest in this period and a recuperation of the significance of domestic spaces that was heralded by Young in the company of many other domestic novelists. As global networks and transnationalism rapidly transform our lives, it is surely time to turn to the everyday and the home and to locate the construction of identities and subjectivities from within daily life. After all, as Young remarked 'Here, in little, were most of the emotions, preoccupations and duties common to mankind'.

Notes

[1] Quoted by Marilyn Yalom, 'Introduction', George Sand, *Indiana*, 1993: vii.

[2] *The Oxford Dictionary of New Words*, 1997 defines 'Aga saga' as 'A *saga* of family life set against a comfortable background typified by possession of a kitchen with an *Aga* stove, notionally an emblem of middle-class life, and representing a sustained cosiness' (9). See also Deborah Philips, 'Keeping the Home Fires Burning: The Myth of the Independent Woman in the Aga-Saga', 1996: 48–54.

Bibliography

Adam, Ruth (1975), *A Woman's Place 1910–1975*, London: Chatto and Windus.

Anonymous, (undated), Letter to E.H. Young, Young Papers.

Ardener, Shirley (1993), *Women and Space*, Oxford: Berg.

Ardis, Ann, L. (1990), *New Women, New Novels: Feminism and Early Modernism*, New Brunswick, NJ: Rutgers University Press.

Armstrong, Nancy (1987), *Desire and Domestic Fiction: A Political History of the Novel*, New York: Oxford University Press.

Attfield, Judy and Pat Kirkham, eds (1995), *A View from the Interior: Women and Design*, London: The Women's Press.

Austen, Jane (1811, 2001), *Sense and Sensibility*, Peterborough, Ontario: Broadview Press.

—— (1813, 2002), *Pride and Prejudice*, Peterborough, Ontario: Broadview Press.

—— (1814, 2001), *Mansfield Park*, ed. June Sturrock, Peterborough, Ontario: Broadview Press.

—— (1818, 1934), *Persuasion*, London: J.M. Dent.

—— (1979), *Jane Austen's Letters*, ed. R.W. Chapman, Oxford: Oxford University Press.

Bachelard, Gaston (1954, 1994), *The Poetics of Space*, trans. M. Jolas. Boston: Beacon Press.

Bagnold, Enid (1938, 1987), *The Squire*, London: Virago.

Baines, Phil (2005), *Penguin by Design: A Cover Story 1935–2005*, London: Allen Lane, Penguin Books.

Bakhtin, M.M. (1981), *The Dialogic Imagination: Four Essays*, ed. Michael Holquist, trans. Caryl Emerson and Michael Holquist, Austin: University of Texas Press.

Bal, Mieke (1985), *Narratology: Introduction to the Theory of Narrative*, Toronto: University of Toronto Press.

Bammer, Angelika (1992), 'Editorial: The Question of "Home"', *New Formations*, 17 (Summer): vii–xi.

Baudrillard, Jean (2002), 'Structures of Interior Design [1968]', in Ben Highmore, ed., *The Everyday Life Reader*, London: Routledge: 309–18.

Baxendale, John and Christopher Pawling (1996), *Narrating the Thirties. A Decade in the Making: 1930 to the Present*, London: Macmillan.

Bayley, John (1988), 'Introduction', *William* by E.H, Young, London: Virago: v–xv.

Beauman, Nicola (1983), *A Very Great Profession: The Woman's Novel, 1914–1939*, London: Virago.

170 *Domestic Modernism, the Interwar Novel, and E.H. Young*

Beauman, Sally (1984), 'Introduction', *Miss Mole* by E.H. Young, London: Virago: v–xi.

—— (1985a), 'Introduction', *The Misses Mallett* by E.H. Young, Garden City, NY: Dial Press: vii–xvi.

—— (1985b), 'Introduction', *Jenny Wren* by E.H. Young, London: Virago: v–xv.

Beckwith, F. C. (1925), Review of *William* by E.H. Young, *New York Literary Review*, 29 August: 2.

Beddoe, Deidre (1989), *Back to Home and Duty: Women Between the Wars 1918–1939*, London: Pandora.

Beetham, Margaret (1996), *A Magazine of Her Own: Domesticity and Desire in the Woman's Magazine, 1800–1914*, London: Routledge.

Benjamin, David, ed. (1995), *The Home: Words, Interpretations, Meanings, and Environments*, Aldershot: Avebury.

Benjamin, Walter (1973), 'Louis-Philippe or the Interior', in *Charles Baudelaire: A Lyric Poet in the Era of High Capitalism*, trans. Harry Zohn, London: NLB: 167–9.

Bennett, Arnold (1899), 'Mr. George Gissing. An Enquiry', *Academy* 57 (July–December): 224.

—— (1908, 1988), *The Old Wives' Tale*, Harmondsworth: Penguin.

—— (1909), *Literary Taste: How to Form it, with Detailed Instruction for Collecting a Complete Library of English*, London: New Age Press.

—— (1911), *Hilda Lessways*, London: Methuen.

—— (1914), *The Author's Craft*, London: Hodder and Stoughton.

—— (1971), *The Journals*, ed. Frank Swinnerton, Harmondsworth: Penguin.

Bennett, Tony and Diane H. Watson, eds (2002), *Understanding Everyday Life*, Oxford: Blackwell.

The Bentleian 1.4 (Mid-Summer 1950): 13.

Bentley, Phyllis (1934), *A Modern Tragedy*, London: Victor Gollancz.

Berry, Paul and Alan Gordon Bishop, eds (1985), *Testament of a Generation: The Journalism of Vera Brittain and Winifred Holtby*, London: Virago.

Best, Victoria (2002), 'Between the Harem and the Battlefield: Domestic Space in the Work of Assia Djebar', *Signs* 27.3: 873–9.

Betjeman, John (1933, 1970), *Ghastly Good Taste or, a Depressing Story of the Rise and Fall of English Architecture*, London: Anthony Blond.

Bhabha, Homi K. (1997), 'The World and the Home', in Anne McClintock, Aamir Mufti and Ellen Shohat, eds, *Dangerous Liaisons: Gender, Nation, and Postcolonial Perspectives*, Minneapolis: University of Minnesota Press: 445–55.

Bibesco, Elizabeth (1928), Review of *The Vicar's Daughter* by E.H. Young, *The New Statesman*, 20 October: 52–3.

Bird, Jon (1995), 'Dolce Domum', in James Lingwood, ed., *House*, London: Phaidon: 110–25.

Birdwell-Pheasant, Donna and Denise Lawrence-Zuñiga (1999), 'Introduction: Houses and Families in Europe', in Donna Birdwell-Pheasant, ed., *House Life: Space, Place and Family in Europe*, UK: Berg: 1–35.

Bibliography

Blain, Virginia, Patricia Clements and Isobel Grundy, eds (1990), *The Feminist Companion to Literature in English: Women Writers from the Middle Ages to the Present*, London: Batsford.

Blanchot, Maurice (1987), 'Everyday Speech', trans. Susan Hanson, *Yale French Studies* 73: 12–20.

Booker, Michael (2000), Letter to Kathy Mezei, 2 February.

—— (2002), Letter to Kathy Mezei, 10 January.

The Bookseller, Thursday, 8 August 1935.

Borden, Mary (1998), 'Preface', *The Diary of a Provincial Lady* by E.M. Delafield, Chicago: Academy Chicago Publishers: ix–xi.

Boston, Anne, ed. (1994), *Wave Me Goodbye: Stories of the Second World War*, London: Virago.

Bourdieu, Pierre (1990), *The Logic of Practice*, trans. Richard Nice, Cambridge: Polity Press.

Bowen, Elizabeth (1927), *The Hotel*, London: Constable and Co.

—— (1929, 1982), *The Last September*, Harmondsworth: Penguin.

—— (1932, 1999), *To the North*, London: Vintage Classic.

—— (1935), *The House in Paris*, London: Gollancz.

—— (1938, 1949), *The Death of the Heart*, London: Readers Union and Jonathan Cape.

—— (1942, 1964), *Bowen's Court*, London: Longmans, Green and Co.

—— (1980), *The Collected Stories of Elizabeth Bowen*, London: Jonathan Cape.

Boys, Jos (1998), 'Beyond Maps and Metaphors? Re-thinking the Relationships Between Architecture and Gender', in Rosa Ainley, ed., *New Frontiers of Space, Bodies and Gender*, London and New York: Routledge: 203–17.

Bracco, Rosa Maria (1993), *Merchants of Hope: British Middlebrow Writers and the First World War, 1919–1939*, Providence: Berg.

Braybrooke, Neville and June Braybrooke (2004), *Olivia Manning: A Life*, London: Chatto and Windus.

Briganti, Chiara and Kathy Mezei (1999), 'Domestic Novel', in Lorna Sage, ed., *The Cambridge Guide to Women's Writing in English*, Cambridge: Cambridge University Press.

—— (2004), 'House Haunting: The Domestic Novel of the Inter-war Years', *Home Cultures* 1.2: 147–68.

Brontë, Charlotte (1911), *Jane Eyre*, Edinburgh: John Grant.

Bryden, Inga and Janet Floyd, eds (1999), *Domestic Space: Reading the nineteenth-century interior*, Manchester and New York: Manchester University Press.

Buck-Morss, Susan (1989), *The Dialectics of Seeing: Walter Benjamin and the Arcades Project*, Cambridge, MA: MIT Press.

Burnett, John (1986), *A Social History of Housing: 1815–1985*, London: Methuen.

Busch, Akiko (1999), *Geography of Home: Writings on Where We Live*, New York: Princeton Architectural Press.

172   *Domestic Modernism, the Interwar Novel, and E.H. Young*

Cadogan, Mary and Patricia Craig (1978), *Women and Children First: The Fiction of Two World Wars*, London: Gollancz.

Callil, Carmen (2000), E-mail to Chiara Briganti, 6 March.

Cambridge, Elizabeth (1933, 2003), *Hostages to Fortune*, London: Persephone Books.

Cameron, Maude (undated), Letter to E.H. Young, Undated Young Papers.

Cameron, Ronald (1991), *Appeasement and the Road to War*, Glasgow: Pulse Publications.

Carey, John (1992), *The Intellectuals and The Masses: Pride and Prejudice among the Literary Intelligentsia, 1880–1939*, London: Faber and Faber.

Carsten, Janet and Stephen Hugh-Jones, eds (1995), *About the House: Levi-Strauss and Beyond*, Cambridge: Cambridge University Press.

Cather, Willa (1936), 'The Novel Démeublé', *Not Under Forty*, London: Cassell.

Cavaliero, Glen (1977), *The Rural Tradition in the English Novel: 1900–1939*, Totowa, NJ: Rowman and Littlefield

Chandler, Marilyn R. (1991), *Dwelling in the Text: Houses in American Fiction*, Berkeley: University of California Press.

Chapman, R.W, ed. (1979), *Jane Austen's Letters to her Sister Cassandra and Others*, Oxford: Oxford University Press.

Chapman, Tony and Jenny Hockey (1999), 'The Ideal Home as it is Imagined and as it is Lived', in Tony Chapman and Jenny Hockey, eds, *Ideal Homes? Social Change and Domestic Life*, London: Routledge: 1–13.

Christie, Agatha (1930), *The Murder at the Vicarage*, Glasgow: William Collins Sons and Co.

Coggin, Joan (1944, 2003), *Who Killed the Curate?*, Boulder, CO: Rue Morgue Press.

Cohen, Debra Rae (2002), *Remapping the Home Front: Locating Citizenship in British Women's Great War Fiction*, Boston: Northeastern University Press.

Collignon, Beatrice, and Jean-François Staszak (2002), 'Espaces domestiques/ Domestic Spaces Conference', Paris, 17–20 September, <http://www.Cybergeo. presse.fr/actualit/colloq/domspa.htm>.

—— eds (2004), *Espaces domestiques: construire, habiter, représenter*, Paris: Bréal.

Compton-Burnett, Ivy (1925, 1952), *Pastors and Masters*, London: Gollancz.

—— (1951), *A House and Its Head*, London: Eyre and Spottiswoode.

—— (1955), *Mother and Son*, London: Gollancz.

Comyns, Barbara (1950, 2000), *Our Spoons Came from Woolworths*, London: Virago.

Cooper, Lettice (1936, 1987), *The New House*, London: Virago.

Cooperman, Jeannette Batz (1999), *The Broom Closet: Secret Meanings of Domesticity in Postfeminist Novels by Louise Erdrich, Mary Gordon, Toni Morrison, Marge Piercy, Jane Smiley, and Amy Tan*, New York: Peter Lang.

Craig, Patricia, and Mary Cadogan (1981), *The Lady Investigates: Women Detectives and Spies in Fiction*, London: Victor Gollancz.

Bibliography

Cronin, A.J. (1931), *Hatters Castle*, London: Victor Gollancz.

Crowley, John E. (2000), *The Invention of Comfort: Sensibilities and Design in Early Modern Britain and Early America*, Baltimore, MD: The Johns Hopkins University Press.

Cuddy-Keane, Melba (2003), *Virginia Woolf, the Intellectual, and the Public Sphere*, Cambridge: Cambridge University Press.

Danielewski, Mark Z. (2000), *House of Leaves*, London: Anchor.

Davenport, Basil (1934), 'A Writer of Sense and Sensibility', Review of *The Curate's Wife* by E.H. Young, *Saturday Review of Literature*, 17 November: 291.

Davidoff, Leonore (1979), 'The Separation of Home and Work? Landladies and Lodgers in Nineteenth and Twentieth-Century England', in Sandra Burman, ed., *Fit Work for Women*, London: Croom Helm: 64–93.

Davidoff, Leonore, Jean L'Esperance, and Howard Newby (1976), 'Landscape with Figures: Home and Community in English Society', in Juliet Mitchell and Ann Oakley, eds, *The Rights and Wrongs of Women*, Harmondsworth: Penguin: 139–75.

De Beauvoir, Simone (1949,1993), *The Second Sex*, trans. and ed. H.M. Parshley, New York: Alfred A. Knopf.

De Certeau, Michel (1984), *The Practice of Everyday Life*, trans. Steven Rendall. Berkeley: University of California Press.

Deen, Stella (1993), 'Gender Skepticism in Twentieth-Century British Women's Fiction: Developments in and Away from the Domestic Novel', dissertation, University of Virginia.

—— (2000), 'Dream Houses and Twisting Passages: Domestic Consciousness in E.H. Young's *Celia*', in Stella Deen, ed., *'A Great Adventure Enlivened by Countless Minor Episodes': The Life and Work of Emily Hilda Young*, Proceedings of E.H. Young International Conference, June 2000: 21–9.

—— (2001), 'Emily Hilda Young's *Miss Mole*: Female Modernity and the Insufficiencies of the Domestic Novel', *Women's Studies: An Interdisciplinary Journal*, 30.3 (June): 351–68.

—— ed. (2002a), *Challenging Modernism: New Readings in Literature and Culture, 1914–45*, Burlington, VT: Ashgate.

—— (2002b), '"There is No Ordinary Life": Privacy and Domesticity in E.H. Young's *Celia* and Elizabeth Bowen's *The Death of the Heart*', in Stella Deen, ed., *Challenging Modernism: New Readings in Literature and Culture, 1914–1945*, Burlington, VT: Ashgate: 97–114.

—— (2003), '"So Minute and Yet So Alive": Domestic Modernity in E.H. Young's *William*', *Tulsa Studies in Women's Literature*, 22.1 (Spring 2003): 99–120.

—— (2004), 'E.H. Young' in *Dictionary of National Biography*, Oxford University Press, <http://www.oxforddnb.com/view/article/56897>.

Delafield, E.M. (1919, 2000), *Consequences*, London: Persephone Books.

—— (1923), *Messalina of the Suburbs*, London: Hutchinson and Co.

—— (1927), *The Way Things Are*, London: Hutchinson.

174 *Domestic Modernism, the Interwar Novel, and E.H. Young*

—— (1930, 1998), *The Diary of a Provincial Lady*, Chicago: Academy Chicago Publishers.

—— (1932, 1989), *Thank Heaven Fasting*, London: Macmillan; Virago.

—— (1934), Review of *The Curate's Wife* by E.H. Young, *Now and Then* (Winter): 34.

—— (1939), *Three Marriages*, London: Macmillan.

Delany, Paul (2004), *Bill Brandt: A Biography*, London: Jonathan Cape.

Denny, Norman (1947), *Sweet Confusion*, London: John Lane [The Bodley Head].

Derrida, Jacques (1994), *Specters of Marx: The State of the Debt, the Work of Mourning, and the New International*, trans. Peggy Kamuf, London: Routledge.

—— (1997), 'Architecture Where the Desire May Live (Interview)', in Neil Leach, ed., *Rethinking Architecture: A Reader in Cultural Theory*, London: Routledge: 319–23.

Després, Carole (1991), 'The Meaning of Home: Literature Review and Directions for Future Research and Theoretical Development', *Journal of Architectural and Planning Research. Special Issue: The Meaning and Use of Home*, guest ed. Roderick J. Lawrence, 8.2 (Summer): 96–115.

De Wolfe, Elsie (1913), *The House in Good Taste*, New York: Century Co.

Dickens, Charles (1853), *Bleak House*, London: Bradbury and Evans.

Dickinson, Emily (1955), *The Poems of Emily Dickinson*, Vol. II, ed. Thomas H. Johnson, Cambridge: Harvard University Press.

Disraeli, Benjamin (1845, 1853), *Sybil, etc.*, Paris: A. and W. Galignani and Co; London: David Bryce.

Donald, Moira (1999),'Tranquil Havens? Critiquing the Idea of Home as the Middle-class Sanctuary', in Inga Bryden and Janet Floyd, eds, *Domestic Space: Reading the nineteenth-century interior*, Manchester and New York: Manchester University Press: 103–20.

Douglas, Mary (1991), 'The Idea of a Home: A Kind of Space', *Social Research* 58.1 (Spring): 287–307.

Douglas, Roy (1977), *In the Year of Munich*, New York: St Martin's Press.

Drew, Elizabeth (1935), *The Enjoyment of Literature*, New York: W.W. Norton & Co.; Cambridge: Cambridge University Press.

Du Maurier, Daphne (1938), *Rebecca*, New York: Doubleday.

Duncan, James (1981), 'From Container of Women to Status Symbol: The Impact of Social Structure on the Meaning of the House', in James S. Duncan, ed., *Housing and Identity: Cross-cultural Perspectives*, London: Croom Helm: 36–59.

Eckersley, A. (1910), Review of *A Corn of Wheat* by E.H. Young, *Punch* 17 August: 108.

Eliot, George (1871–72, 1956), *Middlemarch*, Cambridge, MA: The Riverside Press.

Ellmann, Maud (2001), 'Elizabeth Bowen: The Shadowy Fifth', in Rod Mengham and N.H. Reeve, eds, *The Fiction of the 1940s: Stories of Survival*, London: Palgrave: 1–25.

Bibliography 175

—— (2003), *Elizabeth Bowen: The Shadow Across the Page*, New York: Columbia University Press.

Fallows, Christopher (2005), E-mail correspondence with Kathy Mezei, 1 August.

Felski, Rita (1999), 'The Invention of Everyday Life', *New Formations* 39 (1999–2000): 15–31.

Fish, Stanley (1980), *Is There a Text in This Class? The Authority of Interpretive Communities*, Cambridge: Harvard University Press.

Flanders, Judith (2003), *The Victorian House: Domestic Life From Childbirth to Deathbed*, London: Harpers Perennial.

Ford, Boris, ed. (1988), *The Cambridge Guide to the Arts in Britain*, Cambridge: Cambridge University Press.

Forster, E.M. (1910, 1921), *Howards End*, Garden City, NY: Garden City Publishing Company.

—— (1924, 1931), *A Passage to India*, London: Arnold.

Forty, Adrian (2002), *Objects of Desire: Design and Society Since 1750*, London: Thames and Hudson.

Foucault, Michel (1997), 'Of Other Spaces: Utopias and Heterotopias', in Neil Leach, ed., *Rethinking Architecture: A Reader in Cultural Theory*, London: Routledge: 350–56.

Fowler, Bridget (1997), *Pierre Bourdieu and Cultural Theory: Critical Investigations*, London: Sage.

Frank, Ellen Eve (1979), *Literary Architecture: Essays Towards a Tradition, Walter Pater, Gerard Manley Hopkins, Marcel Proust, Henry James*, Berkeley: University of California Press.

Freud, Sigmund (1916–1917, 1973), *Introductory Lectures on Psychoanalysis*, trans. James Strachey, Harmondsworth: Penguin.

—— (1955), 'The Uncanny', *The Standard Edition of the Complete Psychological Works of Sigmund Freud*, ed. and trans. James Strachey. 24 vols. Vol. 17 (1917–19), London: Hogarth Press, pp. 217–52.

Fritz, Meike (2001), 'The Apostle of Quiet People: Die Schriftstellerin E.H. Young', dissertation, Berlin Technical University.

—— (2002), *The Apostle of Quiet People: Die Schriftstellerin E.H. Young und ihre Romane als Beispiel populärer Frauenliteratur der englischen Mittelschicht in der ersten Hälfte des 20 Jahrhunderts*, Frankfurt am Main: Peter Lang.

Fuss, Diana (1998), 'Interior Chambers: The Emily Dickinson Homestead', *Differences: A Journal of Feminist Cultural Studies*, 10.3: 1–46.

—— (2004), *Four Rooms and the Writers That Shaped Them*, New York and London: Routledge.

Fussell, Paul (1980), *Abroad: British Literary Travelling Between the Wars*, New York: Oxford University Press.

Gale, Maggie B. (2000), 'Women Playwrights of the 1920s and 1930s', in Elaine Aston and Janelle Reinelt, eds, *The Cambridge Companion to Modern British Women Playwrights*, Cambridge: Cambridge University Press: 23–37.

176   *Domestic Modernism, the Interwar Novel, and E.H. Young*

Gale, Matthew (2004), 'Still Life/Object/Real Life Suite', 'Art of the Everyday' Collection, Tate Modern, December.

Gamelin, Lionel (1945), Producer, 'The Way You Look At It', BBC 'Home Life', Monday 12 November, Gladys Young Files, 1945–6, BBC Written Archives.

Garber, Marjorie (2000), *Sex and Real Estate: Why We Love Houses*, New York: Pantheon Books.

Gaskell, Elizabeth (1853, 1993), *Cranford*, Ware: Wordsworth Editions.

Gasiorek, Andrzej (1995), *Post-War British Fiction: Realism and After*, London: Edward Arnold.

Genette, Gèrard (1980), *Narrative Discourse*, trans. Jane E. Lewin, Ithaca, NY: Cornell University Press.

George, Rosemary Marangoly (1996), *The Politics of Home: Postcolonial Relocations and Twentieth-Century Fiction*, Cambridge: Cambridge University Press.

Gibbons, Stella (1932, 2000), *Cold Comfort Farm*, Harmondsworth: Penguin.

—— (1934, 1946), *Bassett*, London: Longmans, Green and Co.

—— (1938), *Nightingale Wood*, London: Longmans, Green and Co.

—— (1944), *The Bachelor*, London: Longmans, Green and Co.

—— (1946), *Westwood, or the Gentle Powers*, London: Longmans, Green and Co.

Giles, Judy (1995), *Women, Identity and Private Life in Britain, 1900–50*, London: Macmillan.

—— (2004), *The Parlour and the Suburb: Domestic Identities, Class, Femininity and Modernity*, Oxford: Berg.

—— and Tim Middleton, eds (1995), *Writing Englishness 1900–1950: An Introductory Sourcebook on National Identity*, London: Routledge.

Gill, Richard (1972), *Happy Rural Seat: The English Country House and the Literary Imagination*, New Haven: Yale University Press.

Giltrow, Janet (1995), *Academic Writing: Reading and Writing Across the Disciplines*, Peterborough, Ontario: Broadview Press.

Girard, René (1976), *Deceit, Desire, and the Novel*, trans. Yvonne Freccero, Baltimore, MD: The Johns Hopkins University Press.

Goldsmith, Oliver (1766, 1908), *Vicar of Wakefield*, London: J.M. Dent.

Gornick, Vivian (1997), *The End of the Novel of Love*, Boston: Beacon Press.

Gotch, David (1969 or 1970), Letter to Glen Cavaliero, 2 June.

Gouldner, Alvin W. (1975), 'Sociology and the Everyday Life', in Lewis A. Coser, ed., *The Idea of Social Science*, New York: Harcourt Brace Jovanovich: 417–32.

Grant Charlotte, 'Reading the House of Fiction: From Object to Interior 1720–1920', *Home Cultures, Special Issue: The Domestic Interior in British Literature*, guest ed. Charlotte Grant, 2:3 (November 2005): 233–49.

Graves, Robert (1934), *I, Claudius*, London: Barker.

—— and Alan Hodge (1941), *The Long Week-end: A Social History of Great Britain, 1918–1939*, Macmillan: New York.

Green, Henry (1948), *Loving: A Novel*, London: Hogarth Press.

Greene, Graham (1934), Review of *The Curate's Wife* by E.H. Young, *The Spectator*, 7 September: 336.

Bibliography

Grierson, John, *Fortnightly Review*, August 1939, quoted in Forsyth Hardy, ed. (1966), 'Introduction', *Grierson on Documentary*, London: Faber and Faber.

Gunn, Kirsty (2005), 'Cooking up a Storm', *The Guardian*, 26 March, G2: 36.

Hall, Radclyffe (1924, 1981), *The Unlit Lamp*, London: Virago.

Hamilton, Cicely (1909, 1981), *Marriage as a Trade*, London: The Women's Press.

Hamon, Philippe (1989), *Expositions: Littérature et Architecture au XIXe Siècle*, Paris: José Corti.

Hanson, Claire (1990), 'Introduction to Katherine Mansfield', in Bonnie Kime Scott, ed., *The Gender of Modernism: A Critical Anthology*, Bloomington: Indiana University Press: 298–305.

—— (2000), *Hysterical Fictions and the Woman's Novel in the Twentieth Century*, Basingstoke: Macmillan.

Hapgood, Lynne and Nancy L. Paxton, eds (2000), *Outside Modernism: In Pursuit of the English Novel, 1900–30*, New York: St Martin's Press.

Harbison, Robert (2000), *Eccentric Spaces*, Cambridge: MIT Press.

Hardy, Forsyth, ed. (1966), 'Introduction', *Grierson on Documentary*, London: Faber and Faber.

Hardy, Thomas (1896), *Jude the Obscure*, New York: Harper.

Hare, Steve, ed. (1995), 'The War Broadcasts', *Penguin Portrait: Allen Lane and the Penguin Editors, 1935–1970*, London and New York: Penguin.

Hareven, Tamara K. (1991), 'The Home and the Family in Historical Perspective', *Social Research*, 58.1: 1–46.

Harris, Steven (1997), 'Everyday Architecture', in Steven Harris and Deborah Berke, eds, *Architecture of the Everyday*, New York: Princeton Architectural Press: 1–8.

Hartley, Jenny, ed. (1994), *Hearts Undefeated: Women's Writing of the Second World War*, London: Virago.

—— (1997), *Millions Like Us: British Women's Fiction of the Second World War*. London: Virago.

Hartley, L.P. (1930), Review of *The Voyage Home* by Storm Jameson, *Saturday Review*, 1 February 1930: 144.

Haughton, Hugh (1999), 'Introduction', *To the North* by Elizabeth Bowen, London: Vintage Classic: vii–xix.

Hastings, Selina (2002), *Rosamond Lehmann*, London: Chatto and Windus.

Head, Alice M, ed. (1932), *Twelve Best Stories from Good Housekeeping*, London: Ivor, Nicholson and Watson.

Hecht, Anat (2001), 'Home Sweet Home: Tangible Memories of an Uprooted Childhood', in Daniel Miller, ed., *Home Possessions: Material Culture Behind Closed Doors*, Oxford: Berg: 123–45.

Hegglund, Jon (1997), 'Defending the Realm: Domestic Space and Mass Cultural Contamination in *Howards End* and *An Englishman's Home*, *English Literature in Transition* 40:4: 398-401.

Heidegger, Martin (1997), 'Building, Dwelling, Thinking', in Neil Leach, ed., *Rethinking Architecture: A Reader in Cultural Theory*, London: Routledge: 100–109.

178   *Domestic Modernism, the Interwar Novel, and E.H. Young*

—— (1997), '… Poetically Man Dwells …', in Neil Leach, ed., *Rethinking Architecture: A Reader in Cultural Theory*, London: Routledge: 109–19.

Heller, Agnes (1984), *Everyday Life*, London: Routledge.

Henderson, Ralph (1950), 'E.H. Young – An Appreciation', *The Bentleian*, 1C.4 Mid-Summer: 11.

—— (n.d.), 'E.H. Young as a Mountaineer', Young Papers.

—— (n.d.), '*E.H. Young*, her Muse, her Method & her Message', ts. 8 pp, Young Papers.

Hewlett, Maurice Henry (1898), *The Forest Lovers: A Romance*, London: Macmillan.

Highmore, Ben (2002a), *Everyday Life and Cultural Theory*, London: Routledge.

—— ed. (2002b), *The Everyday Life Reader*, London: Routledge.

Higonnet, Anne (1992), *Berthe Morisot's Images of Women*, Cambridge: Harvard University Press.

Hodgson, Vere (1976,1999), *Few Eggs and No Oranges: A Diary Showing How Unimportant People in London and Birmingham Lived Through the War Years 1940– 45, Written in the Notting Hill Area of London*, London: Persephone Books.

Holtby, Winifred (1924), *The Crowded Street*, London: John Lane.

—— (1931, 1985), *Poor Caroline*, London: Virago.

—— (1935), 'What We Read and Why We Read It', *The Left Review* 1.4 (January): 111–14.

—— (1936), *South Riding: An English Landscape*, London: Collins.

Home Cultures, Special Issue: The Domestic Interior in British Literature, guest ed. Charlotte Grant, 2:3 (November 2005).

hooks, bell (1991), 'Homeplace: A Site of Resistance', *Yearning: Race, Gender, and Cultural Politics*, London: Turnaround.

Howard, Elizabeth Jane (1990–1995), *The Cazelet Chronicle*, 4 vols (*The Light Years*, 1990; *Marking Time*, 1991; *Confusion*, 1993; *Casting Off*, 1995), London: Macmillan.

Howard, Michael S. (1971), *Jonathan Cape, Publisher*, London: Jonathan Cape.

Howell, Signe (2003), 'The House as Analytic Concept: A Theoretical Overview', in Stephen Sparkes and Signe Howell, eds, *The House in Southeast Asia: A Changing Social, Economic and Political Domain*, London: Routledge Curzon: 16–33.

Hudson, Derek (1964), 'Reading', in Simon Nowell-Smith, ed., *Edwardian England*, Oxford: Oxford University Press: 303–26.

Humble, Nicola (2001), *The Feminine Middlebrow Novel: 1920s to 1950s: Class, Domesticity and Bohemianism*, Oxford: Oxford University Press.

Humphreys, Helen (2002), *The Lost Garden*, Toronto: HarperFlamingoCanada.

Huxley, Aldous (1923, 1997), *Antic Hay*, Normal, IL: Dalkey Archive Press.

Huxley, Elspeth (1968), *Love Among the Daughters: Memories of the Twenties in England and America*, New York: William Morrow.

Huyssen, Andreas (1986a), *After the Great Divide: Modernism, Mass Culture, Postmodernism*, Bloomington: Indiana University Press.

Bibliography

—— (1986b), 'Mass Culture as Woman: Modernism's Other', in Tania Modleski, ed., *Studies in Entertainment: Critical Approaches to Mass Culture*, Bloomington: Indiana University Press: 188–207.

H.W.E. (1933), Review of *Jenny Wren* by E.H. Young, *Boston Evening Transcript*, 25 February: 1.

Ingman, Heather (1998), *Women's Fiction Between the Wars: Mothers, Daughters, and Writing*, Edinburgh: Edinburgh University Press.

Ishiguro, Kazuo (1989), *The Remains of the Day*, New York: Knopf.

Jackson, Margaret (1994), *The Real Facts of Life: Feminism and the Politics of Sexuality, 1850–1940*, London: Taylor and Francis.

James, Henry (1917), *Portrait of a Lady*, New York: P.F. Collier and Son.

—— (1957), *The House of Fiction: Essays on the Novel*, ed. and with intro. Leon Edel, London: R. Hart-Davis.

Jameson, Frederic (1999), 'Is Space Political?', in Neil Leach, ed., *Rethinking Architecture: A Reader in Cultural Theory*, London: Routledge: 255–69.

Jameson, Storm (1924), *The Pitiful Wife*, London: Constable.

—— (1926), *Three Kingdoms*, London: Constable.

—— (1927), *The Lovely Ship*, London: Heinemann.

—— (1929), *The Georgian Novel and Mr. Robinson*, London: Morrow.

—— (1931) *A Richer Dust*, London: Heinemann.

—— (1933, 1982), *A Day Off*, London: Virago, 1982.

—— (1933), *No Time Like the Present*, London: Cassell.

—— (1934), *Company Parade*, London: Cassell.

—— (1935), *Love in Winter*, London: Cassell.

—— (1936), *None Turn Back*, London: Cassell.

—— (1938), *The Moon Is Making*, London: Cassell.

—— (1939), *The Voyage Home*, London: Heinemann.

—— (1945), *The Journal of Mary Hervey Russell*, New York: Macmillan.

—— (1969, 1984), *Journey from the North* I, London: Virago.

Jenkins, David Fraser and Chris Stephens, eds (2004), *Gwen John and Augustus John*, London: Tate.

Jesse, F. Tennyson (1934, 1979), *A Pin to See the Peepshow*, London: Virago.

Joannou, Maroula (1995), *'Ladies, Please Don't Smash These Windows': Women's Writing, Feminist Consciousness and Social Change, 1918–1938*, Oxford and Providence: Berg.

—— ed. (1999), *Women Writers of the 1930s*, Edinburgh: Edinburgh University Press.

Johnson, George M. (1998), *Dictionary of Literary Biography*, Vol. 191, Detroit: Gale Research.

Johnson, Lesley (1996), 'As Housewives, We Are Worms', *Cultural Studies* 10.3: 449–63.

Jung, C.G. (1963), *Memories, Dreams, Reflections*, trans. Richard and Clara Winston, New York: Pantheon Books.

180   *Domestic Modernism, the Interwar Novel, and E.H. Young*

Kaplan, Alice and Kristin Ross (1987), 'Introduction', *Yale French Studies: Everyday Life* 73: 1–4.

Kaplan, Caren (1987), 'Deterritorializations: The Rewriting of Home and Exile in Western Feminist Discourse', *Cultural Critique* 6 (Spring): 187–98.

Kaplan, Carola M, and Anne B. Simpson, eds (1996), *Seeing Double: Revisioning Edwardian and Modernist Literature*, New York: St Martin's Press.

Kaye-Smith, Sheila (1916), *Sussex Gorse*, London: Nisbet and Co.

Kemp, Sandra, C. Mitchell, and D. Trotter, eds (1997), *Edwardian Fiction: An Oxford Companion*, Oxford: Oxford University Press.

Keith, Rhonda (1985), 'Flora Macdonald Mayor', in *Dictionary of Literary Biography* 36 'British Novelists, 1890–1929: Modernists', ed. Thomas F. Staley, Detroit, MI: Bruccoli Clark: 169–71.

Kennedy, Margaret (1925), *The Constant Nymph*, Garden City, NY: Doubleday.

King, Mary (1925), Letter to E.H. Young, 16 October, Young Papers.

Kipling, Rudyard (1917), 'Mary Postgate', *The Works of Rudyard Kipling*, Vol. XXVI, New York: Scribner's: 489–513.

—— (1926), 'The Janeites', *The Writings in Prose and Verse of Rudyard Kipling*, Vol. XXXI, New York: Scribner's: 159–89.

Kirkpatrick, D.L. (1976), *Contemporary Novelists: The Longman Companion to Twentieth Century Literature*, ed. James Vincent, New York: St Martin's Press.

Knapp, Bettina (1986), *Archetype, Architecture, and the Writer*, Bloomington: Indiana University Press.

Knight, Stephen (2004), *Crime Fiction: 1800–2000*, London: Palgrave.

Kunitz, Stanley J. and Howard Haycraft, eds (1942), *Twentieth Century Authors: A Biographical Dictionary of Modern Literature*, New York: H.W. Wilson.

Kunitz, Stanley J. and Vineta Colby, eds (1955), *Twentieth Century Authors: First Supplement. A Biographical Dictionary of Modern Literature.* New York: H.W. Wilson.

Lacour, Claudia Brodsky (1996), *Lines of Thought: Discourse, Architectonics, and the Origin of Modern Philosophy*, Durham: Duke University Press.

Laing, Stuart (1955), 'Presenting "Things As They Are": John Sommerfield s *May Day* and Mass Observation', in Frank Gloversmith, ed., *Class, Culture, and Social Change: A New View of the 1930s*, Brighton: Harvester Press: 142–60.

Lancaster, Osbert (1939, 1948), *Homes Sweet Homes*, London: John Murray.

Lane, Allen (1935a), 'All About the Penguin Books', *The Bookseller*, 22 May: 497.

—— (1935b), *The Bookseller*, 8 August: 767.

Lane, Maggie (2000), 'E.H. Young Conference', Bristol, UK, 17 June.

Langhamer, Claire (2000), *Women's Leisure in England, 1920–60*, Manchester: Manchester University Press.

Langbauer, Laurie (1999), *Novels of Everyday Life: The Series in English Fiction, 1850–1930*, Ithaca: Cornell University Press.

Lassner, Phyllis (1998), *British Women Writers of World War II: Battlegrounds of Their Own*, London: Macmillan.

Bibliography

Last, Nella (1983), *Nella Last's War: A Mother's Diary, 1939–45*, ed. Richard Broad and Suzie Fleming, London: Sphere.

Laville, Sandra (2005), 'Women Writers: Dull, Depressed and Domestic', *The Guardian*, 23 March: 1.

Lawrence, D.H. (1928, 1994), *Lady Chatterley's Lover*, Harmondsworth: Penguin.

Lawrence, Margaret (1936, 1966), *The School of Femininity: A Book For and About Women As They Are Interpreted Through Feminine Writers of Yesterday and Today*, Port Washington, NY: Kennikat Press.

Lawrence (Greene), Margaret (1937), *We Write As Women*, London: M. Joseph.

Lawrence, Roderick, J. (1991), 'The Meaning and Use of Home', *Journal of Architectural and Planning Research, Special Issue: The Meaning and Use of Home*, guest ed. Roderick J. Lawrence. 8.2 (Summer): 91–5.

—— (1995), 'Deciphering Home: An Integrative Historical Perspective', in David Benjamin, ed., *The Home: Words, Interpretations, Meanings, and Environments*, Aldershot: Avebury: 53–68.

Lawson, Nigella (2000), *How to be a Domestic Goddess: Baking and the Art of Comfort*, London: Chatto and Windus.

Leach, Neil, ed. (1997), *Rethinking Architecture: A Reader in Cultural Theory*, London: Routledge.

Leavis, Q.D. (1932, 1979), *Fiction and the Reading Public*, Harmondsworth: Penguin Books.

Ledger, Sally (1997), *The New Woman: Fiction and Feminism at the Fin de Siècle*, Manchester: Manchester University Press; New York: St Martin's Press.

Lee, Hermione (1981, 1999), *Elizabeth Bowen*, London: Vintage.

Lefebvre, Henri (1971), *Everyday Life in the Modern World*, trans. Sacha Rabinovitch, London: Penguin.

—— (1991), *Critique of Everyday Life*, trans. John Moore, London: Verso.

—— (1997), 'The Everyday and Everydayness', in Steven Harris and Deborah Berke, eds, *Architecture of the Everyday*, New York: Princeton Architectural Press: 32–7.

Lehmann, Rosamond (1927), *Dusty Answer*, New York: Reynal and Hitchcock.

—— (1930), *A Note in Music*, London: Chatto and Windus.

—— (1932, 1975), *Invitation to the Waltz*, New York: Harcourt Brace Jovanovich.

—— (1953), *The Echoing Grove*, London: Collins.

Leverson, Ada (1982), *The Little Ottleys*, (*Love's Shadow* [1908], *Tenterhooks* [1912], *Love at Second Sight* [1916]), London: Virago.

Levy, Andrea (2004), *Small Island*, London: Headline Book Publishing Ltd.

Lewis, Jane (1980), 'In Search of a Real Equality: Women Between the Wars', in Frank Gloversmith, ed., *Class, Culture, and Social Change: A New View of the 1930s*, Sussex: Harvest Press: 208–239.

Lichenstein, Rachel and Iain Sinclair (1999), *Rodinsky's Room*, London: Granta.

Light, Alison (1991), *Forever England: Femininity, Literature, and Conservatism Between the Wars*, London: Routledge.

182 *Domestic Modernism, the Interwar Novel, and E.H. Young*

Lively, Penelope (2001), *A House Unlocked*, London: Viking.

Loveman, Amy (1938), 'An Artist in Living', *Saturday Review of Literature* 17.4 (19 February): 330.

Lucas, John (1974), *Arnold Bennett: A Study of His Fiction*, London: Methuen.

Lukacs, John (1970), 'The Bourgeois Interior', *American Scholar* 39: 616–30.

Luria, Sara (1999), 'The Architecture of Manners: Henry James, Edith Wharton and The Mount', in Inga Bryden and Janet Floyd, eds, *Domestic Space: Reading the nineteenth-century interior*, Manchester and New York: Manchester University Press: 189–90.

Lyotard, Jean-François (1999), '*Domus* and the Megalopolis', in Neil Leach, ed., *Rethinking Architecture: A Reader in Cultural Theory*, London: Routledge: 271–9.

McAleer, Joseph (1992), *Popular Reading and Publishing in Britain 1914–1950*, Oxford: Clarendon Press; New York: Oxford University Press.

Macaulay, Rose (1921, 1985), *Dangerous Ages*, London: Methuen

—— (1926), *Crewe Train*, New York: Boni and Liveright.

—— (1928), *Keeping up Appearances*, London: W. Collins.

McCaffey, Larry and Gregory Sinda (2003), '*Haunted House*: An Interview with Mark Z. Danielewski', *Critique* (Winter) 44.2: 99–135,

Macdonald, Myra (2004), 'From Mrs Happyman to Kissing Chaps Goodbye: Advertising Reconstructs Femininity', in C. Carter and L. Steiner, eds, *Critical Readings: Media and Gender*, Maidenhead: Open University Press: 41–67.

McDowell, Linda (1999), *Gender, Identity, and Place: Understanding Feminist Geographies*, Cambridge: Polity Press.

—— (2002), 'Unsettling Naturalisms', *Signs* 27.3 (March): 815–22.

McEwan, Ian (2001), *Atonement*, London: Jonathan Cape.

Mackail, Denis (1925), *Greenery Street*, London: Heinemann.

McKeon, Michael (1987), *The Origins of the English Novel, 1600–1740*, Baltimore: The Johns Hopkins University Press.

McLeod, Mary (1997), 'Henri Lefebvre's Critique of Everyday Life: An Introduction', in Steven Harris and Deborah Berke, eds, *Architecture of the Everyday*, New York: Princeton Architectural Press: 9–29.

Macheski, Cecilia (1988), 'Elizabeth Taylor, The Novelist, Of Course', *Barbara Pym Newsletter*, 5 June.

Mallet-Joris, Françoise (1970), *La maison de papier*, Paris: Grasset.

Mansfield, Katherine (1954), *Journal of Katherine Mansfield*, ed. J. Middleton Murry, London: Constable.

—— (2002), *Selected Stories*, ed. and with intro. Angela Smith, Oxford: Oxford University Press.

Marcus, Clare Cooper (1995), *House as a Mirror of Self: Exploring the Deeper Meaning of Home*, Berkeley: Conari Press.

Marcus, Sharon (1999), *Apartment Stories: City and Home in Nineteenth-Century Paris and London*, Berkeley: University of California Press.

Bibliography

Martin, Biddy and Chandra Talpade Mohanty (1986), 'Feminist Politics: What's Home Got to Do With It?', in Teresa de Lauretis, ed., *Feminist Studies/Cultural Studies*. Bloomington: Indiana University Press: 191–212.

Maslen, Elizabeth (2001), *Political and Social Issues in British Women's Fiction, 1928–1968*, London: Palgrave.

Mass-Observation (1943), *Enquiry into People's Homes* [*A Report prepared by Mass-Observation for The Advertising Service Guild*], London: John Murray.

Maugham, W. Somerset (1932, 1967), 'For Services Rendered', *Modern Plays*, London: Dent: 291–354.

Mayor, F.M. (1918, 1980), *The Third Miss Symons*, London: Virago.

—— (1924, 1987), *The Rector's Daughter*, London: Virago.

—— (1929, 1987), *The Squire's Daughter*, London: Virago.

Mendelson, Cheryl (1999), *Home Comforts: The Art and Science of Keeping House*, New York: Prentice Hall.

Mengham, Rod (2000), 'Innervisions', in Iwona Blazwick and Simon Wilson, eds, *Tate Modern Handbook*, London: Tate Publishing.

—— (2001a), 'Bourgeois News: Humphrey Jennings and Charles Madge', *New Formations* 44 (Autumn): 26–33.

—— (2001b), 'Broken Glass', in Rod Mengham and N.H. Reeve, eds, *The Fiction of the 1940s: Stories of Survival*, London: Palgrave: 124–33.

Meyers, Jeffrey (2004), *Somerset Maugham: A Life*, New York: Alfred A. Knopf.

Meynell, Viola (1910), *Martha Vine: A Love Story of Simple Life*, London: Herbert and Daniel.

—— (1911), *Cross-in-Hand Farm*, London: Herbert and Daniel.

—— (1913), *Lot Barrow*, London: Secker.

—— (1914), *Modern Lovers*, London: Badger.

Mezei Kathy, with Mark Ihnat and Wendy Thompson, <http://www.sfu.ca/domestic-space>.

Mezei, Kathy and Chiara Briganti (1999a), 'Domestic Novel', in Lorna Sage, ed., *The Cambridge Guide to Women's Writing in English*, Cambridge: Cambridge University Press: 197.

—— (1999b), 'E.H. Young', in Lorna Sage, ed., *The Cambridge Guide to Women's Writing in English*, Cambridge: Cambridge University Press: 686.

—— (2000a), 'Reading the House: A Literary Perspective', *Signs* 27.3: 837–46.

—— eds (2000b), 'Forum: Domestic Space', *Signs* 27.3 (March): 813–900.

—— (2001), '"She Must be a Very Good Novelist", Re-reading E.H. Young (1880–1949)', *English Studies in Canada* 27: 303–31.

Milburn, Clara (1981), *Mrs. Milburn's Diaries: An Englishwoman's Day-to-Day Reflections 1939–45*, ed. Peter Donnelly, London: Fontana/Collins.

Miller, Betty (1941, 2000), *Farewell to Leicester Square*, London: Persephone Books.

—— (1945, 1985), *On the Side of the Angels*, London: Virago.

Miller, Daniel, ed. (2001), *Home Possessions: Material Culture Behind Closed Doors*, Oxford: Berg.

184   *Domestic Modernism, the Interwar Novel, and E.H. Young*

Miller, Jane Eldridge (1994), *Rebel Women: Feminism, Modernism and the Edwardian Novel*, London: Virago.

Mitchell, Juliet and Ann Oakley, eds (1976), *The Rights and Wrongs of Women*, Harmondsworth: Penguin.

Mitchison, Naomi (1986), *Among You Taking Notes: The Wartime Diary of Naomi Mitchison, 1939–1945*, ed. Dorothy Sheridan, Oxford: Oxford University Press.

Modleski, Tania (1982), *Loving with a Vengeance*, Hampden, CT: Archon Books.

Montefiore, Janet (1996), *Men and Women Writers of the 1930s: The Dangerous Flood of History*, London: Routledge.

Mooney, Bel (1987), 'Afterword', *Chatterton Square*, London: Virago: 369–78.

Moorhouse, Paul (2000), 'Still Life/Object/Real Life', in Iwona Blazwick and Simon Wilson, eds, *Tate Modern Handbook*, London: Tate Publishing: 58–73.

Moran, Joe (2004), 'Housing, Memory and Everyday Life in Contemporary Britain', *Cultural Studies* 18.4 (July): 607–27.

Morgan, Geneviève Sanchis (1997), 'The Hostess and the Seamstress: Virginia Woolf's Creation of a Domestic Modernism', in Elizabeth Jane Harrison and Shirley Peterson, eds, *Unmanning Modernism: Gendered Re-Readings*, Knoxville: University of Tennessee Press: 90–104.

Morley, David (2000), *Home Territories, Media, Mobility and Identity*, London: Routledge.

Muthesius, Hermann (1904, 1979), *The English House*, trans. J. Seligman, London: Crosby, Lockwood Staples.

Nesbitt, Jennifer Poulos (2005), *Narrative Settlements: Geographies of British Women's Fiction between the Wars*, Toronto: University of Toronto Press.

Norquay, Glenda, ed. (1999), *R.L. Stevenson on Fiction: An Anthology of Literary and Critical Essays*, Edinburgh: Edinburgh University Press.

Norwood, Gilbert (1929), Review of *The Vicar's Daughter* by E.H. Young, *The Canadian Forum* 9.104 (May): 288.

Obituary (1949), 'Miss E.H. Young', *The Times*, Wednesday 10 August: 3.

O'Brien, Edward J., ed. (1933), *The Best Short Stories: 1933*, London: Jonathan Cape.

O'Brien, Kate (1931), *Without My Cloak*, London, Heinemann.

Oliphant, Margaret (1986), *Chronicles of Carlingford*, London, Virago.

Oliver, Paul, Ian Davis and Ian Bentley (1981), *Dunroamin: The Suburban Semi and its Enemies*, London: Barrie and Jenkins.

Olson, Liesl M. (2002–2003), 'Virginia Woolf's "Cotton Wool of Daily Life"', *Journal of Modern Literature* 26.3 (Winter): 42–65.

Orwell, George (1935, 1986), *A Clergyman's Daughter, The Compete Works of George Orwell*, Vol. 3, ed. Peter Davison, London: Secker and Warburg.

—— (1936, 1962), *Keep the Aspidistra Flying*, Harmondsworth: Penguin Books.

—— (1968), 'Review of Penguin Books', *The Collected Essays, Journalism and Letters of George Orwell: An Age Like This, 1920–1940*, Vol. 1. *(New English Weekly* 5 March 1936), ed. Sonia Orwell and Ian Angus, New York: Harcourt Brace and World: 165–7.

Bibliography

—— (1968), 'The English People', *The Collected Essays, Journalism and Letters of George Orwell: As I Please, 1943–1945*, Vol. III, ed. Sonia Orwell and Ian Angus. New York: Harcourt Brace and World: 1–38.

Osborne, Peter (1995), *The Politics of Time: Modernity and Avant-Garde*, Verso: London.

Oxford Dictionary of New Words (1997), ed. Elizabeth Knowles and Julia Elliott, Oxford and New York: Oxford University Press.

Pain, G.C. (1943), *Surplus Women*, London: John Gifford.

Panter-Downes, Mollie (1947, 1985), *One Fine Day*, London: Virago.

Papastergiadis, Nikos (1998), *Dialogues in the Diasporas: Essays and Conversations on Cultural Identity*, London: Rivers Oram Press/Pandora.

Parker, Peter, ed. (1994), *The Reader's Companion to the Twentieth-Century Novel*, London: Fourth Estate/Helicon.

Pater, Walter (1889,1967), *Appreciations, With an Essay on Style*, Oxford: Blackwell.

Paxton, Nancy L. (2000), 'Eclipsed by Modernism', in Lynne Hapgood and Nancy L. Paxton, eds, *Outside Modernism: In Pursuit of the English Novel, 1900–30*, Basingstoke: Macmillan: 3–21.

Pellin, Henry (1968), *Popular Politics and Society in Late Victorian Britain*, London: Macmillan.

Philips, Deborah (1996), 'Keeping the Home Fires Burning: The Myth of the Independent Woman in the Aga-Saga', *Women: A Cultural Review* 7.1: 48–54.

Pink, Sarah (2004), *Home Truths: Gender, Domestic Objects and Everyday Life*, Oxford: Berg.

Plain, Gill (1996), *Women's Fiction of the Second World War: Gender, Power and Resistance*, Edinburgh: Edinburgh University Press.

Platt, William (1932), *The Passionate Spinster: A Psychological Novel*, London: Eric Partridge.

Playfair, Jocelyn (1944, 2002), *A House in the Country*, London: Persephone Books.

Poe, Edgar Allan (1840), 'The Philosophy of Furniture', *Burton's Gentleman's Magazine* (May): 243–5.

Pollard, Wendy (2004), *Rosamond Lehmann and Her Critics*, London: Ashgate.

Porteous, J. Douglas (1976), 'Home: The Territorial Core', *The Geographical Review*, 66.4 (October): 383–90.

Post, Emily (1930), *The Personality of a House: The Blue Book of Home Design and Decoration*, New York: Funk and Wagnalls Company.

Pritchett, V.S. (1932), Review of *Jenny Wren* by E.H. Young, *New Statesman and Nation*, 26 November: 660–62.

—— (1934), Review of *The Curate's Wife* by E.H. Young, *New Statesman and Nation*, 8 September: 296.

—— (1937), Review of *Celia* by E.H. Young, *New Statesman and Nation*, 13 November: 800–802.

186   *Domestic Modernism, the Interwar Novel, and E.H. Young*

Pykett, Lyn (1995), *Engendering Fictions: The English Novel in the Early Twentieth Century*, London: Edward Arnold.

Pym, Barbara (1950, 1978), *Some Tame Gazelle*, London: Jonathan Cape.

—— (1955, 1985), *Less Than Angels*, London: Panther.

—— (1987), *The Sweet Dove Died*, New York: Perennial Library.

Radford, Jean (1991), *Dorothy Richardson*, London: Harvester.

Radner, Hilary (1989), 'Extra-curricular Activities: Women Writers and the Readerly Text', in Mary Lynn Broe and Angela Ingram, eds, *Women's Writing in Exile*, Chapel Hill: University of North Carolina Press: 252–67.

—— (1995), *Shopping Around: Feminine Culture and the Pursuit of Pleasure*, New York: Routledge.

Radway, Janice (1997), *A Feeling for Books: The Book-of-the-Month Club, Literary Taste, and a Middle-class Desire*, Chapel Hill: University of North Carolina Press.

Raitt, Suzanne (2000), *May Sinclair: A Modern Victorian*, Oxford: Oxford University Press.

Raitt, Suzanne and Trudi Tate, eds (1996), *Women's Fiction and the Great War*, Oxford: Clarendon Press.

Reed, Christopher, ed. (1996), *Not at Home: The Suppression of Domesticity in Modern Art and Architecture*, London: Thames and Hudson.

Reed, Christopher (2004), *Bloomsbury Rooms*, New Haven: Yale University Press.

Reid, Helen and Lorna Brierly (2001), *Go Home and Do the Washing: Three Hundred Years of Pioneering Bristol Women*, London: Broadcast Books.

Renault, Mary (1944, 1985), *The Friendly Young Ladies*, London: Virago.

Review of *A Corn of Wheat* by E.H. Young, *Times Literary Supplement*, 20 June 1910: 226.

Review of *A Corn of Wheat* by E.H. Young, *Punch*, 17 August 1910: 108.

Review of *Yonder* by E.H. Young, *The Nation*, 6 March 1913: 232.

Review of *Yonder* by E.H. Young, *American Library Association Booklist*, 9 March 1913: 301.

Review of *Yonder* by E.H. Young, *Times Literary Supplement*, 1 August 1912: 307.

Review of *Moor Fires* by E.H. Young, *Times Literary Supplement*, 7 December 1916: 587.

Review of *William* by E.H. Young, *Boston Transcript*, 2 September 1925: 6.

Review of *William* by E.H. Young, *New York Literary Review*, 29 August 1925: 2.

Review of *William* by E.H. Young, *Spectator*, 30 May 1925: 896, 898.

Review of *William* by E.H. Young, *The New Republic*, 9 September 1925: 78.

Review of *William* by E.H. Young, *Times Literary Supplement*, 30 April 1925: 298.

Review of *Misses Mallet* by E.H. Young, *Springfield Republican*, 4 September 1927: 7 f.

Review of *Misses Mallet* by E.H. Young, *The Spectator*, 12 February 1927: 253.

Review of *Miss Mole* by E.H. Young, *Outlook and Independent*, 8 October 1930: 230.

Bibliography

Review of *Jenny Wren* by E.H. Young, *New Statesman and Nation*, 26 November 1932: 660–662.

Review of *Jenny Wren* by E.H. Young, *New York Times Book Review*, 19 February 1933:7.

Review of *Jenny Wren*, Boston Evening Transcript, 25 Feb. 1933:1.

Review of *Jenny Wren* by E.H. Young, *Times Literary Supplement*, 1 December 1932: 920.

Review of *The Curate's Wife* by E.H. Young, *New Statesman and Nation*, 8 September 1934: 296.

Review of *The Curate's Wife* by E.H. Young, *The Commonweal*, 4 January 1935: 296.

Rice, Charles (2004), 'Rethinking Histories of the Interior', *The Journal of Architecture* 9 (Autumn): 275–97.

Richardson, Dorothy (1938), *Pilgrimage*, London: Dent.

Rimmon-Kenan, Shlomith (1983), *Narrative Fiction: Contemporary Poetics*, London: Methuen.

Robertson, E. Arnot (1928, 1989), *Cullum*, London: Virago.

—— (1933, 1982), *Ordinary Families*, London: Virago.

Robinson, Charlotte, 'A Brief Portrait of a Publisher – Jonathan Cape – Part I', <http://www.ibooknet.co.uk/archive/news_june03.htm>.

Romines, Ann (1992), *The Home Plot: Women, Writing and Domestic Ritual*, Amherst: University of Massachusetts Press.

Rose, Gillian (1993), *Feminism and Geography: The Limits of Geographical Knowledge*, London: Blackwell, Polity.

Rosner, Victoria (2005), *Modernism and the Architecture of Private Life*. New York: Columbia University Press.

Ross, Mary (1928), Review of *The Vicar's Daughter* by E.H. Young, *New York Herald Tribune*, 21 October: 5–6.

—— (1930), Review of *Miss Mole* by E.H. Young, *New York Herald Tribune*, 28 September: 6.

—— (1934), 'Vermeer-like Quality of E.H. Young' (review of *The Curate's Wife*), *New York Herald Tribune*, 21 October: 8.

Rowse, A.L. (1961), *Appeasement: A Study in Political Decline 1933–1939*, Norton: New York.

Rubin, Joan Shelley (1992), *The Making of Middle/brow Culture*, Chapel Hill: University of North Carolina Press.

Rubenstein, Roberta (2001), *Home Matters: Longing and Belonging, Nostalgia and Mourning in Women's Fiction*, London: Palgrave.

Rudkin, L.S. (2005), 'Home is Where Art Is', 'Letters', *Review*, *The Guardian*, 2 April: 8.

Russell, Bertrand (1968), *The Autobiography of Bertrand Russell, 1914–1944*, Vol. II, London: George Allen and Unwin.

Rybczynski, Witold (1986), *Home: A Short History of An Idea*, New York: Viking.

188   *Domestic Modernism, the Interwar Novel, and E.H. Young*

Sackville-West, Vita (1931), *All Passion Spent*, London: Hogarth Press.

Sand, George (1832,1993), *Indiana*, trans. Eleanor Hochman, New York: Signet Classic.

Sassoon, Siegfried (1928, 1931), *Memoirs of a Fox-Hunting Man*, Leipzig: Tauchnitz.

Scannell, Paddy with Cardiff, David (2002), *A Social History of British Broadcasting Vol. 1: Serving the Nation*, Maiden: Blackwell.

Scholes, Robert (1990), 'In the Brothel of Modernism: Picasso and Joyce', *Crossing the Disciplines: Cultural Studies in the Nineties*, The University of Oklahoma, Norman, 19–21 October, <http://www.modcult.brown.edu/people/scholes/Pic_Joy/Part_1_340.html>.

Schulkind, Jeanne, ed. (1976), *Virginia Woolf: Moments of Being Writings*, New York: Harcourt Brace Jovanovich.

Schwenger, Peter (2002), 'Still Life: A User's Manual', *Narrative* 10.2; 140–55.

Sedgwick, Eve Kosofsky (1985), *Between Men: English Literature and Male Homosocial Desire*, New York: Columbia University Press.

Seymour, Beatrice Kean (1928, 1938), *Youth Rides Out*, Harmondsworth: Penguin.

Shaw, Marion (1998), 'The Making of a Middle-Brow Success: Winifred Holtby's *South Riding*', in Judy Simons and Kate Fullbrook, eds, *Writing: A Woman's Business: Women, Writing and the Marketplace*, Manchester: Manchester University Press: 31–80.

Sheridan, Dorothy, ed. (1990), *Wartime Women: A Mass-Observation Anthology 1937–1945*, London: Heinemann.

Shields, Carol (2002), *Unless*, London: Fourth Estate.

—— (2003), 'Narrative Hunger and the Overflowing Cupboard', in Edward Eden and Dee Goertz, eds, *Carol Shields, Narrative Hunger, and the Possibilities of Fiction*, Toronto: University of Toronto Press: 19–36.

Shone, Richard (1995, 2000), 'A Cast in Time', in James Lingwood, ed., *House/Rachel Whiteread*, London: Phaidon Press: 50–61.

—— (1999), *The Art of Bloomsbury*, London: Tate Gallery.

Sidlauskas, Susan (1996), 'Psyche and Sympathy: Staging Interiority in the Early Modern Home', in Christopher Reed, ed., *Not at Home: The Suppression of Domesticity in Modern Art and Architecture*, London: Thames and Hudson: 65–80.

Simmel, Georg (1997), 'Bridge and Door', in Neil Leach, ed., *Rethinking Architecture: A Reader in Cultural Theory*, London: Routledge: 66–9.

Simons, Judy and Kate Fullbrook, eds (1998), *Writing: A Woman's Business: Women, Writing and the Marketplace*, Manchester: Manchester University Press.

Sinclair, May (1913), *The Combined Maze*, London: Hutchinson and Co.

—— (1914), *The Three Sisters*, London: Hutchinson and Co.

—— (1919, 1972), *Mary Olivier: A Life*, Westport, CT: Greenwood Press.

—— (1922), *The Life and Death of Harriett Frean*, New York: Macmillan.

—— (1925), *The Rector of Wyck*, London: Hutchinson and Co.

Bibliography

Smith, Alys Pearsall (1894), 'A Reply from the Daughters, II', *Nineteenth Century* 35 (1894): 446–50.

Smith, Angela, (2002), 'Introduction', *Selected Stories* by Katherine Mansfield, Oxford, Oxford University Press, pp. ix–xxxii.

Smith, Dodie (1949, 1998), *I Capture the Castle*, New York: St. Martin's Press.

Smith, Dorothy E (1987, 2002) 'A Feminist Methodology', in Ben Highmore, ed., *The Everyday Life Reader*, London: Routledge: 271–2.

Smith, Stevie (1936), *Novel on Yellow Paper; or, Work it Out for Yourself*, London: Jonathan Cape.

Smith-Rosenberg, Carroll (1985), *Disorderly Conduct: Visions of Gender in Victorian America*, New York: A.A. Knopf.

St John, John Richard (1990), *William Heinemann: A Century of Publishing, 1890–1990*, London: Heinemann.

Stevenson, Robert Louis (1999), 'A Gossip on Romance', in Glenda Norquay, ed., *R.L. Stevenson on Fiction*, Edinburgh: Edinburgh University Press.

Struther, Jan (1939, 1989), *Mrs. Miniver*, London: Virago.

Tate, Trudi (1998), *Modernism, History and the First World War*, Manchester: Manchester University Press.

Taylor, Elizabeth (1945), *At Mrs. Lippincote's*, London: P. Davies.

—— (1995), *A View from the Harbour*, London: Virago.

T.B.E. (1927), Review of *Misses Mallet* by E.H. Young, *Spectator*, 12 February: 253.

Thompson, Belinda (1998), *Post-Impressionism*, Movements in Modern Art Series, London: Tate Gallery Publishing.

Tickner, Lisa (1999), 'Vanessa Bell: *Studland Beach*, Domesticity, and "Significant Form"', *Representations* 65 (Winter): 63–92.

—— (2004), '"Augustus's Sister": Gwen John: Wholeness, Harmony and Radiance', in David Fraser Jenkins and Chris Stephens, eds, *Gwen John and Augustus John*, London: Tate.

Tiersten, Lisa (1996), 'The Chic Interior and the Feminine Modern: Home Decorating as High Art in Turn-of-the-Century France', in Christopher Reed, ed., *Not at Home: The Suppression of Domesticity in Modern Art and Architecture*, London: Thames and Hudson: 18–32.

Tristram, Philippa (1989), *Living Space in Fact and Fiction*, London; New York: Routledge.

Trodd, Anthea (1998), *Women's Writing in English: Britain 1900–1945*, London: Longman.

Trollope, Anthony (1938), *Barchester Towers*, London: Dent.

Van Doren, Carl. (1927), Review of *Moor Fires* by E.H. Young, *New York Herald Tribune*, 9 October: vii 6–7.

Van Lennep, D.J. (1987), 'The Hotel Room', in Joseph J. Kockelmans, ed., *Phenomenological Psychology: The Dutch School*, Dordrecht: Martinus Nijhoff: 209–15.

190   *Domestic Modernism, the Interwar Novel, and E.H. Young*

Vicinus, Martha (1985), *Independent Women: Work and Community for Single Women, 1850–1920*, Chicago: Chicago University Press.

Vidler, Anthony (2000), *Warped Space: Art, Architecture and Anxiety in Modern Culture*, Cambridge, MA: MIT Press.

Vinson, James, ed. (1983), *20th-Century Fiction*, with intro. by George Woodcock, London: Macmillan.

Vitruvius (1999), *Ten Books on Architecture*, trans. Ingrid D. Rowland, Cambridge: Cambridge University Press.

Von Arnim, Elizabeth (1914), *The Pastor's Wife*, Garden City, NY: Doubleday, Page and Co.

Wall, Cynthia (1993), 'Gendering Rooms: Domestic Architecture and Literary Acts', *Eighteenth-Century Fiction*, 5.4 (July): 349–72.

Walkowitz, Judith R. (1992), *City of Dreadful Delight: Narratives of Sexual Danger in Late-Victorian London*, London: Virago.

Wallace, Diane (1999), 'Revising the Marriage Plot in Women's Fiction of the 1930s', in Maroula Joannou, ed. (1999), *Women Writers of the 1930s*, Edinburgh: Edinburgh University Press: 63–75.

—— (2000), *Sisters and Rivals in British Women's Fiction, 1914–1939*, New York: St. Martin's Press.

Waller, Jane and Michael Vaughan-Rees (1987), *The Role of Women's Magazines 1939–1945*, London: Macdonald.

Ward, A.C., ed. (1975), *Longman Companion to Twentieth Century Literature*, London: Longman.

Warner, Sylvia Townsend (1926), *Lolly Willowes: Or the Loving Huntsman*, New York: Viking Press.

Watson, Winifred (1938, 2000), *Miss Pettigrew Lives for a Day*, London: Persephone Books.

Watt, Ian (1964), *The Rise of the Novel: Studies in Defoe, Richardson, and Fielding*, Berkeley: University of California Press.

Waugh, Evelyn (1929), *Decline and Fall*, New York: Grosset and Dunlap.

—— (1930), *Vile Bodies*, Boston: Little, Brown.

—— (1945), *Brideshead Revisited*, London: Chapman and Hall.

—— (1934, 1951), *A Handful of Dust*, Harmondsworth: Penguin.

Webb, Mary (1917), *Gone to Earth*, London: Constable.

—— (1922, 1932), *Seven for a Secret: A Love Story*, London: Hutchinson.

—— (1924, 1981), *Precious Bane*, Harmondsworth: Penguin.

West, Katharine Leaf (1949), *Chapter of Governesses: A Study of the Governess in English Fiction, 1800–1949*, London: Cohen and West.

West, Rebecca (1918), *The Return of the Soldier*, New York: The Century.

—— (1929, 1980), *Harriet Hume: A London Fantasy*, New York: The Dial Press.

Westacott, Mary (1944, 1963), pseud. Agatha Christie, *Absent in the Spring*, New York: Dell.

Bibliography

Wharton, Edith and Ogden Codman Jr (1902), *The Decoration of Houses*, New York: W. W. Norton & Co.

Wharton, Edith (1933), *The House of Mirth*, New York: Scribner.

Whipple, Dorothy (1930, 1946), *High Wages*, London: John Murray; Harmondsworth: Penguin.

—— (1932), *Greenbanks*, London: John Murray.

White, Cynthia L. (1970), *Women's Magazines: 1693–1968*, London: Michael Joseph.

Wigley, Mark (1992), 'Heidegger's House: The Violence of the Domestic', *Public*: 93–118.

—— (2001), *White Walls, Designer Dresses: The Fashioning of Modern Architecture*. Cambridge, MA: MIT Press.

—— (2002), *The Architecture of Deconstruction: Derrida's Haunt*, Cambridge, MA: MIT Press.

Wilhide, Elizabeth (1999), *Bohemian Style*, London: Pavilion.

Williams, Tony (2000), 'Thresholds of Desire and Domestic Space in Nineteenth-Century French Fiction', in Fran Lloyd and Catherine O'Brien, eds, *Secret Spaces Forbidden Places: Rethinking Culture*, New York: Berghahn Books: 39–49.

Wilson, Elizabeth (1991), *The Sphinx in the City: Urban Life, the Control of Disorder, and Women*, London: Virago.

Winslow, Rosemary (1932/33), 'E.H. Young', Letter Club Fonds, Rare Books and Special Collections, University of British Columbia, Vancouver, Canada, 15.

Woodcock, George (1947), Review of *Chatterton Square* by E.H. Young, *New Statesman and Nation*, 6 August: 134.

Woolf, Leonard (1927), *Hunting the Highbrow*, London: Hogarth Press.

—— (1967), *Downhill All the Way: An Autobiography of the Years 1919–1939*, London: Hogarth Press.

Woolf, Virginia (1915), *The Voyage Out*, New York: Harcourt Brace and World.

—— (1917), 'The Mark on the Wall', London: Hogarth Press.

—— (1919), *Night and Day*, London: Duckworth.

—— (1925, 1992), *Mrs. Dalloway*, Oxford: Oxford University Press.

—— (1927, 1994), *To the Lighthouse*, London: Routledge.

—— (1928), 'Introduction to *Mrs. Dalloway*', *Mrs. Dalloway*, New York: Modern Library: v–ix.

—— (1928, 1965), *A Room of One's Own*, Harmondsworth: Penguin.

—— (1937, 1968), *The Years*, Harmondsworth: Penguin.

—— (1938), *Three Guineas*, London: Hogarth Press.

—— (1941), *Between the Acts*, New York: Harcourt Brace.

—— (1947), 'Middlebrow', in *The Death of the Moth and Other Essays*, London: Hogarth Press: 112–19.

—— (1958), 'Phases of Fiction' in *Granite and Rainbow: Essay*, New York: Harcourt Brace.

192 *Domestic Modernism, the Interwar Novel, and E.H. Young*

—— (1975), *The London Scene: Five Essays*, New York: Frank Hallman.

—— (1978), *The Pargiters: the Novel-Essay Portion of 'The Years'*, ed. Mitchell A. Leaska, London: Hogarth Press.

—— (1980), *The Letters of Virginia Woolf, 1936–41*, Vol. VI, ed. Nigel Nicholson and Joanne Trautmann, New York: Harcourt Brace Jovanovich.

—— (1982), *The Diary of Virginia Woolf*, Vol. IV: 1931–1935, ed. Anne Oliver Bell. London: Hogarth Press.

—— (1906, 1989), 'Phyllis and Rosamond', in *The Complete Shorter Fiction of Virginia Woolf*, ed. Susan Dick, London: Hogarth Press: 17–29.

—— (1988), 'Character in Fiction', *The Essays of Virginia Woolf*, Vol. III: 1919–1924, ed. Andrew McNeillie, London: Hogarth Press: 420–38.

Worboise, Emma (1858, 1906), *The Wife's Trials*, London: H.R. Allenson.

—— (1863, 1872), *Married Life, or, The Story of Philip and Edith*, London: James Clarke and Co.

Wright, Frank Lloyd (1992), *Frank Lloyd Wright: Collected Writings*, ed. Bruce Brook Pfeiffer, New York: Rizzoli/Frank Lloyd Wright Foundation.

Wyatt, E.V.R. (1947), Review of *Chatterton Square* by E.H. Young, *The Commonweal*, 24 October: 51.

Young, E.H. (1910), *A Corn of Wheat*, London: Heinemann.

—— (1912), *Yonder*, London: Heinemann.

—— (1913), 'The Cow's Tail', *The English Review*, 53 April: 30–63.

—— (1916), *Moor Fires*, London: John Murray.

—— (1922), *A Bridge Dividing*, London: Heinemann.

—— (1922, 1927, 1984), *The Bridge Dividing*, London: Heinemann, as *The Misses Mallett*, London: Jonathan Cape; London: Virago.

—— (1923), 'Lena Maude', *Time and Tide*, 7 April: 775–6.

—— (1924), 'An Artist', *Time and Tide*, 18 January: 60–61.

—— (1925, 1988), *William*, London: Virago.

—— (1928, 1992), *The Vicar's Daughter*, London: Virago.

—— (1930, 1984), *Miss Mole*, London: Virago.

—— (1932, 1985), *Jenny Wren*, London: Virago.

—— (1932, 1933), 'The Stream', *Good Housekeeping* 21.3 (May): 6–9, 104: 106–15; rpt. as *Twelve Best Stories from Good Housekeeping*, ed. Alice M. Head, London: Ivor Nicolson and Watson: 11–43; *The Best Short Stories: 1933. I. English*, ed, Edward J. O'Brien, London: Jonathan Cape: 272–304.

—— (1933), 'To Miss Atkinson', 5 February, E.H. Young files, Jonathan Cape Correspondence, Archives and Manuscripts, Reading University Library.

—— (1934, 1985), *The Curate's Wife*, London: Virago.

—— (1937, 1990), *Celia*, London: Virago.

—— (1940), *Caravan Island*, London: A. and C. Black.

—— (1947, 1987), *Chatterton Square*, London: Virago.

—— (1935), as E.H. Daniell, 'Reminiscences', *The Climbers' Club Journal* 6: 25–9 (courtesy of Maggie Lane).

Bibliography 193

—— (1941), *William*, 'The Press of the Readers Club' edition with a foreword by Carl Van Doren.

—— (1942), *River Holiday*, London: A. and C. Black.

—— (1948), 'The Grey Mare', 'Mid-Morning Story', 17 February, read by Gladys Young, E.H. Young, Scripts, BBC Written Archives Centre, Caversham Park, Reading.

—— (1950), 'The Cow's Tail', 20 September, read by Gladys Young, E.H. Young, Scripts, BBC Written Archives Centre, Caversham Park, Reading.

—— (n.d.), 'On Empty Houses', Young Papers.

—— (n.d.), 'On Window Curtains', Young Papers.

—— (n.d.), 'The Sacrifice' source unknown, courtesy of Stella Deen and the Sharp family.

Young, Francis Brett (1935), *White Ladies*, London: W. Heinemann.

Young, Iris Marion (1997), *Intersecting Voices: Dilemmas of Gender, Political Philosophy, and Policy*, Princeton: Princeton University Press.

Archival Sources

ADD 63230, Society of Authors Papers, British Library, UK.

Box 35, File 2, Harry Ransom Humanities Research Center, University of Texas at Austin, Texas, USA.

E.H. Young Files, Jonathan Cape Correspondence, Archives and Manuscripts, Reading University Library, Reading, UK.

Letters Club Fonds, Vol. 15, 1932/33, Rare Books and Special Collections, University of British Columbia, Vancouver, Canada.

Mass-Observation Archive, University of Sussex, UK.

P.E.N. Archive, Department of Special Collections, University Archives, McFarlin Library, University of Tulsa, Oklahoma, USA.

Ref. RCONT1 Gladys Young Files: File 4a, 1944; 1945–1946, File 5, 1947–1944; T32/360 1950 (Women of Today), BBC Written Archives Centre, Caversham Park, Reading, UK.

Young Papers, courtesy of William Saunders, London, UK.

Index

Academy, 12
Adam and Charles Black, 86
Adam, Ruth, 58n
adultery, 8
  advertising, 2, 4, 9, 29, 75–6, 77–8, 84, 86, 85 (fig.)
aesthetic value, 9, 12, 75–80, 86–9; *see also* literary valuation
  of the everyday, 166
  standardization of, 86
aesthetics, 13, 166
  Bloomsbury, 55–6
  of the everyday, 53, 103, 138–9
  modernist, 12
  romantic, 13
  transcendental, 13
Aga sagas, 14, 168, 168n
agency 48, 134
  of houses, 52, 118
  women's, 33
  alternative domesticities, 8, 28, 48, 65, 72, 95, 101–3, 107, 111–30, 144, 163, 165
Altman, Robert, 168
angels of the house, 11, 19
appeasement, 155–8
architecture, 7, 13, 16n, 52, 93n, 99, 143, 167
  architectural metaphors, 7, 23–6, 70, 113, 136, 139–40, 154–5
  gender and, 118
  literature and, 7, 18, 22, 38n
  modernism and, 108n
  as symbolic conversation, 140
  writing and, 22, 26, 38n
Armstrong, Nancy, 15n
art of living, 128, 139, 165, 166
attics, 140, 144
audiobooks, 91
Austen, Jane, 17, 46, 49, 88, 112
  comparison of Young, to, 89, 91, 128
  Emma, 114, 128
  influence on Young, 95
  Mansfield Park, 23, 26–7

  Persuasion, 124, 128
  Pride and Prejudice, 124
  Sense and Sensibility, 78, 122
avant-garde, 33, 55

Bachelard, Gaston, 10, 22, 24, 39n, 115, 129n, 136
Bagnold, Enid, 18
  The Squire, 11
Bainbridge, Beryl, 168
Bakhtin, Mikhail, 22, 38n
Balzac, Honoré de, 54
Bammer, Angelika, 18
Barnes, Djuna, 8
Baudrillard, Jean, 10, 26, 52, 134, 135, 138
Bayley, John, 90, 100
BBC radio, 2, 4, 46, 52, 57n, 91, 114, 156
BBC television, 91
Beaton, Cecil, 109n
beau ideal, 1, 14n, 111
Beauman, Nicola, 9
Beauman, Sally, 57n, 70, 73, 90
Beddoe, Deidre, 163n
bedrooms, 115, 140
beds, 50, 131
being, 7, 23, 24
Bell, Vanessa, 55, 57
belonging, 7, 18, 61, 117, 120, 154–5, 163
Benjamin, David, 20
Benjamin, Walter, 24, 39n
Bennett, Arnold, 12, 16n, 54, 56, 70, 131
  Anna of the Five Towns, 26
  The Author's Craft, 12
  Hilda Lessways, 54, 148
  Literary Taste, 12
  The Old Wives' Tale, 148
Benson, Stella, 79
Bentley, Phyllis, *A Modern Tragedy* 47
Betjeman, John, *Ghastly Good Taste*, 22
Bhabha, Homi, 18, 22, 163
Blanchot, Maurice, 10
Bloomsbury
  aesthetics, 55–6
  artists, 11, 16n, 55

196 *Domestic Modernism*

boarding houses; *see* lodging-houses
boarding schools, 19
bodies, 50
 houses as, 21, 48, 50, 63
 of wounded soldiers, 160–61
bohemianism, 13, 56–7, 98, 100, 101
Bonnard, Pierre, 57
Book Guild, 77
Book Society, 77, 78
Booker, Michael, 58n
Book-of-the-Month Club, 77
Books; *see* novels; publishing
books on tape, 91
Borden, Mary, 131
borders, 19, 48
Bottome, Phyllis, 4
Bourdieu, Pierre, 10, 19, 22, 35, 88
bourgeois culture, 13, 34
Bourgeois, Louise, 57
Bowen, Elizabeth, 1, 9, 18, 25, 26, 28, 29,
 39n, 49, 62, 76, 77, 124, 167, 168
 Bowen's Court, 22, 27
 children's books by, 164n
 The Death of the Heart, 51
 The Hotel, 51
 The House in Paris, 11
 The Last September, 28, 51, 59n
 'The New House', 11, 51
 To the North, 29, 108n, 136
 'The Return', 59n
 studies on, 92n
Boys, Jos, 117–18
Bracco, Rosa Maria, 92n
Brandt, Bill, 29
Braque, Georges, 57
bridges, 69, 70, 117
British Federation of University Women, 76
Brittain, Vera, 6
Brontë, Charlotte, 88
 Jane Eyre, 78, 102
Brontë sisters, 61
Brookner, Anita, 168
brows, battle of the, 75–80, 93n
Brunel Bridge, 70
Bryden, Inga, 10, 22, 29, 50
Burnett, John, 2
Burney, Fanny, 17

Butland, Alan, 91

Callil, Carmen, 36n, 90, 91
Cambridge, Elizabeth, *Hostages to Fortune*,
 47, 66, 67, 124, 132
Cameron, Maud, 88
canon formation, 9, 13, 30, 76, 79, 86–9, 93n
capitalism, 24
cars, 19
Cather, Willa, 90
 'The Novel Démeublé', 54
Cavaliero, Glen, 61, 62, 91
celibacy, 8, 64
Cézanne, Paul, 55, 165
Chamberlain, Neville, 156, 157
character, reciprocity with home, 99, 126
characters, 23, 116
 communication of, 126
 complexity of Young's, 145
 consciousness of, 13
 houses and, 52
 objects and, 72, 126
 psychology of, 51–2
 stock, 113, 120
Chesterton, G.K., 112
childhood, 24, 27
Christianity, 125
Christie, Agatha, 18, 35, 40n, 49, 78, 108n,
 151n
 home of, 81
 The Murder in the Vicarage, 35, 112, 124
church, the, 111–16, 125, 128; *see also*
 clerical settings; vicarages
cinema; *see* film
cisterns, 125, 144, 151n
 cities, 24, 28, 29, 35, 47, 48, 69, 117; *see*
 also urbanism
 rural world and, 70
citizenship 24, 163n
class, 7, 49, 50, 102, 105, 118, 119–21, 129,
 167
claustrophobia, 64
cleaning, 32
clerical settings, 111–16
Coates, Wells, 40n, 93n
Coggin, Joan, *Who Killed the Curate?*, 112,
 124

Index 197

Coke, Sir Edward, 29
Coleridge, Samuel Taylor, 63, 71
colonies, 29
colours, 56–7, 98–9
comedy, 18
comfort, 18, 23, 37n
commodification, 77
communication
  ritualization of, 50–51
  through objects, 126
communities, 155
  meaning of, 52
  memory and, 26
  of women, 65
Compton-Burnett, Ivy, 1, 9, 18, 25, 34, 35,
    36, 36n, 88, 124
  A House and Its Head, 35, 100
  Mother and Son, 35, 102–3
  Pastors and Masters 111
Comyns, Barbara, *Our Spoons Came from
    Woolworths*, 56
Connolly, Cyril, 33
Conrad, Joseph, 1
consciousness, 20–21, 25, 48, 108, 118, 125,
    167
  of characters, 13
  domesticity and, 123
conservative modernism, 138
'conservative modernity', 77
consumption, 2, 24, 29
control, 18–19, 50, 55, 115, 133, 135
Cooper, Lettice, 6, 9, 25, 49, 98, 148, 168
  The New House, 11, 19, 50, 138, 167
Corbusier, Le, 11, 40n, 55, 108n
  anti-home, of 16n
Corder, Robert, 112, 113
Cronin, A.J., *Hatter's Castle*, 78
Cuddy-Keane, Melba, 78
'cult of the house', the, 11
curates, 49, 111–16, 125
curtains, 50, 52–3, 123
customs, 53–4

Dane, Clemence, 36n
Danielewski, Mark Z., *House of Leaves*, 23,
    38n

Daniell, Emily Hilda, 15n; *see also* Young,
    Emily Hilda
Daniell, John Arthur, 8, 41, 58n
Daniell, Lily, 15n; *see also* Young, Emily
    Hilda
daughters, 8, 11
Davenport, Basil, 88, 128
Dawson, Geoffrey, 161
de Beauvoir, Simone, *The Second Sex*, 10
de Certeau, Michel, 10, 32
de Hooch, Pieter, 53
de la Mare, Walter, 58n
de la Roche, Mazo, 91
Deen, Stella, 33, 40n, 91, 101, 140, 150n
deferral, 34, 50
Delafield, E.M., 1, 2, 6, 8, 9, 13, 18, 31, 32,
    34, 76, 78, 87, 91, 106, 129, 131, 132,
    165, 168
  Diary of a Provincial Lady, 8, 11, 88, 124,
    149
  Messalina of the Suburbs, 8, 47
  reception of Young's novels, 88
  Thank Heaven Fasting, 50, 148, 149
  Three Marriages, 98
Delany, Paul, 29
delay, 34, 50
Delft, 53
Dell, Ethel, 78
Denny, Norman, *Sweet Confusion*, 157,
    158
Depression, the, 48, 129
Derrida, Jacques, 13, 16n
description, 54–5
design, 59n; *see also* interior decoration
Design Museum, London, 81
desire, 51
Després, Carole, 20
detail, 54–5, 56
detective novels, 18, 29, 35, 36n, 78, 79,
    111–12
Dial Press of New York, the, 90
dialogue, 2, 7, 32, 33, 35, 89, 96, 115, 125
diary form, 31
Dickens, Charles, 16n
Dickinson, Emily, 102, 105
dislocation, 27, 29
Disraeli, Benjamin, 161

198   *Domestic Modernism*

'dissertation novel', 93n
divorce, 146
documentary film movement, 14n, 31
dole office practices, 2
doll's houses, 50, 55, 131, 136, 144
domestic artistry, 105, 122, 126, 128, 135–6, 159, 165
domestic metaphors, 154–5
domestic modernism, 33–4, 40n, 62, 88, 165, 167, 168
  turn to, 95–109
domestic novels, 1, 6, 7, 9, 13, 17–40, 46–7, 54–5, 76, 111–12, 167
  contemporary rewriting of, 14
  definition of the, 13, 17–18
  families in, 108
  fathers in, 101
  interwar, 17–40, 54–5
  marriage in, 108
  modernism and, 55–6
  readers of, 78
  reading and, 148–9
  reception of, 76–7
  rise of the, 2
  titles of, 130n
domestic space, 1, 4, 6, 11–13, 14n, 18, 50, 62, 63, 119, 141, 150n, 154, 159, 165, 167–8
  control over, 18–19, 133, 135
  defining, 19–22
  hybrid public/private, 13
  material aspects of, 19
  memory and, 26–7
  metaphors of, 139–40
  modernity and, 22
  psychological aspects of, 19
  relation to literature, 14n
  securization of, 19
  self and, 7
  social aspects of, 19
  spiritual aspects of, 19
  status of, 10
  subjectivity and, 7
domestic values, 2
domesticity, 7, 33, 75, 91, 119, 139, 144, 153, 167
  aesthetics of, 166

alternative domesticities, 8, 28, 48, 65, 72, 95, 101–3, 107, 111–30, 144, 163, 165
  comforts of, 53
  confinement of, 53, 63, 64
  consciousness and, 123
  cult of, 11, 21, 72, 155
  debate about, 10
  defense of, 10
  degradation of, 10, 13, 87
  epistemology of, 13
  escape from, 61
  families and, 57
  feminism and, 11, 164n
  human relations and, 133
  language of, 26, 55, 125, 165
  meaning of, 96
  modernism and, 13, 55, 101
  modernity and, 33–6, 163
  nature and, 65
  oppressiveness of, 33
  reading and, 74n
  reorganization of after WWI, 154
  representation of, 88
  turn to, 13
  urban, 47
  Young's vision of 101
Donald, Moira, 39n
doors, 13, 49, 50, 116, 129n, 141, 150n, 166; *see also* doorsteps; locks; thresholds
  locked, 50
doorsteps, 49, 162; *see also* 'drama of the doorstep'
Douglas, Mary, 18–19, 37n
Drabble, Margaret, 131, 168
'drama of the doorstep', 14n, 30–32, 118, 158–60
dream houses, 136, 144
dreaming, 24
Drew, Elizabeth, *The Enjoyment of Literature*, 76
du Maurier, Daphne, *Rebecca*, 26, 78, 102
Dubuffet, Jean, *Matière et mémoire*, 57
Duckworth, 2, 84
Duncan, James, 32
Dutch painting, 53–7
dwelling, 23, 24
dwellings, 18; *see also* architecture; houses

Index 199

eavesdropping, 34, 49, 124, 140
economic change, 17
Eden, Emily, 88
Edgeworth, Maria, 17
Edwardian novel, 12, 79
Eliot, George, 23, 61, 88
   Middlemarch, 38n
Ellis, Alice Thomas, 131, 168
Ellman, Maud, 26, 51
empire, 23, 69, 154, 167
enclosures, 21, 102
Engel, Claire, 41
England, 153–64; *see also* Englishness;
   nationhood
   as homeland, 154, 155, 163
English Review, The, 78
Englishness, 2, 13, 29, 35, 89, 119, 153–5,
   161, 167
entering, 48, 141
epistemology, 7, 13
Equal Franchise Act, 139
erotic triangulation, 71–2, 74n
Ertz, Susan, 4
escapism, 61, 76
ethnicity, 7
everyday, the, 1, 11, 13, 17, 30–33, 48, 55,
   89, 91, 118–20, 124–5, 159
   aesthetic value of, 166
   aesthetics of, 53, 103, 138–9
   gender and, 166
   heroism of the, 13, 126, 131–51, 165
   modernity and, 33
   pleasure and, 166
   as site of social transformation, 34
exiting, 48, 141
experimentalism, 55
exteriority, 19, 49, 116, 123
   and interiority, 105–106

Fallows, Christopher, 45, 46
families, 18, 48, 57, 63, 95, 134, 140, 141,
   144, 154, 155, 163
   alternative, 165
   continuity of, 144–5
   gender and, 36n
   idea of, 115
   interior life of, 48

   intimacy and, 143
   meaning of, 52
   memory and, 26
   modernity and, 22
   private space and, 39n
   representation of, 90
   urban, 48
fathers, 95–7
Felski, Rita, 10, 33, 164n
female society, 65
feminine, the, 33, 35
femininity, 64, 76, 89, 101, 160–61, 165
   identification with interiority, 102
   value of, 139
feminism, 27, 33, 164n, 168
   domesticity and, 10, 11
   home and, 11
   New Feminism, 2
   Old Feminism, 2
   second-wave, 10
   World War II and, 157
feminization, 2
fetishism, 50
film, 2, 14, 158, 168
   documentary film movement, 14n
First World War; *see* World War I
Fish, Stanley, 89
Fitzgerald, Penelope, 168
Flanders, Judith, 39n
Florin Books, 84
Floyd, Janet, 10, 22, 29, 50
focalization, 2, 7, 33, 35, 40n, 71, 72, 101,
   116, 118, 122–3, 125, 133, 140–41,
   145, 155, 163
foreign, the, 29; *see also* travel
Forlini, Stefania, 39n
Forster, E.M., 12, 18, 78, 88, 107
   Howards End, 65, 154
   A Passage to India, 86
Foucault, Michel, 19, 33
Fowler, Bridget, 8, 80, 88
free indirect discourse, 25, 32, 33, 34, 71,
   106, 123
French, Marilyn, 33
Freud, Sigmund, 20–21, 31, 37n
   'Introductory Lectures on
      Psychoanalysis', 20–21

200   *Domestic Modernism*

Fried, Michael, 58n
friendship, 8
Fry, Roger, 55
furniture, 21, 37n, 50–51, 115, 122–3, 126, 134
Fuss, Diana, 38n, 102, 105

Gale, Maggie, 36n
Garber, Marjorie, 21
Gardam, Jane, 168
gardens, 19
Garnett, Edward, 84, 114
Gasiorek, Andrzej, 35
Gaskell, Elizabeth, 17, 23, 88
gaze, the, 33, 49, 116, 118, 119, 143, 165
  feminine, 97
gender, 21, 27, 34, 49, 50, 86–92, 102, 154, 166, 167
  architecture and, 118
  families and, 36n
  power and, 36n, 133
  relations, 4
  roles, 7, 11, 35, 50, 64–5, 167
genre, 86–9
genre painting, 13
George, Rosemary Marangoly, 23, 27
Gibbons, Stella, 4, 9, 18, 34, 48, 76, 119, 168
  The Bachelor, 29–30, 153
  Bassett, 22, 47, 119, 119–20, 129n
  Cold Comfort Farm, 62, 66, 108n, 115, 154
  Nightingale Wood, 79
  Westwood, or the Gentle Powers, 79, 97
Giles, Judy, 10–11, 33–4, 151n, 153–4, 163n
Girard, René, 74n
Goldsmith, Oliver, *Vicar of Wakefield*, 112
Good Housekeeping, 6, 45, 78
Gornick, Vivian, 108
Gotch, Cyssely, 45
Gotch, Mervyn, 45
Gothic, the, 21, 61
Grant, Duncan, 55, 57
Graves, Robert, 78
  I, Claudius, 86

Green, Henry, 35
Greene, Graham, 87, 125
  reception of Young's novels, 89
Grierson, John, 14n, 158
Gunn, Kirsty, 10

habitus, 19, 102
Hall, Radclyffe, 90
  The Unlit Lamp, 11
halls, 50, 140, 166
Hamilton, Cicely, 6
Hamon, Philippe, 22, 140, 150n
handbooks, 49
Hanson, Claire, 76–7
Harcourt Brace, 78, 86
Hardy, Thomas, 13, 22, 61, 88
  Jude the Obscure, 65, 69
Harrisson, Tom, 31
Hartley, L.P., 28
Harwood, Harold, 36n
Haughton, Hugh, 29
Heidegger, Martin, 16n, 23–4, 39n
Heinemann, 44, 70, 78, 81
Heller, Agnes, 162
Hemingway, Ernest, 78, 160
Henderson, Beatrice (Mansfield), 8, 44, 46
Henderson, John Ralph, 44
Henderson, Ralph, 8, 34, 44, 46, 47, 58n, 61, 112, 156, 157, 159
  'E.H. Young – An Appreciation', 41
  'E.H. Young as a Mountaineer', 45
  '*E.H. Young*: her Muse, her Method & her Message', 44, 114
  The Four Witnesses, 44
heterodiegetic realism, 7, 8
heterosexuality, 13, 72, 163, 165
heterotopias, 19
Heyer, Georgette, 78
high modernism, 7, 18, 33, 34
highbrow culture, 12, 35, 77, 78
history, 26–7
'History of Modern Design in the Home' exhibit, Design Museum, London, 81
Holtby, Winifred, 2, 18, 76, 77, 81, 160–61
  The Crowded Street, 8, 98
  Poor Caroline, 148
  South Riding, 86

Index

home, 2, 4, 6, 7, 13, 48, 89, 125, 163
  bohemian, 13
  bourgeois, 13, 18, 29
  defining, 19–22, 37n
  distinction from house, 37n
  Edwardian, 64
  epistemology of the, 167
  escape from, 61
  feminism and, 11, 164n
  grammar of the, 126
  handbooks on the, 49
  human relations and, 46, 47, 48, 51–2, 73
  idea of, 53–7, 111, 115, 140, 153–5, 158, 163
  identity and, 59n
  meaning of, 13, 17–40, 36n, 52, 95, 155
  memory and, 26–7, 59n
  nation and, 23
  non-traditional ideas of, 19
  nuclear family, 23
  power of, 28
  reciprocity with character, 99, 126
  relation to houses, 7
  relation to nation, 7
  relation to political ideologies, 7
  relation to society, 7
  representation of, 111
  significance to literature, 10
  symbolism of, 117
  travel and, 27–30
home culture, 1, 7, 14n
home ownership, 163n
homeland, 154, 155, 163
homelessness, 117, 119; *see also* transience
homemakers, 25, 131–51, 163
  as artists, 55
homemaking, 4, 6, 21, 55, 159, 165, 5 (fig.);
  see also housework
  compared to authorship, 18
  control and, 18
homesickness, 13, 24, 61, 117–24, 136, 161
homosociality, 8, 74n, 90, 145–6
hooks, bell, 27, 28
house
  definition of, 19–20, 37n
  distinction from home, 37n
house portraiture, 23

households, 37n
  household systems, 18, 100
  hybrid public/private, 111
  housekeepers, 101–3
housekeeping, 101–3; *see also* cleaning;
  housework
houses, 7, 13, 16n, 49
  agency of, 52, 118
  anthropomorphized, 116, 118
  association with interiority, 102
  as bodies, 21, 48, 50, 52, 63
  Celia's house, 142 (fig.)
  characters and, 52
  childhood and, 24
  compared to novels, 7, 13, 16n, 18, 22–6, 118, 153
  death and, 61
  defining, 19–22
  detached, single-family, 2, 111, 153
  doll's houses, 136, 144
  dream, 136
  dreaming and, 24
  embodied, 118
  as expressions of mental states, 48–9, 63, 72–3
  feminist attitudes toward, 164n
  gendering and sexualizing of, 21, 48
  grammar of, 140–41
  haunting of, 61–74
  human relations and, 118
  images of, 21
  as living beings, 52
  as markers of socio-economic change, 22
  memory and, 24, 26–7, 51, 61
  in miniature, 136
  mothers and, 107
  personality and, 26, 48–9, 52, 99, 116
  as psyches, 48, 63, 72–3
  representation of, 18
  and the self, 20, 51, 108
  significance to literature, 10
  structure of, 21
  symbolism of, 52, 95, 117, 136, 140
  trope of, 14
  urban, 48
  Woolf's treatment of, 56

202   *Domestic Modernism*

housewives, 131–51, 165; *see also*
  homemakers
  as artists, 135–6
housework, 10, 21, 29, 148, 165; *see also*
  homemaking
housing, 153–4, 163n
housing projects, 2, 117, 153, 163n
Howard, Elizabeth Jane, 131, 168
Howard, Michael, 86
human relationships, 132, 135, 139
Humble, Nicola, 4, 9, 77, 98, 148–9, 151n
humour, 18
Humphrey, Helen, 168
Huyssen, Andreas, 33, 40n
hybrid public/private spaces, 111, 112,
  120

'Ideal Home Exhibitions', 4
Ideal Home, The, 3 (fig.), 5 (fig.)
ideologies, 7, 27, 62–3, 167
Impressionism, 57
Ingman, Heather, 11
Ingram, Monica, 149
initials, adoption of by women writers, 8
insularity, 29
interior decoration, 22, 29, 37n, 48, 50–53,
  55, 72–3, 115, 126, 135–6, 138, 166
  as a form of agency, 134
  modernist, 56–7
  modernity and, 98–9
interior design; *see* interior decoration
interior monologue, 32, 165
interiority, 19, 23–6, 49, 50, 116, 123,
  140–41, 163
  association with houses, 102
  and exteriority, 105–6
  identification with femininity, 102
  psychic, 21, 62
  public sphere and, 118
  representation and, 138
  sexual, 21
interiors, 116, 118, 122–3, 135–6, 166, 167
  bourgeois, 134, 135
  destabilization of, 134
  domestic, 1, 2, 7, 13, 23–6, 27, 97–101,
  108
  patriarchal, 134, 135

  psychological; *see* interiority
  representation of, 119
intertextuality, 128
interwar context, 13; *see also* World War I;
  World War II
intimacy, 49, 120, 134, 140, 143
irony, 18, 32, 89, 91, 106, 139, 140, 163
Ishiguro, Kazuo, 168
Isokon, 84 (fig.)
Ivory, James, 168

Jacob, Naomi, 78
James, Henry, 17, 38n
  The House of Fiction, 22, 118
James Tait Black Fiction Prize, 76, 86
Jameson, Frederic, 22
Jameson, Storm, 6, 9, 16n, 18, 28–9, 39n,
  62, 76, 160
  Company Parade, 28
  A Day Off, 24
  Love in Winter, 28
  The Lovely Ship, 28
  'Mirror in Darkness' trilogy, 28, 39n, 108n
  The Moon Is Making, 62
  None Turn Back, 28–9, 39n
  The Pitiful Wife, 62
  A Richer Dust, 28
  Three Kingdoms, 4, 79
  The Voyage Home, 28
Jennings, Humphrey, 31, 158
Jesse, F. Tennyson, 8, 36n
  indictment of the English class system,
  121
  A Pin to See the Peepshow, 7, 8, 47, 121,
  151n
Joannou, Maroula, 10, 91
John, Augustus, 55, 57
John, Gwen, 57
John, Ida, 36n
John Murray, 78
Johnson, Lesley, 10, 27
Jonathan Cape, 2, 41, 70, 77–8, 81, 84, 86,
  114
Joyce, James, 1, 12, 32
  Ulysses, 31
Jung, C.G., 20, 37n
  Memories, Dreams, Reflections, 20

Index 203

Kaplan, Alice, 32
Kaplan, Caren, 27
Kaye-Smith, Sheila, 4, 61, 78
   Sussex Gorse, 62
Kennedy, Margaret, 6, 76, 91
   The Constant Nymph, 98
keys, 50, 141, 150n
King, Mary, 88
kinship systems, 18
Kipling, Rudyard, 'Mary Postgate', 147
Knight, Stephen, 36n

Lady, The, 4
Lancaster, Osbert, 23
Landy, Michael, 59n
Lane, Allen, 2, 4, 81
Lane, Maggie, 15n
Langharn, James, 52
Larsen, Thorlief, 90
Lawn Road Flats, 40n, 81, 93n
Lawrence, D.H., 1, 54, 62
Lawrence (Green), Margaret, 91
Lawrence, Roderick J., 37n
Lawrence, T.E., 78
Leavis, Q.D., 86
Lee, Hermione, 28, 39n
Lefebvre, Henri, 10, 32, 34, 40n, 141, 159
   Everyday Life in the Modern World, 31
Lehmann, Rosamond, 9, 18, 76, 77, 90, 91,
     124, 165, 168
   Dusty Answer, 8, 98, 163
   The Echoing Grove, 98
   Invitation to the Waltz, 90
   A Note in Music, 132
   studies on, 92n
Les nouvelles littéraires, 41
lesbianism, 8, 163
Letters Club, the, 90
Leverson, Ada, 18, 150
   The Little Ottleys, 51, 96
Levy, Andrea, 168
Lewis, Sinclair, 78
Lewis, Wyndham, 97
libraries, 34, 77, 80
Lichenstein, Rachel, 49
Light, Alison, 9, 10, 15n, 77
liminal spaces; *see* thresholds

literary classification, 76–7, 80; *see also*
   genre
literary valuation, 9, 12; *see also* aesthetic
   value
literature
   architecture and, 7, 18, 22–6, 38n
   commercialization of, 86
   domestic space and, 14n
   significance of house and home to, 10
Litt, Toby, 10
Lively, Penelope, 27
location, 27
locks, 141; *see also* doors; keys
lodging-houses, 13, 119–24
London, 29, 47
   literary scene of, 79
   reception of Young's novels in, 76
love, 107–8, 118, 125; *see also* romance
Loveman, Amy, 'An Artist in Living',
   150n
Lukacs, John, 23
Luria, Sara, 38n

Macauley, Rose, 6, 9, 76, 124, 161
   Crewe Train, 54, 65, 79–80
   Dangerous Ages, 151n
   Keeping up Appearances, 80, 120–21
Macdonald, Myra, 10
Macheski, Cecilia, 89
Madge, Charles, 31
magazines, 2, 4, 6, 15n, 29
   family, 34
   popular, 34
   women's magazines, 2, 4, 6, 15n, 29
male writers, 147
manhood; *see* masculinity
Mannin, Ethel, 4
Manning, Olivia, 92n
Mansfield, Katherine, 1, 8, 9, 12, 18, 25, 28,
     29, 33, 34, 36, 54, 58n, 62, 77, 90, 149,
     165, 167
   'At the Bay', 167
   'Bliss', 166
Marcus, Sharon, 73n
marketing, 9, 75, 77–8, 84, 86, 85 (fig.); *see*
   also advertising
Marr, Andrew, 79

marriage, 8, 13, 17–18, 72, 101, 107–8, 122,
124–9, 133–6, 138, 140, 144–6, 163,
167–8
  debates about, 91
  equality in, 17
  problematization of, 64, 65
  reality of, 165
  representation of, 90, 111
marriage bar, 2, 4
Marsh, Ngaio, 18
Martin, Biddy, 27
Marx, Karl, 21
masculinity, 49, 89, 90, 97, 101, 118, 139,
143, 155, 160–61
  construction of, 13
mass culture, 33, 78
  feminization of, 34, 40n
mass media, 2
mass production, 2, 81
Mass-Observation (M-O) diarists, 6, 31, 47,
78, 148, 156–7, 158–9
  Enquiry into People's Homes, 153
material culture, 14n
material culture, journals on, 14n
maternity; *see* motherhood
Maugham, W. Somerset, 'For Services
Rendered', 151n
Mayor, F.M., 8, 9, 18, 88, 147, 148
  The Rector's Daughter, 111, 149
  The Third Miss Symons, 70
McCaffey, Larry, 38n
McEwan, Ian, 168
McNeill, Dorelia, 36n
memory, 24, 26–7, 162
  houses and, 51
  objects and, 51
Mengham, Rod, 57, 60n
mental states, 63
metaphors
  architectural, 7, 23–6, 113, 136, 138,
139–40, 154–5
  domestic, 139–40, 154–5
  spatial, 102, 139–40
metonymy, 55; *see also* synecdoche
metropolis; *see also* cities
metropolises, 4
Meyers, Jeffrey, 109n

Meynell, Viola, 4
  Cross-in-Hand Farm, 70
  Lot Barrow, 70
  Martha Vine, 70
  Modern Lovers, 70
middle class, 1, 2, 17, 23, 28, 34, 40n, 48,
75, 119, 167
middlebrow
  middlebrow culture, 13, 34; *see also*
middlebrow fiction
  usage of the term, 92n
middlebrow fiction, 7, 9, 12, 75–80, 86,
87–8
  female, 148–9
  'feminine', 77
  interior decoration and, 98–9
  'progressive', 77
Middleton, Jim, 153–4
Miller, Betty, *On the Side of Angels*, 97, 107
mirrors, 150n, 166
Miss Atkinson, 41
Mitchell, Margaret, *Gone with the Wind*, 78
Mitchison, Naomi, 161
modernism, 7, 9, 11, 30, 32, 135–6
  aesthetic standards of, 12
  conservative, 138
  domestic, 33–4, 40n, 62, 88, 95–109, 165,
167, 168
  domestic novels and, 55–6
  domesticity and, 13, 55, 101
  high, 18, 33, 34
  modernist techniques, 1
modernity, 4, 7, 9, 29, 33, 47, 96, 97, 98,
119, 138, 140, 149, 167
  bohemianism and, 100–101
  'conservative', 77
  domesticity and, 33–6, 163
  the everyday and, 33
  housing and, 153–4
  interior decoration and, 98–9
  nature and, 69
  the New Woman and, 64
  tradition and, 7, 11, 87, 162
  urban, 69
  women and, 153
  women writers and, 163
  of Young's novels, 90

Index

205

Mohanty, Chandra Talpade, 27
Mole, Florence Homer, 109n
Monetfiore, Janet, 157
morality, 53, 64, 69, 98, 113, 125
Moran, Joe, 39n
Morandi, Giorgio, 57
Morgan, Geneviève Sanchis, 40n
Morisot, Bérthe, 57
Morrell, Ottoline, 45, 76
Morris, Robert, 58n
Morris, William, 55
Mortimer, Raymond, *The New Interior Decoration*, 55
motherhood, 6, 139; *see also* mothers
mothers, 8, 61, 139, 163; *see also* motherhood
  houses and, 107
Munich Crisis, 6, 156–7, 164n

Nabis, 56, 57
narrative techniques, 1, 2, 13, 25, 32, 33, 50, 70; *see also* focalization; free indirect discourse; irony
  interior decoration and, 50
  non-linear narrative, 7
  use of dialogue, 96, 125
  use of focalization, 101, 116, 118, 122–3, 125, 133, 140–41, 145, 155, 163
  use of free indirect discourse, 106, 123
  use of irony, 106, 139, 140, 163
narrators, 33, 123
National Insurance Acts, 2
nationalism, 153
nationhood, 1, 111, 153, 155, 163, 167; *see also* England; homeland
  crisis of, 13
  home and, 23
  memory and, 26, 27
  relation to home, 7
nature, 62, 63–4
  domesticity and, 65
  modernity and, 69–70
Nazism, 156
New Feminism, 2, 139
New Woman, 13, 17, 61, 63, 64, 67, 72, 122
novels of the, 28

newspapers, 4
Norwood, Gilbert, 115
nostalgia, 24, 31, 35, 136, 140, 154, 159, 161
novels
  bestselling, 34
  classification of, 76–7, 80
  commercialization of, 86
  compared to houses, 7, 13, 16n, 18, 22–6, 118, 153
  detective, 18, 29, 35, 36n, 111–12
  'dissertation novel', 93n
  domestic, 46, 47, 76–7, 78, 108, 111–12, 130n, 167
  Edwardian, 79
  Gothic, 21
  interwar domestic novels, 17–40
  of manners, 18
  modernist, 32
  'New Woman', 28
  post-World War II, 14, 168
  provincial, 87
  sentimental, 22
  serialized, 34
  traditional, 32
  vicarage, 111–16
  women's, 2, 4, 77, 87

objects, 2, 13, 24, 25–6, 27, 51, 122–3, 131, 163, 167
  as archive of memory, 51
  comparison to characters, 72
  symbolic value of, 126
  viewing of, 34
O'Brien, Kate, *Without My Cloak*, 86
Old Feminism, 2
Oliphant, Margaret, *Chronicles of Carlingford*, 112
Olson, Liesl, 32
Omega Workshops, 11, 13, 55
ontology, 7
order, 135
ordinary, the; *see* everyday, the
ornamentation; *see* interior decoration
ornaments; *see* objects
Orwell, George, 79, 93n, 101, 130n, 150
  A Clergyman's Daughter, 112, 147–8

206 *Domestic Modernism*

Keep the Aspidistra Flying, 54
Owen, Ursula, 36n
Owen, Wilfrid, 90

pacifism, 156
Pain, G.C., 9
   Surplus Women, 47, 55, 56–7, 151n
painting, 13, 134, 165
   Dutch, 53–7
   genre painting, 13
   Impressionism, 57
   Nabis, 56, 57
   Post-Impressionism, 13, 57, 165
Panter-Downes, Mollie, 6, 7
   One Fine Day, 6–7, 55
paperbacks, 2, 77, 81–6, 93n
   paperback revolution, 2–3
'Paris Frocks by Air', 137 (fig.)
passports, 29
pastoral, 4, 61, 63, 117
Pater, Walter, 22, 38n
patriarchy, 11, 33, 35, 102, 163
Paxton, Nancy L., 7
P.E.N., 45, 76
Penguin books, 2–3, 77, 81, 93n, 82 (fig.),
   83 (fig.)
   modern home and, 81
Persephone Books, 9, 36n
perspective, 119, 163, 165
Pharand, Michel, 92n
Picasso, Pablo, 57
Plato, 23
Platonic idealism, 48
Platt, William, 150
   *The Passionate Spinster: A Psychological
     Novel*, 147
Playfair, Jocelyn, *A House in the Country*, 30
playwrights, women, 36n
pleasure, 86–9, 166
Poe, Edgar Allan, 'The Philosophy of
   Furniture', 22
politics, 7, 62–3, 167
   equality in, 17–18
   international, 13
   national, 13
   sexual, 13
Pompili, Graziano, 60n
popular fiction, 9, 12

Porteous, J. Douglas, 168
Post, Emily, 49
postcolonialism, 27
Post-Impressionism, 13, 57, 165
post-war British fiction, 35
power, 133, 155, 167
Pratt, William, *The Passionate Spinster: A
   Psychological Novel*, 147
premarital sex, 8
presence, 16n
Priestley, J.B., 78
prisons, 19
Pritchett, V.S., 87, 122
   reception of Young's novels, 89
privacy, 18, 24, 25, 39n, 49, 115, 117, 141,
   150n
   degradation of, 87
   lack of, 119, 120
   Young's desire for, 41, 76
private room, 38n
private sphere, 1, 19, 23, 25, 49, 50, 52–3,
   97, 105–6, 112, 115, 117, 118
privatization, 2
propaganda, 6, 72, 153
psyche, the, 20, 21, 63
   house as, 48
psychoanalysis, 20–21, 31, 50
public sphere, 1, 19, 24, 47, 49, 50, 52, 87,
   105–6, 112, 118, 157
publicity, 122
publishing, 2, 13, 93n; *see also specific
   publishing houses*
   advertising and, 75–6
   American, 78, 87, 89, 93n
   audiobooks, 91
   books by subscription, 17
   British, 78, 87
   changes in, 9
   circulating libraries and, 17
   commercialization of, 78
   electronic, 91
   mass marketing and, 75–6
   paperbacks, 2–3, 81–6
   women writers and, 92n
Punch, 78
Pym, Barbara, 49, 77, 87, 112, 168
   Some Tame Gazelle, 148

Index

207

The Sweet Dove Died, 37n

Queen, The, 4
quotidian, the; *see* everyday, the

race, 27
Radcliffe, Ann, 17
Radford, Jean, 59n
Radner, Hilda, 77
Raverat, Gwendolen, 87
Raymond, Ernest, 78
readers, 33, 75, 77–8, 119, 148–9
 categories of, 87
 education and, 78
 female, 77, 80, 148–9, 151n
 highbrow, 79
 male, 89, 90
 middle class, 78, 81
 middlebrow, 77, 78, 79, 151n
 working class, 78, 81
reading, 74n, 76, 77–8, 148–9, 151n
 commercialization of, 86
 modes of, 87
 reading pleasure, 86–9
realism, 7, 8, 12, 33, 48, 54, 61
 creation of, 23
 dispossession and, 163
 domestic, 163
 'multiplicity of', 35
 social, 18, 128
rebellion, 18, 98
recession, 156
reconstruction, 156
Reed, Christopher, 33, 55, 88
Renault, Mary, *The Friendly Young Ladies*,
 163
representation, 18
 symbolic *versus* descriptive, 95
repression, 51, 61, 64, 65, 106, 147
Reprint Society, 78
reprints, 2
reproduction, 21; *see also* sexuality
resistance, 50
rest homes, 19
Rhys, Jean, 8, 28, 29, 119
Richardson, Dorothy, 12, 18, 28, 29, 35, 54,
 165

influence on Young, 90
 Pilgrimage, 28, 59n
rituals, 2, 13, 17, 21, 48, 50, 53–4, 119, 120,
 139, 144
Robertson, E. Arnot, 4, 8, 9, 155
 Cullum, 8, 32
 Ordinary Families, 8, 65
romance, 90, 107–8, 118; *see also* love
Romanticism, 61
rooms, 27, 108, 116; *see also* interiors
rootlessness, 10, 105, 158; *see also*
 transience
Roper, Maurice, 1, 7, 113
Rose, Gillian, 27
Ross, Kristin, 32
Ross, Mary, 53, 75
Rubin, Joan Shelley, 93n
Ruck, Bertha, 79
rural world, 48, 63, 69, 91, 117
 cities and, 70
Rybczynski, Witold, 23

Sackville-West, Vita, 4, 76, 91
 All Passion Spent, 63
sagas, 18; *see also* Aga sagas
Sand, Georges, 166
Sanderson, Norah, 41, 42 (fig.)
Sargent, John Singer, 134
Sassoon, Siegfried, 90
 Memoirs of a Fox-Hunting Man, 86
Sayers, Dorothy, 18, 79
Schwenger, Peter, 58n
Second World War; *see* World War II
secularization, 19
Sedgwick, Eve Kosofsky, 74n
self, 1, 23–6, 27, 69, 71, 116, 141
 compromising of the, 144
 construction of, 7, 61–2
 development of the, 108
 dislocation of the, 158
 feminine, 4, 165
 home and the, 158
 houses as symbols of the, 20, 108
 interiority of the, 50
 inviolability of the, 50
 loss of, 64
 other and, 48

society and the, 48
self-reflection, 49, 73, 115, 125, 139
sensation novels, 17
sentimental novels, 22
serialized novels, 34
servants, 39n
sexual freedom, 64
sexual politics, 167
sexual purity movement, 64
sexuality, 8, 13, 35, 50, 62, 64, 65, 72, 145, 163, 165
  female, 21, 62–3, 64, 147
  illicit, 90, 98, 120, 140
  male, 118
  repressed, 61, 106
Seymour, Beatrice Kean, 4
Sharp, Harold, 41
Shaw, Marion, 77
Sherahazade, 107
Shields, Carol, 9, 31
shilling railway editions, 81
Shone, Richard, 53
shopping, 29
Sidlauskas, Susan, 134
Simmel, George, 10, 31, 70, 116, 141
Simmons, Gary, 59n
Simpson, Helen, 76
Sinclair, Iain, 49
Sinclair, May, 9, 12, 18, 34, 92n, 148
  The Combined Maze, 47
  The Life and Death of Harriett Frean, 11, 70
  Mary Olivier: A Life, 65, 73n
  The Rector of Wyck, 111
  The Three Sisters, 111
Sinda, Gregory, 38n
sisters, 8
sitting rooms, 140
'sixpenny blacks', 81
Skye, Stephanie, 91
Smith, Ali, 10
Smith, Dodie, 4, 18, 36n
Smith, Stevie, 18, 34, 165
  Novel on Yellow Paper, 8
Smith-Rosenberg, Carroll, 67
social change, 159–60
social policy, 154

social relationships, 7, 17, 18, 27, 48, 128, 140–41, 167
  control over, 20
  staircases as representing, 50
Society of Authors, 45, 76
soldiers, 29, 153
  feminization of, 90
  returning, 154
  wounded, 90, 94n, 160–61
space, 50, 115
  communal, 115, 120
  domestic, 62, 63, 119, 141, 154, 165, 167, 168
  inner *versus* outer, 49
  masculine, 49
  memory and, 27
  organization of, 19, 24, 38n
Spicer, Harriet, 36n
spinsters, 53, 70–71, 103–104, 119, 122, 146–50, 165, 167
  in vicarage novels, 112, 113
staircases, 13, 50
Stamp, Gavin, 150n
'standpoint', 12–13
Staszak, Jean-François, 37n
Stern, G.B., 8, 36n
still lifes, 53–7, 165
stock characters, 113, 120
Struther, Jan, 13, 18, 31, 76, 131, 134, 168
  Mrs. Miniver, 124, 155
subjectivity, 7, 23–6, 48, 140–41
  decentered, 34
  female, 33, 165
  interiority and, 119
  male, 97, 101
  modernist, 34
  shifting, 118
suburban sprawl, 3 (fig.)
suburbs, 28
suffrage movement, 17, 62–3, 139
surveillance, 105–106, 112, 116
symbolism, 54–5, 95, 116, 117, 126
synecdoche, 50
'synthetic impressionism', 54, 165

Talbot, Laura, 119
taste, 86; *see also* aesthetic value

Index

Tate, Trudi, 160
Taylor, Elizabeth, 77, 89, 131, 168
 Mrs. Lippincote, 135
 A View from the Harbour, 135
Taylorism, 21
technology, 29
The Guardian, 9–10
The Publisher and Bookseller, 78, 84
theatricality, 58n
thinking, 7
Thirkell, Angela, 4, 18
Thompson and Bywaters case, 8
Thompson, Wendy, 150n
thresholds, 13, 49, 65, 118, 140
Tiersten, Lisa, 166
time, 20
 space and, 19, 26
Time and Tide, 2, 45, 78
Times Literary Supplement, 78
titles, 130n
 Todd, Dorothy, *The New Interior
  Decoration*, 55
Tolstoi, Count Lev Nikolayevich, 54
tradition, 20
 modernity and, 7, 11, 87, 162
traditional novels, 32
tranport, 29
transcendental aesthetic, 13
transience, 24, 28, 119, 120
travel, 27–30
Travellers' Library, 78, 84
Treaty of Versailles, 156
Tristram, Philippa, 18
Trodd, Anthea, 91
Trollope, Anthony, 17, 88, 127, 168
 Barchester Towers, 112
Twentieth Century Authors, 76

'U.F. (Unnecessary Female)', 147
uncanny, the, 13, 37n, 61, 65, 126, 127
unconscious, the, 20–21
upper classes, 50, 119
urban housing, 117
urbanism, 10, 28, 29, 47, 48, 69, 117, 119;
 see also cities

values, 17
Van Doren, Carl, 68, 86, 87

verisimilitude, 33
Vermeer, Johannes, 53
vicarage novels, 111–16
vicarages, 13, 111–16, 125
vicars, 49
Virago Press, 9, 36n, 57n, 90–91
vision, 49, 116, 118, 143, 163, 165
Vitruvius, 21
von Arnim, Elizabeth, *The Pastor's Wife*,
 111, 125
voyeurism, 34, 49, 71, 114, 115, 118, 123,
 140
Vuillard, Edouard, 57, 134

Wallace, Diana, 91, 107
Wallace, Edgar, 78
walls, 150n
Walpole, Hugh, 76, 78, 79, 87
war effort, 2
Warner, Sylvia Townsend, 4, 8, 48
Watson, Winifred, *Miss Pettigrew Lives for
 a Day*, 104
Waugh, Evelyn
 Brideshead Revisted, 154
 Decline and Fall, 108n
 Handful of Dust, 154
Webb, Mary, 4, 13, 61
 Gone to Earth, 62
 Precious Earth, 62
 Seven for a Secret, 62
Wells, H.G., 12, 76, 79
Wesley, Mary, 168
West, Algernon, 109n
West, Katharine Leaf, 109n
West, Rebecca, 25, 161
 Harriet Hume, 21
 The Return of the Soldier, 154
Westacott, Mary, *Absent in the Spring*, 151n
Wharton, Edith, 17
 Decoration of Houses, 22, 38n
Whipple, Dorothy, 6, 9
 Greenbanks, 149
 High Wages, 47, 54, 149
Whistler, James Abbott McNeill, 134
white surfaces, 108n
Whiteread, Rachel, 57, 59n
Wigley, Mark, 36, 39n, 108n

Wilson, Elizabeth, 28, 168
windows, 13, 49, 50, 116, 118, 123, 140, 143, 150n
Winslow, Rosemary, 94n
Wolfe, Elise de, 49
'woman's novel', 77
women, 48
  access to higher education, 78
  agency of, 33
  communities of, 65, 70
  discourse of interiority and, 26
  homosociality and, 145–6
  independent, 138, 139
  middle-aged, 133–4
  modern, 56, 96, 138
  modernity and, 153
  representation of, 18, 78, 163
  subjectivity of, 33
women writers
  history of, 76
  the marketplace and, 92n
  modernity and, 163
  reception of, 76–7
  recognition of, 92n
  women novelists, 1, 4, 7, 9, 13, 33, 34, 35
  women playwrights, 36n
  World War II and, 157
women's magazines, 2, 4, 6, 15n, 29
women's novels, 2, 4, 77, 87
Woodcock, George, 77, 87, 164n
Woolf, Leonard, 27, 56, 93n
Woolf, Virginia, 1, 6, 7, 8, 9, 12, 18, 19, 25, 30, 32, 33, 34, 36, 49, 56, 62, 81, 90, 161, 164n, 165, 167
  advocacy of the 'common reader', 78
  anxiety about the middlebrow, 78–80, 93n
  on Arnold Bennett, 148
  Between the Acts, 14, 50, 125, 135, 154, 155, 156, 158, 159, 162, 163
  'Character in Fiction', 54, 79
  compared to Young, 55, 88
  design and, 59n
  To the Lighthouse, 11, 25, 52, 53, 107, 124, 131, 167
  Mrs. Dalloway, 11, 26, 29, 131
  Night and Day, 56, 61, 63
  The Pargiters, 164n

'Phyllis and Rosamond', 11
'Portrait of a Londoner', 155
reception of Young's novels, 75, 76, 78–9
A Room of One's Own, 22, 146
Three Guineas, 155
'Time Passes', 52
treatment of houses by, 56
The Voyage Out, 61, 63
on women, 164n
World War I and, 159
The Years, 11, 14, 154, 155, 159, 162, 163
Worboise, Emma, Married Life, 103
Wordsworth, William, 63
  Tintern Abbey, 26
work, 2, 4, 6, 21, 58n
work spaces, 24
working class, 6, 29, 128
World War I, 4, 22, 29, 153, 156, 157
  aftermath of, 13
World War II, 48
  imminence of, 13
Wright, Frank Lloyd, 'The Cardboard House', 21
writing, architecture and, 22–6, 38n

'yellow backs', 81
Yonge, Charlotte, 17
Young, Emily Hilda, 1, 6, 18, 25, 34, 88
  'An Artist', 45, 103–4
  BBC radio and, 52
  biography of, 7–8, 41–6, 57n, 127, 139
  'The Blunts', 113
  The Bridge Dividing, 70
  bust of, 42 (fig.)
  Caravan Island, 86
  Celia, 9, 13, 28, 29, 46, 47–8, 50, 54, 55, 73n, 76, 78, 90, 124, 131–44, 150n, 151n, 153, 155, 160, 161, 166, 167
  Chatterton Square, 6, 14, 27, 28, 29, 30, 49, 55, 57n, 61, 65, 76, 77, 78, 86, 90, 91, 108, 114, 124, 132, 139, 144–6, 149, 155, 155–63, 167
  children's books by, 86
  'Collected Works', 70, 86
  compared to Woolf, 55, 88
  construction of masculinity by, 13
  A Corn of Wheat, 8–9, 28, 44, 47, 61,

63–5, 66, 67, 68, 81–2, 86, 89, 139
'Cow's Tail', 44, 46
The Curate's Wife, 13, 49, 55, 57n, 88–9, 90, 91, 108, 111, 112–13, 114, 118, 119, 124–9, 139, 144, 151n, 167
desire for privacy, 76, 122
early novels of, 61–74
effect of World War II upon, 156
feminism of, 72
gender identity of, 89
'The Grey Mare', 46
home and domesticity and, 27–8, 46–53
house of, 43 (fig.)
interest in Romantic poetry, 61
interest in the Gothic, 61
interest in the pastoral, 61
interior decoration and, 50
Jenny Wren, 13, 28, 50, 55, 88, 90, 111, 117–24, 150
later novels of, 90, 108, 139, 165–6
'Lena Maude', 45, 103–4
letters of, 15n
literary status of, 94n
Miss Mole, 46, 53, 55, 57n, 65, 78–9, 84, 86, 91, 92n, 95, 101–8, 114, 139, 147, 160, 161, 167, 85 (fig.)
The Misses Mallett, 47, 54, 57n, 62, 65, 70–73, 84, 86, 91
modernity and, 61, 90
Moor Fires, 44, 47, 61, 62, 68–70, 84, 86, 87
names of, 15n
narrative techniques and style of, 34–5, 50, 61, 71, 73, 73n, 89, 96, 101, 106, 116, 117, 118, 122–3, 123, 125, 133, 139, 140–41, 145, 155, 163, 165, 166–7
'On Empty Houses', 52
'On Window Curtains', 52–3, 144
pastoral idealism of, 106
personal situation of, 127

philosophical vision of, 48, 58n, 61
portrayal of the rural world by, 69
publication and reception of, 13, 75–94
representation of social change, 159–60
retrospective views of, 90–91
reviews of, 53, 78–9, 86, 87–8, 89, 123–4, 164n
River Holiday, 86
romanticism of, 65
'The Sacrifice', 11, 45
scholarly attention to, 91–2
self-representation of, 139
shift toward human relationships, 132, 163
signature of, 15n
'The Stream', 45
in *Time and Tide*, 2
use of dialogue, 96, 125
use of focalization, 2, 7, 33, 35, 40n, 71, 72, 101, 116, 118, 122–3, 125, 133, 140–41, 145, 155, 163
use of free indirect discourse, 106, 123
use of irony, 18, 32, 89, 91, 106, 139, 140, 163
The Vicar's Daughter, 45, 46, 55, 84, 86, 91, 111, 113–16, 124, 158
Virginia Woolf and, 30, 75, 76
vision of herself as artist, 53
William, 4, 28, 40n, 41, 46, 47, 57, 57n, 58n, 68–70, 75, 81, 84, 86, 87, 90, 91, 95–101, 107, 114, 82 (fig.)
Yonder, 28, 44, 47, 61, 65–7, 68, 77, 86, 87, 89
Young, Frances Venning, 41
Young, Iris Marion, 10, 27, 28, 164n
Young, Margery, 41
Young (West), Gladys, 41, 44, 52, 57n, 91, 109n
Young, William, 41